"As a musician, I often look at The Beatles for inspiration musically or stylistically. They are the high-water mark, after all. But Dan Absher's book presents a whole other way to view the band: as a case study in building successful teams, businesses, and organizations, highlighting the importance of group unity and creating a situation wherein everyone is on the same page and working together. I also love that the book uses Beatles songs to help build this narrative, with playlists at the end of each chapter to drive home the lesson. As the host of the podcast *Ranking The Beatles*, I'm fortunate to get to read a lot of books about the band. Dan's book offers something fresh and unique that I really enjoyed. It's a fun and entertaining way to learn the band's story and the blueprint for building dynamic teams."

— JONATHAN PRETUS, musician and songwriter; cohost, *Ranking The Beatles* podcast

"Dan Absher's *The Fab Four Pillars of Impact* is a joyful reminder that leadership, like music, is about connection, creativity, and harmony. By drawing on timeless wisdom from The Beatles, Absher shows how anyone can find their unique voice while contributing to something greater than themselves. This book reminded me that the best way forward is to lead with heart, embrace collaboration, and leave behind a legacy that truly matters. A must-read for dreamers, doers, and changemakers alike."

— DEANNA OPPENHEIMER, chair, IHG Hotels and Resorts

"Dan is a lifelong learner on the DNA of successful teams, businesses, and leaders. Now add in his epic passion and encyclopedic knowledge of The Beatles phenomenon, and the result is a compelling and fun leadership playbook for building successful teams."

—JIM WEBER, author, *Running with Purpose*; former chairman and CEO, Brooks Running Company

"What a brilliant concept! Dan Absher weaves the remarkable history of The Beatles into timeless management and leadership principles. This book radiates the same positivity and passion that drives the top performers in any business. Not only does the book outline clear and actionable steps toward organizational excellence, it does so in a fun and refreshing way. I found myself smiling and humming along while learning."

—JOHN OPPENHEIMER, founder and chairman, Columbia Hospitality

THE
FAB FOUR
PILLARS OF IMPACT

BUILDING DYNAMIC TEAMS
THE **BEATLES'** WAY

DAN ABSHER

GREENLEAF
BOOK GROUP PRESS

This publication is designed to provide accurate and authoritative information in regard to the subject matter covered. It is sold with the understanding that the publisher and author are not engaged in rendering legal, accounting, or other professional services. Nothing herein shall create an attorney-client relationship, and nothing herein shall constitute legal advice or a solicitation to offer legal advice. If legal advice or other expert assistance is required, the services of a competent professional should be sought.

This book is not affiliated with, endorsed by, sponsored by, or authorized by The Beatles or its representatives in any way. All trademarks and copyrighted materials mentioned in this book are the property of their respective owners. They are used in this book for informational and commentary purposes only. No affiliation with or endorsement by the trademark or copyright holders is intended or implied, and should not be inferred.

Published by Greenleaf Book Group Press
Austin, Texas
www.gbgpress.com

Distributed by Greenleaf Book Group

For ordering information or special discounts for bulk purchases, please contact Greenleaf Book Group at PO Box 91869, Austin, TX 78709, 512.891.6100.

Design and composition by Greenleaf Book Group
Cover design by Greenleaf Book Group
Cover images used under license from ©stock.adobe.com

Publisher's Cataloging-in-Publication data is available.

Print ISBN: 979-8-88645-438-3

eBook ISBN: 979-8-88645-439-0

To offset the number of trees consumed in the printing of our books, Greenleaf donates a portion of the proceeds from each printing to the Arbor Day Foundation. Greenleaf Book Group has replaced over 50,000 trees since 2007.

Printed in the United States of America on acid-free paper

25 26 27 28 29 30 31 32   10 9 8 7 6 5 4 3 2 1

First Edition

CONTENTS

PREFACE

"IN MY LIFE"

On February 9, 1964, when I was just five years old, my family gathered around a black-and-white television to watch *The Ed Sullivan Show* to get our first glimpse of The Beatles. Seeing my older sisters' reaction certainly had an impact, but not as much as what I saw on the television. The sound, energy, and charisma emanating from those four lads from Liverpool blew me away.

My older brother, Tom, and cousin Mike were similarly smitten. Being older, they immediately became "John" and "Paul," while I embraced the role of "Ringo." (Sorry, George—there were only three of us.) Thus began my lifelong fascination with the enduring excellence of the Fab Four.

The Beatles have been a part of nearly every significant event in my life: weddings, the birth of my children, anniversaries, birthdays, graduations, and memorial services. In good times and bad, The Beatles have provided a soundtrack for my life. What is miraculous is that this is not unique to me—it is universal. The Beatles have touched lives throughout the world in similar ways.

My Beatles obsession takes many forms:

- With the last name of Absher, my nickname (passed down from my dad and brother) was "Abby." When I was in high school, it evolved to "Abby Road" as a nod to my Beatles obsession.

- When my daughter Larissa was in junior high, one of her teachers was such a Beatles fan that she gave one extra-credit Beatles question on each test. Larissa, of course, always got the extra credit, until one time when she answered "Twist and Shout" to one of the questions. The teacher marked it wrong and said it was a Beach Boys song. She couldn't wait to tell me, so I confirmed for her that it was a Beatles song, and she eventually got her extra credit!

- In our family, turning sixty-four is a milestone birthday—"When I'm Sixty-Four."

- Daria (my wife) and I have taken our kids on family trips to Liverpool to immerse ourselves in Beatles' history, to see Abbey Road in London, and to see the Strawberry Fields memorial to John Lennon in Central Park, New York.

- Our dog's name is Ringo (and my brother's dog's name is Penny Lane).

Throughout college, a brief law career, and my business career, my fascination with enduring excellence became focused on business, leadership, and team-building. Several books influenced my career: *They Call Me Coach* by John Wooden; *In Search of Excellence* by Thomas Peters and Robert Waterman Jr.; *Built to Last* by Jim Collins and Jerry Porras; *Good to Great* by Jim Collins; and *The 7 Habits of Highly Effective People* by Stephen Covey.

When I joined my dad and brother (Tom Sr. and Tom Jr.) at Absher

Construction, the family construction business, the company was already successful, but its systems were a bit antiquated. Fortunately, my brother was an ally as we brought modern technology and strategic planning to the business. With the help of our other partners Greg Helle, Clark Helle Jr., brother-in-law Brad Sayre, and a host of valuable team members, the company grew steadily in our time leading it.

The year 2020 was an eventful one for me, in more ways than one. Of course, the COVID pandemic disrupted life at home and at work. In May of that year, I was in the hospital for back surgery when I went into cardiac arrest. I literally died on the table. Fortunately, there is no better place to have that happen. The doctors applied the defibrillator and, with a couple of jolts, brought me back to life. After a two-hour back surgery in the morning, I had a seven-and-a-half-hour triple bypass heart surgery later that day.

The heart incident motivated me to make some changes: 1) If I didn't resolve the company's ownership succession, it would put a terrible burden on Daria, my family, and the team at Absher Construction; 2) I wanted to spend more time with my wife, family, and friends; and 3) I wanted to spend more time writing, something I had dabbled in since my college days. So, in 2022, my brother, Tom, and I agreed to an employee buyout (an employee stock ownership plan [ESOP])—a transition that my grandfather and father would have wholeheartedly endorsed. A year later, after thirty-two years as CEO, I stepped down from that position.

In the summer of 2020, as I recovered from heart surgery during the COVID pandemic, my good friends Alan Frazier, John Morse, and Michael Melvin (aware of my Beatles obsession) suggested I share with them the history of The Beatles in a socially distant gathering. I agreed on one condition—that we do it the right way, which meant sharing The Beatles' story (and music) from beginning to end.

To put it simply, I got carried away. As I dove back into the dozens of books I had read about The Beatles, I realized I could not do it in one evening. In the end, it took three long evenings to share The Beatles' incredible story and music.

Since that time, I have expanded and polished the curriculum to be a team-building workshop for business groups, a Beatles' history class for retirement communities, and a presentation about communications and dispute resolution for college students.

The reception to the team-building workshop convinced me to dive deeper into the uncanny comparisons between The Beatles' success and the business success I have observed and researched. The Beatles developed a blueprint for excellence that applies universally. Whether it's a basketball team or a multinational business, these lessons apply. In the pages that follow, I'll share what I've learned about the fundamental principles that drove their success—principles that can apply to any team or organization pursuing excellence.

I've incorporated some extra fun for Beatles' fans. Each chapter includes a playlist of songs that enrich the stories from the chapter (including my top ten favorite Beatles' songs). These songs provide more evidence of the connection between the music and the remarkable story of how they achieved such enduring excellence.

I also address a few long-debated Beatles topics: Who was the fifth Beatle? Who broke up The Beatles? If they had stayed together for one more album, what would have (or should have) been on it? What would it have looked like if they had found a way to stay together?

Whether you are an avid Beatles fan or you are interested in understanding what drives excellence in teams, organizations, or individuals, the remarkable story of The Beatles applies. This is the story of the universal keys to The Beatles' enduring brilliance—the Fab Four Pillars and how those pillars provide lessons for creating legendary teams and organizations. What is most compelling for me is that underlying all four pillars is a fundamental commitment to love. Not romantic love, but a deeper commitment to connection, compassion, and shared purpose.

PREFACE PLAYLIST

RANKING MY TOP TEN BEATLES' SONGS

With a nod of appreciation to Jonathan and Julia Pretus, cohosts of one of my favorite podcasts, Ranking the Beatles, I give you my top ten favorite Beatles songs (notice I said favorite—not the greatest or best-selling).

1. **"Strawberry Fields Forever"**—John's psychedelic reflections about his childhood blow me away. The song features unprecedented production techniques that merged two completely different takes. Its dreamlike quality and introspective depth changed the landscape of what rock music could be. When John bares his soul, it is both intimate and universal.

2. **"A Day in the Life"**—The ultimate Beatles collaboration, combining John's dreamlike verses with Paul's energetic middle

section, revolutionary orchestral crescendos, and that iconic final piano chord—redefining the possibilities of popular music in a single track. For me, they were at their best when they collaborated closely.

3. **"In My Life"**—John's mature reflection on memory and relationships marked their evolution from pop sensations to profound songwriters. This is The Beatles song I listen to most. It is a part of every significant event for our family. Pardon the oxymoron, but it has a complex simplicity.

4. **"Here Comes the Sun"**—George Harrison's optimistic gem features intricate acoustic guitar work, unconventional time signatures, and an uplifting message of renewal. At a time when a lot of George's songs were negative or preachy, this is a refreshing journey of optimism and hope. It is the most downloaded/streamed song in The Beatles catalog.

5. **"Here, There and Everywhere"**—Paul's delicate love song demonstrates melodic perfection and harmonic sophistication. Its gentle beauty, complex chord progression, and Beach Boys–inspired vocals created what both Paul and John consider one of Paul's finest compositions. The wonderfully constructed lyrics show Paul at his poetic best.

6. **"While My Guitar Gently Weeps"**—George's philosophical exploration of empathy features Eric Clapton's guitar solo. If I were to select one song to tell The Beatles' story, it would be this one. George once called it "All You Need Is Love, Part Two." While John and Paul were singing (and preaching) about love, they often overlooked those closest to them.

7. **"Penny Lane"**—Paul's nostalgic portrait of Liverpool pairs sunny music with keenly observed details and surreal touches. It is the counterpart to John's "Strawberry Fields Forever." Its sophisticated arrangement, featuring the piccolo trumpet inspired by Bach, elevates seemingly simple pop into art. This song is guaranteed to brighten my mood every time I listen to it.

8. **"I Am the Walrus"**—John's surrealist masterpiece combines nonsensical lyrics with an innovative arrangement. To me, this is John at his creative peak. His affection for the nonsense verse of Lewis Carroll and Edward Lear is evident in this masterpiece. Hidden under the obscure lyrics is a profound antiestablishment message.

9. **"Let It Be"**—Paul's gospel-influenced ballad transcends the band's internal conflicts to become a universal hymn of comfort. Knowing that Paul lost his mother, Mary, as a teenager, makes this song even more poignant.

10. **"If I Fell"**—I cannot get enough of this song. John's delicate handling of the raw insecurity of young love shines. The melody and lyrics are perfectly suited. The harmonies rival the best of the Everly Brothers and Simon & Garfunkel.

Note: This is my list *today*. It has changed and will change frequently. Also, these are *my* favorites, not necessarily an objective list of the "best" Beatles' songs of all time. Any objective list would have to consider "Hey Jude," "Yesterday," "I Want to Hold Your Hand," "Something," "Come Together," and many others.

My model for business is The Beatles. They were four guys who kept each other's kind of negative tendencies in check. They balanced each other, and the total was greater than the sum of the parts.

—STEVE JOBS,
excerpt from a 2003 interview with *60 Minutes*

PART 1

THE FAB FOUR
PILLARS

In part 1, we explore the foundation of The Beatles' fascinating journey from Liverpool to legends and ask the questions: How did they create Beatlemania? What internal and external forces propelled four working-class lads from Liverpool to be wildly successful? Or, in the words of John Lennon, how did they reach "the toppermost of the poppermost"?

I use the term Fab Four Pillars of Impact to describe the essential elements that I have discovered supported The Beatles' ascent to greatness. These four pillars provide a framework for understanding not only their musical achievements but also the universal principles that drive exceptional performance in any field—whether in business, sports, or the arts.

Before we examine those pillars of impact, I will define "wildly successful" in chapter 1. Chapter 2 is a cursory introduction of the band, each of the four members, and a few of the major players in The Beatles empire.

As you dig into this book, remember that The Beatles didn't become a global phenomenon by accident. They set out—with intention—to become "bigger than Elvis." While raw talent played a crucial role, their extraordinary success stemmed from deliberately cultivated attitudes, approaches, and decisions that anyone seeking excellence can learn from and apply.

The Beatles' story offers unique insights because it has both a distinct beginning and a clear end. This allows us to study not only how they achieved phenomenal success but also how that success eventually unraveled—providing a complete life cycle of excellence that few case studies can match.

CHAPTER 1

DEFINING "WILDLY SUCCESSFUL"

W hat does it mean to be wildly successful? What makes a team or organization transcend the ordinary to achieve something truly remarkable? These questions have fascinated me since childhood.

My first conscious encounter with this kind of excellence occurred on February 9, 1964. Like millions of Americans, my family gathered around our black-and-white television for *The Ed Sullivan Show* to witness The Beatles' American debut. The energy, charisma, and pure talent emanating from those four lads from Liverpool left an indelible mark. Seventy-three million people watched that night—the largest television audience in history at that time—and American culture was forever changed.

That single performance captivated me, and I've been enamored with The Beatles ever since. What began as simple fandom deepened over decades into serious analysis. How did four working-class lads from Liverpool, with little formal education and no family connections in the music industry, become the most successful and influential band in history? More importantly, how can their journey illuminate the path for any team or organization to be wildly successful?

"Wildly Successful" Defined

To understand what made The Beatles exceptional, we first need to define what I mean by "wildly successful." I'm not talking about short-term success or a flash of brilliance—I'm talking about enduring, transformative achievement that spans generations. Jim Collins and Jerry Porras describe businesses like this as "visionary companies" in their landmark book *Built to Last*.

Collins and Porras define visionary companies as "premier institutions, the crown jewels in their industries, widely admired by their peers and having a long track record of making a significant impact on the world around them."[1] They are organizations that don't just succeed; they fundamentally change the landscape of their industry.

For purposes of this book, here is my definition of wildly successful: A team or organization is wildly successful when it is not just a leader of an industry but transforms an industry. It achieves a level of enduring excellence through a relentless pursuit of innovation. It emerges when vision, talent, and determination intersect with genuine collaboration to create a high level of achievement and/or brilliance.

You will note that my definition practically mandates multiple individuals to achieve the enduring excellence required to fit my definition of wildly successful. I do not mean to minimize individual excellence. Obviously, some individuals achieve a level of excellence that push the boundaries as much as The Beatles, but my hunch is even those individuals relied on a team of people for them to achieve an enduring level of excellence.

By any measure, The Beatles fit this definition perfectly. More than sixty years after they first performed together, and over fifty years since they broke up, they remain the best-selling music act of all time. Their music continues to reach new generations, their influence on music and culture remains profound, and their commercial appeal endures.

In 2023, with the release of "Now and Then"—marketed as the "last Beatles song"—they had their eighteenth number one single in the UK, setting a record for the longest gap between an artist's first and most recent chart-topper at sixty years and seven months. The song was recorded by John Lennon into a lo-fi boom box. Aided by the magic of artificial intelligence, they were able to isolate John's voice and strengthen it for the ultimate recording.

Consider the evidence:

- In Britain, where they first found fame, ten of the thirteen largest-selling albums of the 1960s were by The Beatles. The other three? *The Sound of Music*, *West Side Story*, and *South Pacific*. They didn't just succeed in rock music; they transformed pop culture.

- In the United States, they claimed eight of the thirteen best-selling albums of the decade. Before The Beatles, only one million-seller single existed in US history: Elvis Presley's "Hound Dog." When The Beatles arrived in the US, "I Want to Hold Your Hand" became a million-seller within a month. In New York City alone, it sold ten thousand copies per day.

- On April 4, 1964, they achieved the unprecedented feat of occupying all five top spots on the *Billboard* Hot 100 chart, along with fourteen positions in the top 100—a record that stood until Taylor Swift claimed all top ten positions in 2022. It should be noted, however, that streaming services have changed the way singles are charted.

- Their concert success was equally remarkable. On August 15, 1965, they played to 55,600 people at Shea Stadium, inventing the stadium concert business that continues to thrive today. At the time, it was the largest crowd in history ever to see a concert.

- Their films weren't just promotional vehicles but artistic achievements. *A Hard Day's Night* made the American Film Institute's list of the top 100 movies of the century and maintains a 98 percent rating on Rotten Tomatoes.

- The Beatles consistently top rankings of the greatest rock bands of all time, and remarkably, they won a Grammy in 2023, spanning Grammy wins over sixty years—the largest time span of Grammy recognition ever.

When I consider The Beatles alongside other examples of sustained excellence—whether it's the UCLA basketball dynasty under John Wooden, Apple under Steve Jobs, Disney under Walt Disney, or Amazon under Jeff Bezos—I see certain common elements that transcend industry, era, and individual personalities. These elements form what I call the Fab Four Pillars of Impact that support truly exceptional achievement.

Beyond Talent: The Formula for Enduring Excellence

Perhaps the most remarkable insight from studying The Beatles is that their extraordinary success wasn't accidental or simply the result of four uniquely talented individuals happening to meet. They set out—with intention—to become the biggest band in the world, and they succeeded through deliberate choices and actions from which any organization can learn. I do not mean to take anything away from their immense talent. All four are (or were) uniquely talented, and those talents blended perfectly.

Throughout my career in construction, law, coaching, and leadership, I've observed that whether it's a basketball team, a construction company, or a rock band, the principles that drive them to be wildly successful remain remarkably consistent. The Beatles exemplify these principles with such clarity that they provide the perfect case study for understanding how to achieve it.

What makes them particularly valuable as a case study is that they have both a distinct beginning and a clear end. Their story unfolds over a defined period—from John and Paul's first meeting in 1957 to their breakup in 1970—allowing us to study not only how they achieved phenomenal success but also how that success eventually unraveled. As I researched why they broke up, I saw how the major causes of their "derailment" universally applied to all teams and organizations—a blueprint, if you will, for avoiding derailment. In their rise and fall, we can see the complete life cycle of excellence.

In the pages that follow, we'll explore the Four Pillars of Impact that supported The Beatles' remarkable journey:

First Pillar—the Train: Right People, Right Seats: How The Beatles assembled the right people for their team and defined clear roles for the members of the group.

Second Pillar—Catalytic Vision: How they created a compelling goal that drove extraordinary commitment. How they complemented that catalytic vision with a series of interim goals.

Third Pillar—Esprit de Corps: How they fostered a unique team spirit that elevated their work through humor and fun.

Fourth Pillar—the Magical Mystery: How they leveraged synergy and serendipity to create something unique that was greater than the sum of its parts.

Together, these four pillars form a framework for understanding and achieving phenomenal success in any field. And while we'll use The Beatles as our primary case study, I'll also share insights from research about organizations and leaders who have achieved a remarkable level of excellence and from my own experiences in business, sports, and leadership that reinforce these principles.

The Elements of Success

As I've studied wildly successful teams and organizations across various domains, I've observed that truly exceptional organizations and teams share certain characteristics. They have clear visions. They assemble the right people and put them in positions to succeed. They foster a culture of both collaboration and healthy competition. And they remain open to unexpected opportunities.

The Beatles exemplified all these characteristics but with a chemistry and approach that set them apart. Their story offers insights not only for music lovers or Beatles fans but for anyone seeking to understand how excellence is achieved and sustained.

In the construction business, we know that a building is only as strong as its foundation. The same principle applies to excellence. The Fab Four Pillars that we'll explore in this book form the foundation upon which The Beatles built their extraordinary success. And just as importantly, when these pillars began to crack, their edifice eventually crumbled. Fortunately, we are left with the enduring excellence of their creations.

Jim Collins, in his seminal work *Good to Great*, wrote: "Greatness is not a function of circumstance. Greatness, it turns out, is largely a matter of conscious choice and discipline."[2] The Beatles consistently made those conscious choices, exercised that discipline, and, as a result, achieved a level of greatness that continues to inspire and instruct.

The Role of Innovation

Transformational success isn't just about achieving momentary excellence; it's about achieving something distinctive, meaningful, and enduring. The Beatles certainly achieved commercial success, but they also changed music forever. They innovated constantly, pushing boundaries and exploring new artistic territory. They influenced not only music but fashion, film, graphic design, and even social attitudes. Their excellence was multidimensional. Innovation was what kept them fresh and relevant. The book *In Search of Excellence* highlights the critical role innovation plays in enduring excellence.[3]

Similarly, in business or any organizational context, true excellence goes beyond financial metrics. It encompasses innovation, impact, and the ability to adapt and evolve over time. It's about creating something that matters and that lasts.

The companies I've admired most throughout my career share these qualities. They don't just perform well financially; they revolutionize their industry, develop strong cultures, and make positive impacts on their communities. They, like The Beatles, understand that excellence is holistic.

Excellence as a Journey, Not a Destination

One of the most important insights from studying The Beatles' trajectory is that enduring excellence is not a static achievement but a dynamic process. The Beatles never stopped evolving, never rested on their laurels. From their early days playing Hamburg clubs to the experimental complexity of their later albums, they constantly pushed themselves to grow and change.

This commitment to evolution is evident in their discography. Their first album, *Please Please Me* (1963), consists largely of energetic rock and roll and covers of American hits. Just six years later, they released *Abbey Road* (1969), a sophisticated masterpiece of songwriting and production that sounds like it could have been made by an entirely different band.

In those six years, they reinvented themselves multiple times, moving from "She Loves You" to "A Day in the Life" to "I Am the Walrus" with remarkable speed and creativity. Each album represented not only new songs but new directions, new ideas, and new challenges they set for themselves.

But what's truly remarkable is that even after achieving mastery, they continued to push themselves. They stopped touring in 1966 to focus exclusively on studio recording, embracing new technologies and techniques that expanded what was possible in popular music. They never stopped learning, never stopped growing.

This principle applies equally to excellent organizations. The most successful companies don't achieve a winning formula and then stick to it rigidly; they continuously innovate and evolve. Apple didn't stop with the original Macintosh computer or even the first iPhone. Disney didn't rest after creating Mickey Mouse or Snow White. Amazon didn't stop at being an online bookstore. Excellence requires not only achieving greatness but sustaining and renewing it over time.

Commitment to Quality

Even after achieving fame, The Beatles' commitment didn't waver. Between 1963 and 1966, they maintained a punishing schedule of recording, touring, and filmmaking. In 1964 alone, they released two original albums, performed dozens of concerts across multiple continents, and starred in their first film, *A Hard Day's Night*.

Their commitment extended to their craft as well. They took songwriting seriously, constantly challenging themselves to improve. When they heard Bob Dylan's sophisticated lyrics, they pushed themselves to write more thoughtful and personal songs. When they heard The Beach Boys' *Pet Sounds*, they responded with *Sgt. Pepper's Lonely Hearts Club Band*, determined not to be outdone.

This level of commitment and competitiveness is a hallmark of excellence in any field. The most successful athletes, artists, and business leaders share this quality—a willingness to dedicate themselves completely to their craft, to make sacrifices others wouldn't make, and to persist through challenges that would defeat less committed individuals.

The Journey Ahead

In the chapters that follow, we'll explore each of the Fab Four Pillars in detail, examining how The Beatles embodied these principles and how other successful organizations and teams have done the same. We'll also look at my own experiences in business, sports, and leadership to see these principles in action across different contexts.

Along the way, we'll confront an essential question: If The Beatles were so excellent, why did they break up? Why couldn't they sustain their success indefinitely? This question leads to important insights about the challenges of maintaining excellence over the long term—insights that are relevant to any organization seeking not only to achieve greatness but to sustain it.

The Beatles' story is not just about four talented young men who changed music; it's about the universal principles that drive exceptional achievement in any field. By understanding these principles—the Fab Four Pillars of Impact—we can apply them to our own pursuits, whether we're leading a business, coaching a team, or simply striving for personal excellence.

Excellence is not accidental or mysterious. It follows patterns and principles that we can study, understand, and implement. The Beatles provide us with one of history's most vivid and compelling examples of these principles in action. Before we turn to our exploration of the Fab Four Pillars of Impact, let's "Meet The Beatles."

CHAPTER 1 PLAYLIST

THE EVOLUTION
OF EXCELLENCE

This chronological journey traces their evolution from pop sensations to musical revolutionaries, demonstrating how their pursuit of excellence transformed not only their own work but all popular music.

1. **"She Loves You"**—With its revolutionary "yeah, yeah, yeahs" and that unforgettable drum intro from Ringo, this early hit launched Beatlemania and displayed their ability to create hooks that were impossible to forget.

2. **"I Want to Hold Your Hand"**—Their first number one hit in America that launched Beatlemania across the Atlantic, featuring perfect vocal interplay between John and Paul with those infectious harmonies that captivated millions.

3. **"And I Love Her"**—Paul's tender ballad showcased their growing sophistication with classical guitar and restrained arrangements,

proving they could create intimate beauty alongside their energetic rockers.

4. **"Ticket to Ride"**—This innovative track, with its driving rhythm, descending guitar lines, and unusually structured melody, marked a significant evolution in their sound, pushing the boundaries of pop music with complex arrangements and emotional depth.

5. **"Norwegian Wood"**—George's sitar introduction brought Eastern influences to Western pop for the first time on this Dylan-influenced song written by John. This song demonstrates their fearless willingness to explore uncharted territory—musically and lyrically.

6. **"For No One"**—Paul's heart-wrenching portrait of a failed relationship demonstrates their evolution toward sophisticated storytelling, featuring a French horn solo that exemplifies their innovative approach to instrumentation in pop music.

7. **"When I'm Sixty-Four"**—This music hall–inspired track showcases their versatility and willingness to incorporate diverse influences, while its nostalgic yet forward-looking perspective mirrors their ability to honor tradition while creating something new.

8. **"Happiness Is a Warm Gun"**—A masterclass in compositional innovation that combines multiple musical sections into a cohesive whole, demonstrating how their commitment to excellence meant constantly reinventing their approach to songwriting.

9. **"Something"**—George's masterpiece represents the group's commitment to nurturing each member's talents, with its flawless melody and arrangement demonstrating how their pursuit of excellence extended to every aspect of their craft.

10. **"The Long and Winding Road"**—This moving ballad, one of their final releases, shows how their quest for musical excellence continued even during their dissolution, leaving listeners with a poignant reminder of their extraordinary journey.

CHAPTER 2

MEET THE BEATLES

We were just four guys. First Paul joined,
and then George joined, and then Ringo joined.
We were just a band that made it very, very big.

—JOHN LENNON

To fully appreciate The Beatles' achievement, we need to understand the historical context from which they emerged. When The Beatles formed, in 1957, just twelve years had passed since the end of World War II. Liverpool, their hometown, had been heavily bombed by the Nazis because of its importance as a port receiving crucial shipments from North America. In 1957, the city was still recovering, one of the last major British cities to be rebuilt after the war.

Many children in Liverpool grew up without fathers or in broken homes due to the war. The city was economically depressed, opportunities were limited, and the cultural climate was bleak. John, Paul, George, and Ringo were products of this postwar environment—working-class boys with little reason to expect extraordinary lives.

Rock and roll was a new genre of music when The Beatles were boys. Many thought it would be a short-term fad. American music, especially rock and roll, provided a welcome escape for the youth of Liverpool. They were ready to leave the war behind and embrace a future with hope. This created the perfect environment for forming a rock and roll band. Not only were musicians enthralled with this new music, but the young fans embraced it.

This context matters because it highlights a common thread among wildly successful teams. Not only does the team have to be right for the moment, but the moment must be right for the team.

These four young men from Liverpool, each with their own distinct personality, background, and talents, formed The Beatles' story. To understand how they created such extraordinary success together, we need to meet them as individuals—to see what each brought to the collaboration and how their unique combination of talents and temperaments created something greater than any of them could have achieved alone.

Meet John Lennon: The Visionary Leader

John Winston Lennon was born on October 9, 1940, during World War II. His birth occurred during an air raid, with the sound of German bombs falling on Liverpool. This dramatic entrance into the world seemed fitting for someone who would later shake the foundations of popular culture.

John's childhood was marked by instability and loss. His father, Alfred Lennon, was a merchant seaman who left when John was just four years old. His mother, Julia, an entertainer in her own right, didn't have the capacity to raise a child on her own. She made the difficult decision to have her sister, Mimi Smith, raise John while Julia stayed involved in his life from a distance.

With Aunt Mimi's influence, John became a voracious reader at an early age. A few of his favorite books were Lewis Carroll's *Alice in Wonderland* and *Through the Looking Glass* and Kenneth Grahame's *The Wind in the Willows*. These books fueled John's passion for wordplay and nonsense verse, which are prevalent in his book *In His Own Write*, published in 1964.

This early abandonment left a lasting impression on John, contributing to both the edge in his personality and the depth in his songwriting. It also likely contributed to his determination to succeed on his own terms—to prove himself in a world that had dealt him a difficult hand from the beginning.

John learned guitar at an early age from his mother, Julia. She was a banjo player, so she taught him banjo chords adapted for guitar. This unconventional introduction to the instrument gave John a unique approach—he initially played guitar with four strings using banjo chords. These unusual early lessons would influence his distinctive rhythm guitar style throughout his career.

Tragedy struck again in 1958, when John was seventeen. His mother, Julia, was hit by a car and killed. This devastating loss occurred just as John was finding his footing as a musician. The double abandonment—first through his parents' separation and then through his mother's death—left deep emotional scars that would often surface in his music and his interactions with others.

These early experiences shaped John into a complex, sometimes contradictory person. He could be abrasive and sarcastic, yet also tender and vulnerable. He was fiercely intelligent but often impatient with formal education. (He attended the Liverpool College of Art but was more interested in music than his studies.) He was both a natural leader and someone who struggled with insecurity about his own worth.

John's visionary leadership and creative brilliance were cut short on

December 8, 1980, when he was tragically murdered outside his New York City apartment building. At just forty years old, John was gunned down by Mark David Chapman as John returned home with his wife, Yoko Ono, from a recording session. The world mourned the loss of not only a musical genius but also a passionate advocate for peace.

In the years before his death, John had stepped away from music to focus on raising his son Sean, only to reemerge with the album *Double Fantasy* shortly before his passing. His death marked the definitive end of any hope for a Beatles reunion and left fans worldwide in shock and grief. Lennon's legacy lives on through his music, his message of peace and love, and the catalytic vision he brought to The Beatles' legend.

Meet Paul McCartney: The Melodic Perfectionist

James Paul McCartney was born on June 18, 1942, to Jim and Mary McCartney. Unlike John, Paul grew up in a stable, loving home environment. His family was musical; his father led Jim Mac's Jazz Band, and the family often sang together around the piano. This early immersion in music gave Paul a strong foundation in melody and songcraft.

Paul was the oldest of two brothers. His mother, Mary, had been a midwife, bringing a steady income to the family. Tragically, she died of breast cancer in 1956, when Paul was just fourteen. This loss created an unexpected bond between Paul and John, as both had lost their mothers at a pivotal age.

Through his father, Paul was exposed to a wide range of music, from traditional jazz and music hall tunes to the contemporary pop of the day. This diverse musical education would later be evident in his compositions, which ranged from straightforward rock and roll to elaborate ballads and experimental pieces.

Today, Paul remains a vibrant force in popular music, defying age as he continues to tour globally well into his eighties. Since The Beatles' breakup, his career has encompassed the acclaimed band Wings, numerous solo albums, classical compositions, movie scores, children's books, and ambitious collaborations with artists across generations.

McCartney's 2023–2024 "Got Back" tour demonstrated his remarkable stamina and lasting appeal, regularly performing nearly three-hour shows featuring Beatles classics along with his post-Beatles work. Despite personal challenges—including the losses of his first wife, Linda, to cancer in 1998, a difficult divorce from Heather Mills, and the deaths of bandmates John and George and Beatles producer George Martin—Paul maintained his creative output with albums like *Egypt Station* (2018) and *McCartney III* (2020), both reaching number one on the charts.

Though his relationship with John was complicated, Paul has become the band's most dedicated custodian, frequently sharing previously untold stories and championing their legacy. Sir Paul (knighted in 1997) has maintained the melodic perfectionism and work ethic that defined his Beatles years, creating a musical legacy unmatched in its breadth, commercial success, and cultural impact.

Meet George Harrison: The Spiritual Seeker

George Harrison was born on February 25, 1943 (though some family members claim he was born just before midnight on February 24). He was the youngest of four children born to Harold and Louise Harrison. As the youngest Beatle, George was only fourteen when he joined John and Paul's early group.

George's father, Harold, worked as a bus driver and had initially been skeptical of his son's musical ambitions. His mother, Louise, however, was supportive from the beginning. This contrast in parental attitudes created a determined streak in the young George—a quiet resolve to prove himself that would serve him well throughout his career.

George's role in the band is perhaps the most complex to navigate. As he matured as a musician and songwriter, he sometimes felt overshadowed by the Lennon–McCartney partnership. Yet his contributions—both musical and spiritual—gave The Beatles a depth and range they might otherwise have lacked.

George's spiritual journey took on profound significance in his later years as he faced mortality with the same quiet dignity that characterized his life. In 1997, he was diagnosed with throat cancer, which he attributed to his years of smoking. With treatment, the cancer initially went into remission.

In December 1999, George faced a terrifying ordeal that would further impact his already fragile health. A mentally disturbed intruder broke into his secluded Friar Park estate in Henley-on-Thames, stabbing him multiple times in the chest. Harrison's wife, Olivia, fought off the attacker by striking him repeatedly with a poker and lamp, likely saving George's life. He downplayed the incident in public with his characteristic dry humor, telling reporters "he wasn't a burglar and he certainly wasn't auditioning for the Traveling Wilburys [the supergroup George formed with Bob Dylan, Tom Petty, Roy Orbison, and Jeff Lynne]."[1] The attack punctured his lung and caused serious internal injuries.

George required emergency surgery and a lengthy recovery period. Many close to him believed this traumatic event significantly weakened his immune system, making him more vulnerable when cancer returned in his final years. The physical and emotional toll of the attack added another layer of suffering for George, who approached this challenge through the lens of his spiritual beliefs, viewing it as part of his karmic journey.

In 2001, he was again diagnosed with lung cancer that had metastasized to his brain. Throughout his illness, George maintained his spiritual practices, spending his final days surrounded by family and friends at a friend's home in Los Angeles. Ever committed to his spiritual path, he arranged his affairs meticulously, ensuring his transition would align with his beliefs. George passed away on November 29, 2001, at the age of fifty-eight. According to his loved ones, he left this world consciously and without fear, having prepared for this transition through decades of spiritual practice.

Meet Ringo Starr: The Steady Anchor

Richard Starkey, known professionally as Ringo Starr, was born on July 7, 1940. He was the only child of Richard and Elsie Starkey, who divorced when he was young.

Ringo's childhood was marked by serious illness. He spent a total of three years in the hospital battling tonsillitis and tuberculosis. These long hospital stays meant that his childhood playmates were often nurses. Many have noted that Ringo became an adult at age three because of these experiences. This early adversity gave him both a resilience and a lack of pretension that would characterize his approach to both music and life.

Due to his extended hospitalization, Ringo's formal education was limited. He left school at an early age, with no academic qualifications. However, he developed a natural empathy and ability to connect with people that would make him a valuable peacemaker within The Beatles.

Before joining The Beatles, Ringo was already established as one of Liverpool's premier drummers, playing with Rory Storm and the Hurricanes. The Beatles knew Ringo from their time in Hamburg, where both bands performed, often socializing with him there and in Liverpool, even though he was in a rival band. He even sat in with them occasionally before joining the band.

Today, at over eighty years old, Ringo—the drummer who many dismissed as "the luckiest man in show business"—has defied all expectations. Ringo remains vibrantly active, touring regularly with his All-Starr Band, a rotating supergroup concept he pioneered in 1989, that continues to delight audiences worldwide. His distinctly positive philosophy—encapsulated in his catchphrase "Peace and Love"—has become his calling card, celebrated annually on his birthday, July 7, when he encourages global moments of "Peace and Love" at noon.

Despite his fame, Ringo has maintained his unpretentious Liverpool charm, approaching celebrity with the same good-natured humility that endeared him to Beatles fans decades ago. His artistic pursuits have expanded beyond music to include painting, photography, and authoring children's books. Knighted in 2018, Sir Richard Starkey's contributions to music and culture have received formal recognition, though his greatest pride remains his family life with his wife of over forty years, Barbara Bach, their children, and their grandchildren.

Ringo is still very active. In early 2025, Ringo released a new country album called *Look Up*. On March 10, 2025, he hosted a CBS television special called *Ringo & Friends at the Ryman* in Nashville. The once-underestimated Beatle has proven himself to be a cultural institution—a steady anchor not only for The Beatles but for the enduring message of peace and love they championed.

The Birth of a Name

Long before they became the most famous band in the world, the band needed a name. Sixteen-year-old John formed a band called The Quarrymen, named after their school, Quarry Bank High School. The evolution from "The Quarrymen" to "The Beatles" wasn't straightforward, but it reflected the band's growing identity and John's playful wit.

At different times they were known as "The Silver Beetles" and "The Silver Beatles." For a brief period, the group performed as "Johnny and the Moondogs" and "Long John and the Silver Beatles," highlighting John as the front man. Even though this was the common structure at the time, John and the band resisted it, preferring a singular group identity without one person elevated above the others. Eventually, they simplified to "The Beatles," establishing the egalitarian ethos that would define their approach to music and performance.

In 1960, Stuart Sutcliffe (John's friend and bandmember) and John conceived the name "The Beetles" as a tribute to Buddy Holly and the Crickets, whose insect-themed band name they admired. Lennon, who loved wordplay, suggested changing the spelling to "Beatles," combining "beat" with "beetles." This clever pun referenced both the insect and the musical "beat" that defined their sound—a fitting name for a band emerging in the "Mersey Beat" scene (Liverpool is on the River Mersey).

In a 1961 *Mersey Beat* magazine article, John offered a far more fanciful explanation: "It came in a vision—a man appeared on a flaming pie and said unto them, 'From this day on you are Beatles with an A.' Thank you, Mister Man, they said, thanking him."[2] This whimsical fabrication perfectly captured his irreverent humor and distaste for self-serious origin stories. Years later, Paul used the name for one of his solo albums, *Flaming Pie*, as a tribute to John's tongue-in-cheek story.

Meet the "Fifth Beatle"

While John, Paul, George, and Ringo formed the core of The Beatles, several key individuals played such pivotal roles in the band's development and success that they earned the unofficial title of "the fifth Beatle." This distinction speaks to their profound influence on the group's sound, image, or business affairs.

Perhaps the most widely recognized "fifth Beatle" was Brian Epstein, the band's manager who discovered them at Liverpool's Cavern Club in 1961. A refined record store owner from a wealthy family, he saw potential in the leather-clad, rough-edged group that many others missed. He transformed their image with matching suits and professional stage presence, secured their first recording contract with EMI, and masterminded their early career strategy. Brian Epstein's unwavering belief in The Beatles and his business acumen were instrumental in their rise to fame. His tragic death from an accidental overdose in August 1967, at just thirty-two years old, marked a turning point for the band, removing the buffer that had often mediated internal conflicts.

While Brian Epstein may be the most widely recognized, my choice for the title of the fifth Beatle goes to George Martin. The Beatles' producer at EMI's Parlophone label was a classically trained musician with experience in comedy recordings. Martin brought sophisticated musical knowledge to the band's raw talent. He also played piano on several early recordings. His arrangements added orchestral elements to songs like "Yesterday" and "Eleanor Rigby," while his patient studio guidance helped translate the band's increasingly complex musical ideas into groundbreaking recordings. Martin's willingness to experiment with unconventional recording techniques proved essential to albums like *Sgt. Pepper's Lonely Hearts Club Band*. His contribution was so significant that Paul once said, "If anyone was the fifth Beatle, it was George."[3]

Stuart Sutcliffe, John's art school friend and The Beatles' original bassist from 1960 to 1961, represents a "fifth Beatle" who might have been. A talented visual artist, Sutcliffe lacked musical proficiency but brought intellectual depth and stylistic influence to the early group. It was Sutcliffe and his German girlfriend Astrid Kirchherr who influenced the band's famous haircuts, transforming their teddy-boy style into the iconic moptop look. Sutcliffe left the band to pursue his art career in Hamburg but died tragically of a brain hemorrhage in April 1962, before The Beatles achieved international fame.

Pete Best, the band's drummer from 1960 until August 1962, held the position prior to Ringo, performing with them during crucial formative years in Hamburg and Liverpool. His dismissal just before the band's commercial breakthrough became one of rock music's most infamous personnel changes, leading some fans to refer to him sympathetically as the "fifth Beatle." The circumstances of his replacement by Ringo remain controversial, with theories ranging from producer George Martin's dissatisfaction with his drumming to personality conflicts within the band.

Others with claims to the title include Neil Aspinall, the band's road manager and later head of Apple Corps, who protected their interests for over forty years; Mal Evans, their loyal roadie and assistant who contributed to some of their recordings; Billy Preston, the keyboardist who performed on "Get Back" sessions during the band's difficult final period; and even Yoko Ono, whose relationship with John significantly influenced the band's later dynamics.

The concept of the "fifth Beatle" ultimately highlights an essential truth about exceptional achievement: Even the most seemingly self-contained group relies on a broader network of support, inspiration, and expertise. The Beatles' journey from Liverpool to legend wasn't solely the work of four talented musicians but rather the product of a remarkable collaborative ecosystem that allowed their genius to flourish.

CHAPTER 2 PLAYLIST

THE BEATLES' EARLY RECORDINGS

Before Beatlemania swept the world, the group recorded several songs that reveal their musical roots and early development. This playlist captures the sound of The Beatles in their formative years, showcasing their evolution from cover band to songwriters finding their own voice.

This collection of recordings documents The Beatles' journey from skiffle-influenced teenagers to the polished professional group on the verge of changing popular music forever. These tracks reveal not only their musical influences and developing skills but the persistence and versatility that would help them achieve excellence in the years ahead. Note the early McCartney–Harrison and Lennon–Harrison songs; they went away from that as the Lennon–McCartney bond became stronger.

1. **"That'll Be the Day"**—Recorded as The Quarrymen (with John, Paul, and George) at Phillips' Sound Recording Service in Liverpool, this Buddy Holly cover represents the earliest known recording of the future Beatles.

2. **"In Spite of All the Danger"**—The flip side of their first recording session as The Quarrymen and the only song credited to McCartney–Harrison. This simple, plaintive ballad reveals early songwriting ambitions and displays the group's rockabilly and doo-wop influences.

3. **"You'll Be Mine"**—This rare home recording captures the playful side of the pre-fame Beatles. Paul's vocals come straight from the '50s, while John hams it up during the spoken part. It's a rare early glimpse into their chemistry and sense of humor.

4. **"Ain't She Sweet"**—Recorded in Hamburg with Pete Best on drums, this old standard from 1927 gets the rock and roll treatment with John delivering a confident, bluesy vocal.

5. **"Cry for a Shadow"**—An instrumental written by George and John during their Hamburg period, imitating the style of British instrumental group The Shadows. This rare Harrison–Lennon composition offers insight into their musical influences before establishing their own sound.

6. **"Sheik of Araby"**—Recorded during their unsuccessful audition for Decca, with Pete Best on drums, this cover of the 1921 standard showcases George's vocals and developing guitar skills. The performance demonstrates their willingness to adapt songs from any era and style.

7. **"Hello Little Girl"**—John's first-ever composition, written around 1957 but recorded during the Decca session. The song

reveals John's early songwriting approach with its simple structure and direct lyrics, influenced by Buddy Holly and American pop music but beginning to show distinctive Lennon–McCartney characteristics.

8. **"Besame Mucho"**—Performed during their successful EMI audition with Pete Best still on drums, this Spanish-language standard had been part of their Hamburg set. Paul's passionate vocal delivery impressed producer George Martin, helping secure their recording contract and marking the beginning of their professional recording career.

9. **"Like Dreamers Do"**—An early Lennon–McCartney original also from the Decca audition, with Paul on lead vocals. Though rejected by Decca, this song demonstrates their emerging songwriting style with its melodic structure and memorable chorus, pointing toward the direction their music would soon take.

10. **"I'll Be on My Way"**—Another early Lennon–McCartney composition that wasn't released as an official Beatles record during the band's active years. It can be found on the *Live at the BBC* recordings, demonstrating their developing songwriting style with its melodic structure and memorable chorus.

CHAPTER 3

PILLAR ONE— THE TRAIN: RIGHT PEOPLE, RIGHT SEATS

In 2002, I was sitting in a business leaders' retreat discussing Jim Collins's book *Good to Great*. As we explored Collins's research on what makes companies exceptional, one concept resonated with me more deeply than others: Good-to-great leaders "first got the right people on the bus, the wrong people off the bus, and the right people in the right seats—and then they figured out where to drive it."[1]

This highlighted a classic dilemma in building wildly successful organizations: Which comes first, the right people or the compelling vision? In *Good to Great*, Jim Collins argues for the primacy of people: "The executives who ignited the transformation from good to great did not first figure out where to drive the bus and then get people to take it there."[2]

While I generally agree with Jim Collins that in most cases it's the people first, in the case of The Beatles, it's a bit of a chicken-or-the-egg situation. For The Beatles, the right people and the vision developed in tandem, each influencing the other. John already had a bold vision of musical greatness when he formed The Quarrymen, but that vision evolved and expanded as Paul, George, and eventually Ringo joined the group.

This interplay between people and vision is the first key insight into how excellence emerges. The right people help shape and refine the vision, while the vision attracts and energizes the right people. It's not a linear process but a dynamic one.

When examining any great team—whether in business, sports, or music—the primacy of finding talented people who can occupy the right seats consistently emerges as the foundation of excellence. Therefore, for the purposes of this book, the first pillar of sustainable success is assembling the right combination of talents, personalities, and roles. Without this foundation, even the most compelling vision or enthusiastic team spirit will eventually falter.

I resisted the urge to use Jim Collins's bus metaphor for this chapter. I considered several modes of transportation: a submarine ("Yellow Submarine"), the bus (the *Magical Mystery Tour* bus), the train (*A Hard Day's Night* opening scene), and even a rocket before deciding on the train. A train—especially a bullet train—embodies the speed at which The Beatles were traveling. Many people are on board the train with different roles, including many passengers. Importantly, I see their breakup as a derailment from the tracks on which they were bound.

The Right People

The Beatles didn't emerge fully formed; they evolved through a deliberate process of finding the right people over time. John had already formed the band The Quarrymen. On July 6, 1957, they performed at

St. Peter's Church fete in Woolton, near Liverpool—a moment that would prove pivotal in music history.

In the audience that day was a fifteen-year-old named Paul McCartney. After the show, a mutual friend, Ivan Vaughan, introduced Paul to John. They moved indoors to the auditorium, where Paul auditioned for John.

Paul borrowed John's guitar, but being left-handed, he turned it upside down and played the Eddie Cochran tune "Twenty Flight Rock" and a couple of other rock and roll songs. Then, as if that weren't impressive enough, he went over to the piano and played a medley of Little Richard songs on the piano. John was duly impressed but didn't immediately invite Paul to join the band. If he brought Paul into the group, he would be bringing in someone who could easily rival him to be the front man.

From Paul's perspective, seeing John perform was a revelation of what could be and a calling to contribute his immense talent to the group. He was impressed when The Quarrymen played "Come Go with Me," which was "fresh off the boat" from America. Years later, Paul reflected, "He was singing something like 'Come, come, come, come, go with me, down to the penitentiary.' Those are definitely not the words, but he must have pulled that from Lead Belly or somebody else. I thought that was pretty ingenious of him."[3] John's ad-libbed lyrics made the song more rebellious and gave it an edge that Paul thought was brilliant.

Ultimately, John decided to do what would be best for the band. Paul's talent was undeniable, so a few weeks later, John invited him to join. Thus began the most successful band and songwriting partnership in history.

When Paul joined The Quarrymen, he suggested another addition: his young friend George, who rode the same school bus and was rarely seen without his guitar. John gave him an audition but was reluctant to invite him to join because of George's youth (he was only fourteen). George's second audition took place during a bus ride across Liverpool, where his guitar-playing impressed John enough to overcome his concerns about George's age.

Three Cool Cats

A dynamic rarely discussed in Beatles history is that John, Paul, and George were in a band together for nearly five years before Ringo joined. Those three formed a bond in their formative years that drove their path to excellence. When Ringo did join, he fit in so seamlessly that it is hard to believe that he was such a late addition to the band.

All the time they spent in the Liverpool and Hamburg clubs paying their dues did not include Ringo. He literally joined the band on the cusp of their fame. This created a dynamic on stage among the three of them that could only be developed over thousands of hours of practice.

One of the songs they played in the early days called "Three Cool Cats" exemplifies how I imagine the three of them were hamming it up on stage in Liverpool and Hamburg. This playful song, with George singing lead, was a vehicle for flirting with the girls and developing rapport with the audience. When listening to the song, the timing and charisma shine through.

The Early Beatles Lineup

By 1960, the group—now called The Beatles—consisted of John Lennon, Paul McCartney, George Harrison, Stuart Sutcliffe, and Pete Best. Sutcliffe was John's best friend from art school, a talented artist who had recently won a prize in an art show. John convinced him to use his winnings to buy a bass guitar, as the band needed a bassist. Sutcliffe had no passion for playing bass and wasn't particularly skilled at it, but he agreed so he could experience life in a rock band and for the chance to hang out with his friends. He eventually left the band in August 1961 and, as noted in chapter 2, tragically died of a brain hemorrhage in April 1962.

Pete Best joined when The Beatles needed a drummer for their first Hamburg gig. His mother, Mona Best, owned the Casbah Coffee Club, a popular music venue where they frequently performed. She agreed to buy him a drum kit if The Beatles would accept him into the band as their drummer. While he was the same age as the others, he wasn't a close friend, and his musical abilities would eventually come into question.

Before the fateful day that The Beatles replaced Pete Best with Ringo, they were already filling out other crucial members of the team. The Beatles' success wasn't solely due to the four band members. Several other people played crucial roles in their growth and success. The two most important "right people"—especially in their early success—were manager Brian Epstein and producer George Martin.

The Supporting Cast: Finding the Right Manager

Brian Epstein discovered The Beatles in November 1961, when they were performing at the Cavern Club. As manager of his family's record store (NEMS), he was well connected in the British music scene. Here's what he said about his first time hearing them: "I was immediately struck by their music, their beat, and their sense of humor on stage. And even afterwards when I met them, I was struck again by their personal charm."[4]

He was so impressed by their talent and charisma, he offered to become their manager, and they accepted. Brian Epstein transformed The Beatles from a rough-edged local band into a professional outfit. He insisted on matching suits instead of leather jackets, eliminated their smoking and eating on stage, and added the synchronized bow at the end of each song. Most importantly, he brought organization and structure to their career.

Mark Lewisohn described this transformation that occurred after Brian Epstein became their manager: "They returned [from Hamburg] to organization, order, and promise . . . he handed each Beatle a large manila envelope . . . these contained the latest *Mersey Beat* (reporting news of their EMI contract) and two typed sheets listing line-by-line their bookings for the next forty days and nights. Weekly bulletins would follow with fuller details and instructions."[5]

Brian Epstein's persistence was crucial in securing their recording contract. After being rejected by Decca Records in January 1962 (one of the most infamous missteps in the history of the music business), he continued approaching record companies until he arranged an audition with EMI, who delegated the audition to its subsidiary Parlophone and young producer George Martin in June 1962.

The Right Producer: George Martin

In George Martin, The Beatles found the perfect producer for their talents. He was classically trained and older than the band members but not so old that he couldn't relate to them (he was in his mid-thirties when they met). George Martin's experience included extensive work on comedy records and experimental sound projects. This combination gave him both technical expertise and openness to innovation—exactly what The Beatles needed.

George Martin's expertise complemented The Beatles' raw creativity. He could translate their ideas into arrangements, suggest instrumental additions, and guide their experimentation in productive directions. In addition, his piano-playing can be heard on several early Beatles recordings. The combination of their innovative spirit and his technical knowledge created a partnership that redefined popular music.

Perhaps most important was George Martin's personality, which blended well with the lads from Liverpool. He was diligent, loyal, patient, a good listener, and he had a sense of humor. All of these traits were needed to navigate the diverse personalities in the band.

The Critical Decision: Finding the Right Drummer

In June 1962, The Beatles auditioned for producer George Martin at EMI's Parlophone label. Though he was intrigued by their potential, he had concerns about Pete Best's drumming, which was unsteady and sometimes problematic. George Martin suggested using a session drummer for recordings—a common practice at the time but a blow to the band's identity as a self-contained unit.

This suggestion provided John, Paul, and George with the excuse they needed to address a long-standing issue. They decided to replace Pete Best with Ringo, widely regarded as the best drummer in Liverpool. Ringo was then playing with Rory Storm and the Hurricanes. The Beatles knew Ringo well from their time performing in Hamburg, where both bands frequented.

Before joining The Beatles, Ringo would occasionally fill in for Pete Best when he was not available. Recalling the first time Ringo played with them, Paul shared a telling memory, "I remember just glancing at the other two guys, and we all had a look in our eyes. It was one of those magical moments."[6]

This decision was painful but necessary for achieving their goals. Unable to deliver the difficult news themselves, John, Paul, and George asked their manager, Brian Epstein, to inform Pete of his dismissal. While their handling of the situation was less than ideal, their decision to prioritize the band's musical quality over personal comfort was crucial to their subsequent success.

The move paid immediate dividends. When they recorded with Ringo on September 4, 1962, his drumming was noticeably superior to Best's. However, George Martin, still concerned based on their previous session, had hired session drummer Andy White as a backup. This led to two versions of "Love Me Do"—one with Andy White on drums and Ringo on tambourine (released as the single) and one with Ringo on drums (included on their first album).

This incident—having a professional drummer replace their chosen bandmate—frustrated the lads but demonstrated their growing determination to control their artistic identity. While they reluctantly accepted George Martin's decision for that session, they remained committed to being a self-contained unit that wrote and performed their own music, which was a revolutionary concept at that time.

The Right Seats: Clearly Defined Roles and Responsibilities

For a team to function at its highest level, each member must understand their role and how it contributes to collective success. The Beatles exemplified this principle, with each member fulfilling a clearly defined function within the group.

How Personalities Helped Define the Roles

London writer June Harris captured the band's dynamic: "George was very sweet and kind, a nice young man, Ringo didn't say much, Paul was sensible and taking things in his stride, and John just got on with it like 'I know where I'm going and what I want to do with this group.' The others were deferential to him. He was the leader and had a sense of direction for all of them, and when he had something to say he said it—and why not?"[7]

This dynamic established both hierarchy and specialization within the group.

John was the visionary leader. He played rhythm guitar, sang lead vocals, occasionally played harmonica, and wrote or cowrote many of their songs. His personality was visionary, creative, passionate, quick-witted, thoughtful, and social. He provided the driving force behind the band's ambition and identity.

Paul was more of a leader in terms of musical direction. He played bass guitar, sang lead vocals, occasionally played keyboard, and wrote or cowrote many of their songs. His personality was driven, perfectionistic, creative, professional, cordial, and outgoing. He brought polish and precision to their music.

George was the lead guitarist, background vocalist, occasional lead vocalist, and occasional songwriter. His personality was introverted, funny, spiritual, kind, flexible, and confident. He provided a grounding influence and introduced new musical elements, particularly from Eastern traditions.

Ringo played drums and percussion and occasionally sang. His personality was steady, reliable, friendly, peaceable, loyal, and down-to-earth. He provided the solid rhythmic foundation that anchored their music and a calming presence that helped balance stronger personalities.

Clearly Defined Roles in Action

The Beatles' path to the top was built on a foundation of clearly defined roles that remained remarkably consistent during their early years. Unlike bands that constantly shifted responsibilities, The Beatles established and maintained specific functions that allowed each member to develop mastery in their field.

In the formative years through June 1966, these roles were not fluid or interchangeable but deliberately specialized. John was firmly established as the band's leader and primary rhythm guitarist. His distinctive voice—capable of tender ballads like "This Boy" and raw rockers like "Twist and Shout"—gave the band its edge. John also handled most of the harmonica parts that distinguished early Beatles recordings like "Love Me Do" and "I Should Have Known Better."

Paul's role as bassist came about not by choice but by necessity after Stuart Sutcliffe left the band. Though initially reluctant, Paul embraced the role and transformed it, creating melodic bass lines that went far beyond the typical root-note playing of early rock bassists. His clear, pitch-perfect vocals provided the perfect counterpoint to John's rougher sound.

George maintained his position as lead guitarist throughout this period, developing a distinctive style that combined rockabilly, country-western, and rhythm and blues. Though rarely stepping into the spotlight as a lead vocalist during these early years, when he did—on songs like "Do You Want to Know a Secret" and "I'm Happy Just to Dance with You"—his voice offered yet another dimension to The Beatles' sound.

Ringo's steady, distinctive drumming style became a signature element of The Beatles' recordings. Unlike many rock drummers of the era who played on top of the beat to drive the song forward, Ringo often played slightly behind the beat, creating the relaxed, confident groove that defined classics like "She Loves You" and "I Feel Fine." His limited but charming vocal contributions on songs like "I Wanna Be Your Man" and "Act Naturally" added yet another color to their palette.

The stability of these roles was reinforced by The Beatles' grueling schedule. Between touring, recording, promotional appearances, and filmmaking, they simply didn't have the luxury to experiment with their established formula. The machine was working brilliantly, and they stuck to what worked.

A snapshot of where they stood on June 1, 1966, tells the story. *Rubber Soul* was their current album. They had just released the double-sided single "Paperback Writer"/"Rain" and they were busy recording their next album, *Revolver*. At this point, they had released an astonishing 101 songs and six albums in just three and a half years. They had achieved seventeen number one hits and starred in two commercially successful films, all while maintaining a relentless performance schedule.

The writing credits at this point reflected their established roles as well. John had written thirty-one songs, Paul had written twenty, and they had cowritten twenty. George contributed just four songs, while the remaining twenty-six were covers (songs written by others but recorded by The Beatles). This division—with John and Paul handling the bulk of the songwriting—remained consistent throughout this early period.

It's worth noting that I simplified the songwriting attribution for clarity. I arbitrarily determined if a song was at least 80 percent written by one, I gave him full credit; if it was less than 80 percent, I considered it cowritten.

In a lesson that applies to any team or organization, these clearly defined roles laid the foundation for their extraordinary success. By knowing exactly what was expected of them, each Beatle could focus on perfecting their contribution rather than competing for territory. The stability of these roles created the reliable structure that enabled their creative explosion—a lesson for any team seeking enduring excellence.

John Wooden's Lessons on Clearly Defined Roles

John Wooden, often considered the greatest college basketball coach of all time, provides an excellent case study in the importance of clearly defined roles for team success. In his book *Wooden on Leadership: How to Create a Winning Organization*, Wooden emphasizes how critical it was for each player to understand and embrace their specific role within the team.[8]

One of Wooden's most significant strategic shifts came after the 1961–1962 season at UCLA, which ultimately led to ten NCAA championships. As he explained, "Starting in 1962–1963, my new policy was to go primarily with seven main players—virtually, seven starters—in both practice and games. My previous goal of doling out playing time in a democratic manner was discarded. I changed a fundamental policy for how I did things." However, he made sure to clearly communicate to every player what their roles would be. "I didn't intend to ignore the eighth to twelfth players, obviously, but I let them know very clearly what their roles in the group would be and for what purpose. More important, I tried very hard to make them understand the great value of their role and how it would contribute to the overall welfare of the team."[9] This clarity of purpose was essential to his team's remarkable success.

This philosophy has direct parallels to The Beatles' early success. Just as Wooden insisted that each player accept their specific role for the betterment of the team, The Beatles maintained clear divisions of responsibility during their formative years.

Personal Reflection: Coach Ed Pepple

Ed Pepple is the winningest basketball coach in Washington state history, with 952 wins. Most of his coaching career was spent at Mercer Island High School, where his teams won twenty-three league championships and four state championships. In addition, his teams placed second in state four times, third in state four times, and fourth in state three times. He was inducted into both the Washington State Coach's Hall of Fame and the national High School Basketball Hall of Fame. In short, Ed Pepple knew a thing or two about achieving excellence.

From 1984 to 1991, I was an assistant coach on Coach Pepple's staff. I learned a lot about enduring excellence and team-building from him. The Fab Four Pillars of Impact that were the foundation of The Beatles' success were the same principles Coach Pepple instilled in his teams. Most notable was his ability to get the right people on the "train" and put them in the right seats.

The Islanders of Mercer Island won the state championship in 1985, after a tough loss in the 1984 state championship game. At one point in the 1985 season, *USA Today* ranked the team number one in the entire country.

The 1984–85 season started with three days of tryouts. Since we returned the nucleus of a team that finished second in state, competition was fierce—not so much for the top spots, but for the eleventh and twelfth roster spots. Choosing the twelfth player proved to be particularly difficult. It came down to two seniors, both of whom were great guys and would have played for most other teams in our state. One was probably the better player but was a shooting guard, and the team was loaded at shooting guard. The other was a likable, hard-working point guard name Jeff Thompson, who made up for a lack of athleticism with court savvy. Because of our lack of depth at point guard, we went with Jeff.

As we prepared for the 1984–85 season, Quin Snyder was being recruited heavily by Duke University. Quin would go on to be the starting point guard for Duke. He seemed like the obvious choice to move over from shooting guard to point guard. The coaches were concerned, however, about moving one of the state's leading scorers to a new position. Quin excelled at the shooting guard role. He had a scorer's mentality, whereas a point guard in Coach Pepple's system was more of a distributor, so it wasn't a natural fit.

We started the season with Quin as the point guard. As we had feared, his scoring suffered and his shooting percentage slumped. Even though we were winning games, the team was not flowing like it should. The issue came to a head at an invitational tournament in Las Vegas over Christmas break. In the semifinals of the tourney, we put our first-in-the-nation ranking up against Flint Hill of Oakton, Virginia. We suffered our only loss of the season, 60–56. Quin was trying to be the pass-first point guard called for in Coach Pepple's system. When we needed him to be a scorer down the stretch, he hesitated—torn between setting up others or taking it himself.

After the game, Coach Pepple likely knew the change he wanted to make when he asked for my input. I was convinced we needed to move Quin back to shooting guard but didn't have a viable solution at point guard. The starting shooting guard was a great shooter but not a primary ball handler, so that bumped him out of the equation. When Coach Pepple suggested we make Jeff Thompson (the one who just barely made the team) the starting point guard, I was taken aback. Coach Pepple saw a potential for chemistry that I had missed.

Jeff did for the team what Ringo did for The Beatles. He had a steady, calming influence on the court. He was exactly what this team needed: a solid ball handler and determined defender who got the ball in the hands of the stars when and where they needed it. Jeff was inserted into the starting lineup and the team never lost another game.

Learning from The Beatles: The Right People Principle

The Beatles' story offers several key lessons about finding the right people and putting them in the right roles:

- **Talent recognition requires both evaluation and vision.** John saw not only Paul's current abilities but his potential to elevate the entire group. Similarly, Coach Pepple recognized in Jeff Thompson qualities that weren't immediately obvious but would prove crucial to team chemistry.

- **Difficult personnel decisions are sometimes necessary.** Replacing Pete Best with Ringo was painful but essential for The Beatles' musical development. In business and sports, similar difficult decisions often mark the transition from good to great.

- **The right role may not be the initially desired role.** Paul didn't want to play bass but eventually redefined what a rock bassist could be. Quin Snyder had all the skills to be a great point guard, but this team needed him to be a scorer. He went on to be the starting point guard for the Duke Blue Devils, but that was not the role his high school team needed him to play.

- **Supporting roles are as crucial as starring ones.** Ringo's steady, ego-free drumming provided the foundation that allowed the others to shine. Jeff Thompson's unselfish play elevated the entire team. Excellence requires recognition that every role, however seemingly minor, contributes to team chemistry and ultimately to overall success.

- **The right team extends beyond the core group.** Brian Epstein and George Martin were critical to The Beatles' success. Building excellence often means finding the right supporters, advisers, and specialists who complement the core team's abilities.

- **Well-defined roles and responsibilities provide stability.** In a similar way to John Wooden's UCLA Bruins basketball teams, The Beatles had clearly defined roles—especially in the beginning.

At this crucial early stage when they became the most popular band in the world, each of them knew what was expected of them. This allowed them to focus on perfecting their role, a key driver to their enduring excellence.

- **Chemistry often trumps individual capability.** The Beatles weren't necessarily the most technically proficient musicians individually, but their chemistry created something greater than the sum of their parts. Similarly, Jeff Thompson wasn't the most talented player on the Mercer Island team, but his presence created the right chemistry for collective success.

Conclusion: Excellence Begins with People

The train provides a powerful framework for understanding the first pillar of excellence. Before vision, before strategy, before execution comes the fundamental question: Do we have the right people on the train, the wrong people off the train, and the right people in the right seats?

The Beatles answered this question definitively through their personnel decisions. They found four members whose talents and personalities created perfect chemistry. They secured a manager who believed in them and provided structure. They partnered with a producer who understood their ambitions and had the skills to help realize them.

These decisions—about who was on the train and where they sat—created the foundation for everything that followed. Without John's leadership, Paul's perfectionism, George's spiritual depth, Ringo's steadiness, Brian Epstein's organization, and George Martin's expertise, The Beatles phenomenon would have certainly looked different and likely would not have redefined excellence in popular music.

As we explore the remaining pillars of impact, remember that they all rest on this foundation. A compelling vision, strong team spirit, and openness to possibility all matter enormously—but they can only flourish when the right people are in the right roles, working together toward something extraordinary.

Applying the Lessons of Chapter 3

Have you ever been part of a team that looked great on paper but somehow didn't click? Or experienced the magic when a seemingly unlikely combination of people created something extraordinary? The difference often comes down to having the right people in the right seats.

When sixteen-year-old John first encountered fifteen-year-old Paul at the St. Peter's Church fete in 1957, he faced a critical decision. Paul had just impressed him with both guitar-playing and piano skills, demonstrating talent that could potentially overshadow John's own. Should he invite this potential rival into his band?

John's decision to welcome Paul's talent rather than feel threatened by it exemplifies the first principle of building excellence: Talent recognition requires both evaluation and vision.

Coach Ed Pepple at Mercer Island High School faced a pivotal moment during the 1984–85 basketball season. After a disappointing loss in a Las Vegas tournament, he needed to reconsider how his team's extraordinary talent was being utilized. The team was stacked with exceptional players, including two returning all-state players—but something wasn't clicking.

When Coach John Wooden simplified the rotation and communicated specific roles for the players, they went on to win ten NCAA championships.

These stories illustrate four key principles for assembling extraordinary teams:

- **Embrace top talent:** When John decided to invite Paul into the band, he set ego aside for the good of the whole. When they added George, and then Ringo, it was to make the band stronger.

- **Find your Ringo:** The Beatles later replaced Pete Best with Ringo despite personal discomfort. When they did, everything gelled. Similarly, when Coach Pepple inserted Jeff Thompson—who had barely made the team—into the starting lineup, the team reached its potential.

- **Clearly define the roles:** As The Beatles climbed to the top of pop music, each of them had clearly defined roles. This allowed them to perfect their craft. Coach Wooden discovered the value of this principle when he changed to a seven-man rotation with clearly defined roles that were well communicated.

- **Extend the team beyond the core group:** Brian Epstein and George Martin fulfilled critical supporting roles for The Beatles, similar to the coaches and critical role players for the UCLA Bruins and the Mercer Island Islanders.

TEAM-BUILDING EXERCISE:
FIND YOUR INNER BEATLE

Exercise Instructions: Divide into small groups of three to five people.

Part 1: The Mirror Moment
(Individual reflection—five minutes)

Each team member privately considers which Beatle they most resemble in their work approach. Use these personality snapshots to find your right seat on the train:

John—the Visionary Leader

- Work style: Big-picture thinker who challenges the status quo
- Strengths: Generates bold ideas, drives ambition, questions everything
- At their best: When inspiring others toward breakthrough thinking
- Challenge area: Can be impatient with details and traditional approaches

Paul—the Producer

- Work style: Detail-oriented perfectionist who makes things happen
- Strengths: Sees the whole picture, polishes ideas into reality, maintains quality standards, drives execution
- At their best: When turning their or others' vision into concrete deliverables
- Challenge area: Can overwhelm others with their intensity and high standards

George—the Specialist

- Work style: Deep expertise with a calm, grounding presence
- Strengths: Brings specialized knowledge, introduces fresh perspectives, stays centered under pressure
- At their best: When providing thoughtful input and innovative solutions

- Challenge area: Not speaking up in a healthy way may build resentment

Ringo—the Steady Foundation

- Work style: Reliable team player who keeps everyone connected
- Strengths: Creates stability, mediates conflicts, supports others' success
- At their best: When providing the consistent backbone that lets others shine
- Challenge area: May avoid conflict for the sake of group harmony

Part 2: The Reveal (Group sharing—twenty minutes)

Round 1: Self-Declaration (ten minutes)

- Each person shares which Beatle they identify with and explains why.
- Give specific work examples: "I'm like George because I tend to quietly research solutions while others are debating, then offer a completely different approach that nobody saw coming."
- No interruptions during individual sharing—just listen and absorb.

Round 2: The Feedback Loop (ten minutes)

- After everyone has shared, the group provides supportive feedback.
- Focus on affirmation: "Yes, I totally see that!" or "That makes perfect sense because . . ."
- Gentle adjustments: "I hear the George in you, but I also see some Paul when you're driving our project deadlines."
- Missing pieces: "Have you considered that you might also have some Ringo qualities when you help us stay focused during heated discussions?"

Part 3: The Harmony Check
(Group analysis—fifteen minutes)

Now look at your team's composition.

Questions to Explore

- Do we have all four "Beatles" represented, or are we missing a crucial seat on our train?
- Are we overweighted in one area? (Three Johns and no Ringo might create chaos!)
- Who naturally collaborates well together? (Paul and John's creative tension? George and Ringo's steady partnership?)
- What does this tell us about how we should structure our work and decision-making?

Part 4: Action Planning (ten minutes)

Creating "Harmony" with the Team

- John types: How can we better channel your big ideas without overwhelming the detail-oriented folks?

- Paul types: How can we harness your drive for excellence while keeping the team energized, not exhausted?

- George types: How can we make sure your expertise gets heard and valued in our regular discussions?

- Ringo types: How can we recognize and celebrate the stability you provide, especially during high-stress periods?

Team commitment: Each person shares one specific way they'll adjust their approach based on today's insights.

CHAPTER 3 PLAYLIST

RIGHT PEOPLE, RIGHT SEATS

This playlist demonstrates how quickly The Beatles established their core identity once they had the right people in the right seats— John, Paul, George, and Ringo each bringing their unique talents to create something greater than the sum of its parts.

1. **"Three Cool Cats"**—Recorded during their Decca audition, this Coasters cover showcases the playful dynamic between John, Paul, and George before Ringo joined. George sings lead, while the John and Paul backing vocals became a vehicle for flirting with girls in the audience during their Hamburg and Liverpool performances, demonstrating their growing stage presence and charismatic interplay.

2. **"Love Me Do"**—Their first official single showcases the original lineup finding their footing, with its simple structure and

memorable harmonica hook from John. The Beatles recorded three versions of this song with three different drummers.

3. **"How Do You Do It"**—Though never officially released by The Beatles (Gerry and the Pacemakers later had a hit with it), this George Martin–suggested cover demonstrates their conviction to write their own material instead of just performing others' songs.

4. **"Please Please Me"**—Their first number one hit in Britain reveals the band hitting their stride with more complex harmonies and arrangements, prompting producer George Martin to say, "Gentlemen, you've just recorded your first number one record."[10] Notice how Paul stays on a single high note during the harmonies—an early example of their innovative vocal approach.

5. **"I Saw Her Standing There"**—This energetic opener to their debut album, written primarily by Paul, with its "One, two, three, FOUR!" count-in captures the raw energy and chemistry of their live performances that made them legends in Liverpool and Hamburg.

6. **"Do You Want to Know a Secret"**—One of George's first lead vocals, showing how the group developed individual roles while maintaining their unified sound. Written by John and inspired by a line in *Snow White*.

7. **"Baby It's You"**—This Shirelles cover demonstrates how The Beatles could take existing material and transform it through their unique chemistry and arrangements, with John's emotive lead vocal showcasing his versatility. It's always been one of my favorites.

8. **"It Won't Be Long"**—The opening track from their second album features those brilliant call-and-response "yeah" vocals between John and Paul, demonstrating how they were perfecting their signature sound through perfect teamwork.

9. **"All I've Got to Do"**—This understated Lennon composition shows their growing sophistication, blending American R&B influences with their own distinctive sound. The intimate vocal performance and subtle backing demonstrate how their roles were becoming more defined.

10. **"Thank You, Girl"**—This B-side to "From Me to You" showcases the Beatles' tight vocal harmonies and compact songwriting, with John and Paul trading lead vocals and sharing harmonies that demonstrate their perfect vocal chemistry.

CHAPTER 4

PILLAR TWO — CATALYTIC VISION

The second pillar of impact is catalytic vision, one so compelling that it drives action and inspires commitment. To truly understand what makes a vision "catalytic," let's begin by defining this often-overlooked concept.

Defining *Catalytic*

In chemistry, a *catalyst* is a substance that increases the rate of chemical reaction without itself being consumed. It provides the energy that makes something happen. Similarly, catalytic vision provides the energy that propels a team forward; it serves as the impetus that drives momentum.

A catalytic vision is more than just "compelling." It's transformative. It doesn't merely suggest action—it demands it. Without it, you wouldn't have the combustion needed to move an organization forward. When a vision is truly catalytic, it creates energy rather than consuming it. It brings clarity to decisions and ignites passion in those who embrace it.

The Beatles' vision was twofold: first, to be the biggest band in the world, and second, to redefine the pop music business so that one band could do it all: write the music, sing the songs, and play the instruments. No one could accuse them of not aiming high enough!

First Part of the Vision: "Toppermost of the Poppermost"

The Beatles possessed a catalytic vision from their earliest days. Their ambition wasn't modest. They wanted to be the biggest band in the world. When spirits flagged during their formative years, John would rally the group with a chant that became their mantra: "Where are we going, fellers?" The others would respond: "To the top, Johnny!" And then: "Where's that, fellers?" "To the toppermost of the poppermost, Johnny!"[1]

This wasn't empty bravado. As John later reflected: "We knew we could make it. We simply wanted to be the biggest. We dreamed of being the British Elvis Presley and we believed it."[2] This vision catalyzed their actions and sustained them through the grueling years playing in Hamburg, Germany, where they would perform for hours on end, seven nights a week.

Second Part of the Vision: The Beatles' Way

Their vision wasn't just to be successful musicians; it was revolutionary. They aimed to redefine what a musical group could be by writing their own songs and playing their own instruments. This might seem obvious today, but in the early 1960s, the music industry operated differently.

The industry clung to a system where people stayed in their lane.

Songwriters pitched their songs to publishers. Publishers, in turn, would pitch the songs to record companies' artists-and-repertoire ("A&R") executives who managed the talent. The A&R executive would record the song with one of his/her artists. A&R executives wielded the power, and performers simply performed what they were told. The singer was often the star and was paired with studio musicians to record the songs.

John, Paul, George, and Ringo had the audacity to believe they could do it all. They wrote their own material, they played their own instruments, and they sang their own songs. They were determined not to be anyone's musical puppets. Another revolutionary aspect of their catalytic vision was creating a new paradigm for popular music, one where the star isn't the individual; the star is the band itself. In George's words in an interview with Brian Matthew for *Live at the BBC*, "I think the bad thing about some groups is, you know, the lead guitarist likes to be the star or the drummer likes to be the star and also the singer out there in the front, you know, who is the star of the group and that's all wrong. I think with us we try, and everybody is a bit of, you know, one whole."[3]

Personal Reflection: Absher Construction

I experienced the power of catalytic vision firsthand at Absher Construction Company. Absher Construction was founded in 1940 by my grandfather, Barney Absher. In the late '50s, my dad, Tom Sr., Uncle Jim, and family friend Clark Helle Sr. took over management and ownership of the company. They grew the company from a small remodeling company into a midsize general contractor specializing in public projects—especially K–12 schools.

In the early '90s a third generation took over: My brother, Tom Jr., brother-in-law Brad, and I were joined by Greg Helle and Clark Helle Jr. Only 12 percent of family businesses survive to a third generation, so we were already beating the odds. Add to this that we were now going into a second generation of a two-family business, so our odds of success were even lower.

When we took over in the early '90s, we had twelve active construction projects. Eleven of those twelve projects were schools. We knew we wanted to do more than build schools, so we focused on other markets in the construction industry, while maintaining our expertise in school construction. This was working well, but we were not excelling. By the mid to late '90s, we were maintaining but not experiencing the growth I knew we could achieve.

My brother and I are both avid readers of books on leadership and team-building. We both read the book *Built to Last* by Jim Collins and Jerry Porras. Collins and Porras define a company's Core Ideology as its Core Purpose and its Core Values.[4] We realized after reading the book that we could not articulate our company's core purpose. And if we couldn't do that, we certainly couldn't expect the rest of our team to know it.

This proved to be an inflection point for our company. We were managing fine day-to-day, but we were missing something. The five owners of the company went away for a retreat, relying primarily on the insights from *Built to Last* to discover and articulate our core ideology. That retreat was the moment at which we aligned behind a single purpose, allowing the company to grow to new heights.

In our search to "discover" and articulate our core purpose, we went back to the history of the company. Why did Grandpa Barney start the company? He did not start the company with the ambition of becoming the biggest general contractor in the country; he started it in response to the needs of others. He put his talents to work to serve his neighbors and his community.

By shifting the focus from grinding it out day-to-day to make a buck, we hit upon the core purpose that drove us throughout our careers. To some it may seem a bit trivial, but it was our driving force. Our core purpose was *to create and build community with vision and compassion*. We shifted our focus to serving our community, and that resonated with us.

Prior to this we had ten company values, a smorgasbord of things we believed. Collins and Porras convinced us that for values to be "core," there should only be three to five. We landed on four:

1. **We Care About People**

   When we say *people*, we mean all people. We honor and respect the intrinsic value of each individual. We foster an environment that is inclusive. We promote initiative, creativity, innovation, and the sharing of ideas. We provide opportunity for personal growth and encourage each person to discover his or her purpose in life.

2. **Servant Leadership**

   We are building community leaders. We embrace a model of leadership called *servant leadership* within the industry and the community. A servant leader is one who

   - is willing to sacrifice for the good of others
   - cherishes teamwork and fellowship
   - displays empathy, patience, and kindness
   - strives for excellence in customer service
   - seeks to encourage and motivate
   - is positive and optimistic
   - communicates easily at all levels
   - provides and encourages feedback
   - is a spokesperson and diplomat

- ◦ is able to see the big picture

- ◦ seeks improvement in self and others

- ◦ emulates the company values

- ◦ embraces the company purpose

3. **Doing Things Right**

   Upon founding Absher Construction Company in 1940, R. L. Absher instilled a simple credo: "If you're going to do a job, do it right." This does not just mean building with top quality but doing it in a certain way; it means doing it safely with respect for the environment and surrounding community. And it means conducting business in a certain way; it means acting with modesty, humility, honesty, integrity, and class.

4. **Doing Right Things**

   We do what is ethical, appropriate, and just. We are charitable in the community. We value the individual and the family. We develop leaders for our company and the community. We plan for our future while respecting our past. We do not lose sight of the important for the sake of the urgent.

This vision—our core purpose and values—shifted our focus from simply making money to something greater; for us, it was catalytic. Our mission became clear—we would pursue projects significant to our community rather than just those solely to generate profit. This vision fundamentally changed how we approached our work and inspired all of us to go "all in."

I am reminded of a classic parable I shared with our team to explain the change in our perspective and commitment that resulted from our retreat.

On a foggy autumn day nearly eight hundred years ago, a traveler happened upon a large group of workers adjacent to the River Avon. Despite being tardy for an important rendezvous, curiosity convinced the traveler that he should inquire about their work. With a slight detour, he moved toward the first of the three tradesmen and said, "My dear fellow, what is it that you are doing?" The man continued his work and grumbled, "I am cutting stones." Realizing that the mason did not wish to engage in a conversation, the traveler moved toward the second of the three and repeated the question. To the traveler's delight, this time the man stopped his work, ever so briefly, and stated that he was a stonecutter. He then added, "I came to Salisbury from the north to work, but as soon as I earn ten quid, I will return home." The traveler thanked the second mason, wished him a safe journey home, and began to head to the third of the trio.

When he reached the third worker, he once again asked the original question. This time the worker paused, glanced at the traveler until they made eye contact, and then looked skyward, drawing the traveler's eyes upward. The third mason replied, "I am a mason, and I am building a cathedral." He continued, "I have journeyed many miles to be part of the team that is constructing this magnificent cathedral."

From the moment of our retreat onward, we were no longer "cutting stones"; we were part of a team that was building a "magnificent cathedral."

Organizations that lack a catalytic vision often struggle to gain momentum. Without that compelling North Star, team members lose focus, commitment wavers, and progress stalls. But with a catalytic vision that's broken down into achievable milestones, even ordinary individuals can achieve extraordinary results.

The Importance of Interim Goals

What made The Beatles' catalytic vision particularly effective was how they broke it down into a series of manageable goals. As Lewisohn recounts: "They had 'specific little aims, a series of goals: to get a record made, to get a number one, etc.'"[5]

The Beatles understood that reaching "the toppermost of the poppermost" required setting and achieving a series of smaller goals along the way. They refused to tour America until they had a number one hit there, knowing that many British acts had flopped when trying to break into the American market. They recognized that success required methodical planning and execution, not just raw talent.

One by one, The Beatles accomplished Lennon's "specific little aims": touring with others, a recording contract, a number one song in England, headlining their own tour, a number one song in America. These were all interim steps on their way to the top.

PERSONAL REFLECTION: THE DAD'S INTERIM GOALS

The first time I saw Chevy Chase's *Vacation*, I experienced déjà vu. It was the summer of 1969, but the part of Clark Griswold was played by my dad, Tom Absher Sr. Affectionately called "The Dad," he was a master at managing a big family (six kids). This was important as he prepared us for a long road trip from Sumner, Washington, to Disneyland.

Each of the six kids were given assigned seats in our Country Squire Station Wagon (yes, the same kind of car the Griswolds had in the movie). Dad and Mom were in the front; Debbie, Denise, and Tom (the three oldest) were in the back seat; and Beth, Lisa, and I were in the "way back," as The Dad called it.

In Jim Collins's lingo, we had a BHAG (big hairy audacious goal)[6] for our *Vacation*, which was Disneyland, but it was several days' drive from our starting point. We were excited about two stops along the way: visiting the Ross cousins in Millbrae, California, and the Granholm cousins in Thousand Oaks, California. Other than that, it seemed like a long, boring drive for my siblings and me.

Six kids between the ages of four and fifteen cramped in close quarters was not a recipe for a stress-free drive, and the two cousin stops were far away. So, he, The Dad, masterfully got us to focus on interim goals, consistently building excitement for the next stop on our road trip.

While I don't remember all of them, a few are etched in my mind forever. As we crossed the Oregon border into California, The Dad began talking up the Nut Tree Inn in Vacaville. "Kids, the Nut Tree Inn is world famous." "They have a gift shop and arcade games." "We'll stop for lunch there—great restaurant!" "Oh, and try the fruit. There is nothing better than fresh fruit in California." When we got there, we hurried to the arcade games, and when we were seated for lunch, several of us ordered fresh fruit plates and The Dad was absolutely right—delicious!

Somewhere between San Francisco and Los Angeles sat the second-biggest destination of the trip (behind only Disneyland)—Pea Soup Andersen's restaurant and gift shop. Of all the things The Dad pulled off, this was the greatest. We all hated split pea soup (what kid doesn't?), but somehow, he talked it up so much that we all eagerly anticipated eating split pea soup. He told us it is so good that "you'll think you'd died and gone to heaven." And, to my surprise, it was very good! Once again, he kept us focused on that interim goal. By the time we arrived, we were so hungry and so eager with anticipation, we loved it.

As we reflected on that *Vacation* in later years, my siblings and I began to realize that Dad embellished the magnitude of those stops quite a bit. In fact, I began to wonder if Dad knew anything about them, other than they were convenient stops along the way. Regardless, by setting those interim goals, he kept us focused and excited about the next leg of the journey—all the while getting closer to our ultimate goal.

After the long road trip south, we finally pulled into our motel near Disneyland. The kids stayed in the car as Mom and Dad went to check us in. There was some problem with the reservation or the motel; we could see it in our parents' frustration. About ten minutes later, they came back, and The Dad told us, "Guess what, we found a better place to stay. It's a space-age motel called The Inn of Tomorrow." Sure enough, when we got there, we were so enthralled by the geodesic dome adjacent to the swimming pool we didn't even notice that it was a low-budget motel.

Years later, when I started working with my dad, I realized he used many of these same techniques with his team at work. He was a master at getting people to focus on interim goals. For many, a BHAG seems unattainable or too far into the future to matter. While my dad wasn't big on long-term goals, he masterfully kept the team (or family) focused on near-term, interim goals. What got buy-in from his team (and family) was his enthusiasm, the import he placed on the goals, and how he kept those goals understandable and within reach.

In a similar way, John kept his bandmates focused on smaller, interim goals on the way to their ultimate vision of being the biggest band in the world. And one by one, they achieved those goals.

10,000 HOURS

The Beatles' catalytic vision drove their commitment to mastering their craft. Malcolm Gladwell, in his book *Outliers*, uses The Beatles as a prime example of the "10,000-hour rule"—the idea that achieving mastery in any field requires approximately 10,000 hours of dedicated practice.[7]

Pete Best, The Beatles' former drummer who played with them in Hamburg, recalled: "Once the news got out that we were making a show, the club started packing them in. We played seven nights a week. At first, we played almost non-stop till twelve-thirty, when it closed, but as we got better, the crowd stayed till two most mornings."[8]

By the time The Beatles performed on *The Ed Sullivan Show* on February 9, 1964, they had already performed approximately 1,200 live performances. In 1961 alone, they gave 349 live performances. Once they started recording, they produced twelve original albums in a little over seven years. By contrast, another of my favorite rock bands, The Who, released their twelfth original album fifty-two years after the release of their first.

In a later interview, John recalled their level of commitment: "We got better and got more confidence. We couldn't help it with all the experience playing all night long. It was handy them being foreign. We had to try even harder, put our heart and soul into it, to get ourselves over."[9]

This dedication wasn't simply about putting in time; it was about pursuing improvement with purpose. Their catalytic vision drove them to practice, perform, write, and innovate at a pace few others could maintain. Without that vision propelling them forward, it's unlikely they would have invested so heavily in developing their craft.

Even after they achieved worldwide fame, they put the hours in. The early albums and singles were recorded in a day or two, and some songs were recorded in one take. As touring became impossible to manage, they shifted more of their effort to the studio. Of course, one of the advantages of their success was the amount of studio time they were allowed to have.

Studio time was expensive, so it was rare to have more than a handful of "takes" of a song. John and George often obsessed over a song trying to get it right, but Paul was the king of multiple takes—a result of his perfectionist tendencies.

"Ob-La-Di, Ob-La-Da" from the White Album, famously took 102 takes to complete. This song drove Paul's bandmates to frustration. As Geoff Emerick recalled, the day Paul announced that he wanted to record the lead vocal yet again, "I saw the grimaces flicker across the faces of George Harrison and Ringo, and I'm quite sure none of us missed the sheer look of disgust on John's."[10]

Other Beatles songs that required an unusually high number of takes include:

- "Not Guilty" (George): 99 takes, and it still didn't make the White Album
- "Sexy Sadie" (John): 67 takes
- "Happiness Is a Warm Gun" (John): 70 takes
- "Maxwell's Silver Hammer" (Paul): 35 takes
- "Get Back" (Paul): 169 takes

Catalytic Vision in Practice

A catalytic vision isn't just a lofty statement—it manifests in practical, everyday decisions. For The Beatles, this was evident in their approach to developing their catalog.

When EMI producer George Martin first worked with The Beatles, he tried to impose the industry's traditional vision by selecting a song called "How Do You Do It?" (written by Mitch Murray) for their first single. Martin told them, "The first priority is to find a hit song for the boys to sing. I knew I had it when Dick James brought me a number written by Mitch Murray called 'How Do You Do It?' After he played it for me, I jumped and said, 'That's it, we've got it. This is the song that's going to make The Beatles a household name.'"[11]

The Beatles, guided by their own vision, pushed back. Martin recalled, "They were not very impressed. They said they wanted to write their own material. So, I read the riot act: when you can write material as good as this, then I'll record it."[12]

This was a pivotal moment. Imagine the courage it took for four young Liverpool musicians to resist their producer's direction—the gatekeeper to their dream. But their catalytic vision demanded they create original material rather than become mere performers of others' songs.

They reluctantly recorded "How Do You Do It?" but also prepared their own songs, "Love Me Do" and "Please Please Me." When Martin heard "Please Please Me," he was impressed enough to say, "Boys, I think you've got your first number one hit."[13]

This exchange illustrates how a catalytic vision provides the courage to take risks and challenge established norms. The Beatles believed so strongly in their vision of being songwriter-performers that they were willing to jeopardize their relationship with their producer to realize it.

Conclusion: A Catalytic Vision Inspires Action

A catalytic vision doesn't just point to a destination, it provides the energy to get there. It transforms ordinary effort into extraordinary achievement. It doesn't merely suggest action; it demands it.

For The Beatles, their vision of becoming "the toppermost of the poppermost" drove them to practice relentlessly, challenge industry norms, and redefine what a musical group could be. For Absher Construction, our vision to "create and build community with vision and compassion" transformed our company from a business that was laying bricks to a business that was building magnificent cathedrals.

Without a catalytic vision, we drift. We may work hard, we may even achieve success by conventional measures, but we won't transform our field or leave a legacy. But with a catalytic vision—one that energizes rather than depletes, that clarifies rather than confuses, that unites rather than divides—even ordinary people can achieve extraordinary results.

For many, the BHAG (big hairy audacious goal) can be overwhelming; that is when a series of smaller, attainable goals can drive a team or organization forward. Whether it's landing the next big project or making it to Pea Soup Andersen's restaurant, it gives people something within reach around which to rally.

This approach to vision—catalytic, milestone-driven, values-based, and transformative—shows how teams, families, and organizations alike can achieve remarkable outcomes through the power of a catalytic vision that inspires action, backed by a series of attainable goals.

Applying the Lessons of Chapter 4

Have you ever been part of an organization that seemed to be merely going through the motions? Or experienced the electric energy of a team driven by a vision so compelling that everyone willingly puts in extraordinary effort? The difference often comes down to having a catalytic vision—one that doesn't just point to a destination but provides the energy to get there.

When John gathered his bandmates and asked, "Where are we going, fellas?," with their enthusiastic response of "To the top, Johnny!" and "To the toppermost of the poppermost!," they weren't just engaging in youthful bravado. They were articulating a catalytic vision that would drive them through countless hours of practice, rejection, and challenges.

Similarly, when the owners of Absher Construction retreated to discover their core purpose—"to create and build community with vision and compassion"—they weren't merely crafting a nice-sounding statement. They were establishing a catalytic vision that transformed their approach to work, shifting from "cutting stones" to "building a cathedral."

The Beatles' story aligns with my research and personal experience to offer four key principles for creating and sustaining a catalytic vision:

1. **Make your vision truly catalytic:** A compelling vision doesn't just describe a destination; it provides the energy to reach it. The Beatles' ambition to be "bigger than Elvis" motivated them through grueling performances in Hamburg and continuous innovation in the studio.

2. **Break your vision into attainable interim goals:** The Beatles' journey to "the toppermost of the poppermost" happened through "specific little aims," much like how "The Dad" masterfully kept six kids focused on exciting interim destinations all the way to Disneyland.

3. **Connect to a deeper purpose:** When Absher Construction shifted from focusing on profit to serving their community, the work itself became more meaningful. As the stonecutter parable reminds us, people who see themselves building a cathedral rather than just cutting stones bring completely different energy to their work.

4. **Visionary commitment demands extraordinary dedication:** The Beatles' 1,200-plus performances before US fame exemplify the "10,000 hours" principle that underpins all forms of excellence, whether in music, construction, or leadership. Be realistic about the effort it will take to accomplish the vision.

TEAM ASSESSMENT TOOL:
THE VISION CLARITY CHECK

This Vision Clarity Check helps teams evaluate whether their current vision has truly catalytic power. By assessing both the compelling nature of the destination and the energy it generates, organizations can identify whether their vision needs refreshing or recalibrating.

For your organization's vision, rate the following on a scale of 1–5:

- **Clear destination:**
  Is the envisioned future specific and vivid? _____

- **Emotional resonance:**
  Does it connect to deeper values and purpose? _____

- **Energy generation:**
  Does it create enthusiasm and motivation? _____

- **Interim milestones:**
  Are there clear steps that build momentum? _____

- **Collective ownership:**
  Do team members feel personally invested? _____

A truly catalytic vision scores high across all dimensions. Lower scores indicate areas needing attention.

IMPLEMENTATION GUIDE:
BUILDING A CATALYTIC VISION

This five-step process provides a structured approach to developing or refreshing a vision that drives action and commitment. Rather than simply crafting a statement, it guides you through creating the kind of catalytic vision that propelled The Beatles from playing Liverpool clubs to achieving worldwide fame.

1. **Purpose discovery:** Facilitate conversations about why your organization exists beyond profit—its contribution to a better world.

2. **Dream session:** Encourage expansive thinking about what's possible—your "toppermost of the poppermost."

3. **Journey mapping:** Define the interim goals that will mark progress toward the ultimate vision.

4. **Create or confirm values:** Establish the core values that will serve as guardrails and decision-making principles in pursuit of the vision—just as Absher Construction did when they identified their four core values.

5. **Confirm amount of effort/work required:** Realistically assess and commit to the level of dedication needed to achieve the vision—understanding that excellence, as The Beatles demonstrated, requires extraordinary commitment and thousands of hours of focused effort.

Remember that a truly catalytic vision should both challenge and inspire. As The Beatles demonstrated, when a vision feels slightly beyond reach but still attainable, it creates the perfect tension to drive extraordinary effort and achievement.

CHAPTER 4 PLAYLIST

CATALYTIC VISION

This playlist illustrates how The Beatles' catalytic vision allowed them to transcend conventional pop music boundaries, incorporating diverse influences from classical to Indian music, while addressing both personal and universal themes that continue to resonate decades later.

1. **"Lucy in the Sky with Diamonds"**—Inspired by John's son Julian's childhood drawing, this psychedelic masterpiece exemplifies The Beatles' vision to push musical boundaries with surreal imagery, innovative studio techniques, and complex arrangements that transformed pop music possibilities. A reminder to "picture yourself" where you want to go.

2. **"The Word"**—John's early philosophical piece about love as the answer to society's problems is the first sign of a change in John's vision for the future. The song demonstrates their evolving vision to use music as a vehicle for deeper messages, positioning themselves as cultural messengers spreading enlightenment.

3. **"Good Day Sunshine"**—Paul's irresistibly upbeat song showcases their vision to blend multiple musical styles (in this case, Motown and ragtime piano influences) into something entirely new, all while making complex musical ideas seem effortless and accessible.

4. **"Tomorrow Never Knows"**—Perhaps their most revolutionary recording, featuring tape loops, reversed guitar solos, and droning Indian-influenced backing. This radical departure from conventional pop music demonstrated their fearless vision to explore uncharted musical territory.

5. **"A Hard Day's Night"**—Written overnight to serve as the film's title track, this song demonstrates their vision-driven ability to deliver extraordinary results under pressure, blending wit, energy, and musical innovation.

6. **"Eight Days a Week"**—Showcases their vision to redefine recording techniques, featuring one of the first fade-in introductions in pop music, illustrating their commitment to innovation even within commercial success. Of course, they did this by working "eight days a week."

7. **"Octopus's Garden"**—Ringo's whimsical underwater fantasy demonstrates his desire to have a safe space to nurture relationships. With a little help from his friends, Ringo created a wonderful world where everyone's creative contributions were encouraged and respected.

8. **"Tell Me What You See"**—This overlooked gem encourages listeners to look beyond surface appearances, mirroring the catalytic vision's purpose of seeing potential beyond current reality.

9. **"Things We Said Today"**—Paul's forward-looking composition demonstrates their vision to create music that contemplates the future while acknowledging the present, mixing melancholy with optimism.

10. **"Glass Onion"**—A self-referential song that playfully acknowledges their own mythology, showing their awareness of how their vision had transformed popular culture while continuing to challenge expectations.

CHAPTER 5

PILLAR THREE— ESPRIT DE CORPS

The third pillar is esprit de corps. Merriam-Webster defines *esprit de corps* as "the common spirit existing in the members of a group instilling enthusiasm, devotion, and strong regard for the honor of the group." British historian F. E. Adcock once noted it's "that typically English characteristic for which there is no English word: esprit de corps."[1]

In the context of The Beatles, this intangible quality manifested in their relationships, their creative process, and their unified identity. It was both the foundation of their success and the magic ingredient that elevated them above their contemporaries. Let's explore three key elements of The Beatles' esprit de corps that any team striving for excellence should emulate.

Setting Egos Aside

One of the most remarkable aspects of The Beatles' rise to prominence was their willingness to set aside individual egos for the betterment of the group. This wasn't always easy, especially among four talented, creative, and ambitious young men.

This spirit of selflessness was established early in their formation. Paul once shared a story that captures the foundation of their esprit de corps: "If John had a chocolate bar, he shared it with me. Not a square or quarter of his chocolate bar, he'd give me half. And that's why The Beatles started right there. Isn't that fantastic? It's the most important story about The Beatles, and it's in none of the books."[2]

This may seem like a small gesture, but it established a precedent of sharing and equality that would become central to the group's identity. From the very beginning, the founding members had to make decisions that prioritized the band's success over individual prominence.

John Invites Paul to Join the Band

As discussed in chapter 3, when John first met Paul at the St. Peter's fete in July 1957, he faced a critical decision. Paul, who had been invited to audition after the show, demonstrated remarkable talent. John was immediately impressed, but he didn't immediately invite Paul to join the band. He had to consider whether bringing in someone who was potentially more talented than himself was the right move. Bringing Paul in would inevitably mean sharing the spotlight. After reflection, John decided that what was best for the band trumped his own ego. He invited Paul to join, setting a precedent for prioritizing the good of the whole over individual prominence.

Similarly, when Paul later introduced George to the group, John initially thought George was too young, at just fourteen years old. But after two auditions, including one aboard a moving bus, John recognized the value George would bring to the band and welcomed him to the group, again placing the band's needs above personal considerations.

This willingness to promote talent, regardless of how it might affect one's own position, extended to the introduction of Ringo as well. In August 1962, after receiving criticism from producer George Martin about Pete Best's drumming, John, Paul, and George made the difficult decision to replace him with Ringo, whom they considered the best drummer in Liverpool. While this decision was painful, it reflected their commitment to the band's quality and success.

Who Is the Front Man?

One of the most significant examples of setting egos aside was The Beatles' approach to the role of front man. In the early 1960s music industry, most groups had a clear star—think Buddy Holly and the Crickets or Smokey Robinson and the Miracles. Industry executives repeatedly tried to promote either John or Paul as The Beatles' front man, but they consistently refused, insisting they were all equal partners.

Set Lists

When they were preparing for their historic appearance on *The Ed Sullivan Show* on February 9, 1964, The Beatles' set list featured primarily Paul's songs or those with Paul on lead vocals: "All My Loving," "Till There Was You," and "I Saw Her Standing There." But "She Loves You" and "I Want to Hold Your Hand" were cowritten and had shared lead vocals. John, despite being the band's leader, willingly stepped back to let Paul take center stage at this pivotal moment in their career.

Think about this for a moment. John, who had worked his tail off for five-plus years to have a chance to make it big in America, did not hog the spotlight. On the contrary, he stepped aside and let Paul shine. It was gestures like this that kept Paul loyal to John and The Beatles.

Something else was also at play. Paul and John both mentioned in interviews that they created their set lists based on what seemed right at the time, not on some equal division of songs. Neither was hung up on getting their share as lead singer.

At their historic Shea Stadium concert in 1965, with 55,600 attendees (the largest concert in history at the time), the dynamic shifted. There, John sang most of the songs: seven to Paul's three, with one each for George and Ringo. This flexibility in spotlight sharing demonstrated their commitment to what served the moment best rather than focusing selfishly on whose turn it was to sing lead.

Sharing Band Profits Equally

The profit-sharing structure of The Beatles further exemplified this egalitarian approach. From the beginning, they shared profits equally. Even when Ringo joined on the eve of their fame, he came in as a 25 percent member of the band, a practice that continued even after the band dissolved. To this day, John's and George's estates have an equal vote with Paul and Ringo, with everyone maintaining veto power over decisions regarding the band's legacy.

There was one notable exception to this equal sharing—songwriting royalties. Since John and Paul were more interested in songwriting early on, they received additional income through songwriting credits. However, this was less a deliberate choice for unequal profit distribution (at the time) and more a reflection of their actual creative contributions.

This prioritization of the collective over the individual is a rare quality, especially in creative fields where personal recognition often drives success. But for The Beatles, it was foundational to their identity and a key factor in their unprecedented achievements.

Friendly Internal Competition

The Beatles' commitment to collective success didn't mean they did not enjoy and benefit from internal competition. Rather, they channeled competitive energy in productive ways, creating "friendly internal competition"—especially between John and Paul.[3]

One of the clearest examples of this productive competition was the creation of "We Can Work It Out" and "Day Tripper." Both songs were written around the same time, with Paul bringing in the framework for "We Can Work It Out" and John developing "Day Tripper." Rather than competing for the single release slot, they decided to innovate by creating a double A-sided single, a departure from the traditional A-side/B-side format of 45 rpm singles.

An even more profound example was the creative exchange that led to "Strawberry Fields Forever" and "Penny Lane." In late November 1966, John came to the studio with "Strawberry Fields Forever," a reflective song about his childhood in Liverpool. Everyone at the studio sat stunned at the depth and beauty of the song. Inspired by John's nostalgic creation, Paul went home and wrote his own reflection on his Liverpool childhood, "Penny Lane."

These two masterpieces reveal much about their creators' different personalities and perspectives. "Strawberry Fields Forever" is melancholic and introspective while "Penny Lane" is upbeat and cheerful. Together, they created two of the most celebrated Beatles' songs, each elevated by the creative tension between their writers.

Another instance of this productive competition occurred when John wrote and recorded "Revolution," which was slated to be the next Beatles single. Before it was released, Paul brought in a new song he had been working on called "Hey Jude." When Paul introduced "Hey Jude," John immediately recognized its superior quality and agreed it should be the A side of the next single. This willingness to acknowledge each other's strengths and defer when appropriate was crucial to maintaining their productive rivalry. "Hey Jude" went on to be the biggest-selling single of all time (at the time).

Movie Soundtracks

The pattern repeated with movie soundtracks. When their first movie, *A Hard Day's Night*, was nearly complete, the director mentioned it needed an upbeat title song. John and Paul took it as a competitive challenge. John returned the next day with the song "A Hard Day's Night," which became the title of the movie and a number one hit. Similarly, for their next film, *Help!*, John again delivered under pressure to come up with a title track, whose title was slated to be "Eight Arms to Hold You" until John came up with the new song.

Our World Satellite Broadcast

Perhaps the most impressive example of their creative competition under pressure came in June 1967, when The Beatles were asked to represent Great Britain in the world's first multinational and multi-satellite broadcast called *Our World*. This broadcast brought together representatives from several countries to share something from their country with the world. For example, the Vienna Philharmonic and the Vienna Choir Boys represented Austria. The broadcast was wildly successful, as an estimated 400–700 million people watched this historic event.

Despite having just released *Sgt. Pepper's Lonely Hearts Club Band* a month earlier, the group was asked to create something new. John rose to the occasion again and wrote "All You Need Is Love," which they performed live for the broadcast (with a backing track). This anthem to universal love became a number one hit, and the version we hear today is from that live recording.

This pattern of friendly competition consistently pushed both songwriters to greater heights. It wasn't about who got more credit or who wrote more songs; it was about creating the best possible music. Their competition served the band rather than their individual egos, making it a productive force rather than a divisive one.

Sense of Humor and Fun

The third essential component of The Beatles' esprit de corps was their remarkable sense of humor and fun. Despite the intensity of their work ethic and the pressures of unprecedented fame (or perhaps because of it), they maintained a playful, often irreverent approach to their career. Andrew Sobel, in an article in *Strategy+Business*, says, "There is an example of a team that learned to deliver the highest level of performance while having fun on a legendary scale. Not coincidentally, it's the most successful team of our time: The Beatles."[4]

Their humor was evident from their earliest recording sessions. George Martin, their producer, recalls their first session: "I wanted to get them involved from the start in the techniques of recording. So, after the first run through, I called them out to the control room to hear a playback and if there's anything you don't like, tell me and we'll try to do something about it."[5] George, the "smart ass," replied, "Well, for a start, I don't like your tie."[6] Everyone erupted in laughter, and even Martin, who was somewhat formal, eventually joined in. This irreverence endeared The Beatles to him and set the tone for their productive working relationship.

The Beatles' cheeky humor extended to formal occasions as well. When they performed at the Royal Command Performance, an annual charity event hosted by the royal family, they were the first rock group ever invited to participate. Before performing "Twist and Shout," John addressed the audience: "For our last number, I'd like to ask for your help. The people in the cheaper seats, clap your hands. And the rest of you, if you'd just rattle your jewelry."[7] This gentle ribbing of the aristocracy was daring for the time but was delivered with enough charm to avoid causing offense.

Their playful approach extended to their lyrics as well. In "Paperback Writer," they sang "Frère Jacques" in the background, a song they had learned as children. In "Taxman," George included several satirical jabs at the British tax system.

They also brought some surreptitious "naughty" humor to some of their songs. Getting these references past the censors was a challenge they gladly accepted. In the song "Girl," the lads sang "dit, dit, dit" in the background—or at least that's what they told George Martin, who could not distinguish between a *D* sound and a *T* sound as they were singing. And there are a few "naughty" references in "Penny Lane," but I will leave it to the reader to try to decipher them.

The Beatles also brought humor to their press conferences. When asked how they accounted for their success, they responded, "We have a press agent."[8]

Asked if they hoped to get haircuts when in America, they quipped, "We had one yesterday."[9]

When questioned about the movement in Detroit to stamp out The Beatles, they countered, "We have a campaign of our own to stamp out Detroit."[10]

And when asked what they thought of Beethoven, Ringo responded, "I love him, especially his poems."[11]

This playful spirit permeated their work environment and contributed significantly to their creative output. It allowed them to take risks, challenge conventions, and maintain their enthusiasm despite grueling schedules and mounting pressures. It was a crucial element of the esprit de corps that bound them together and fueled their revolutionary impact on music and culture.

Incorporating Fun at Work

At Absher Construction, we consciously introduced "fun" into the workplace. At one point, we started a routine of calling Fridays "Good News Friday." By looking for good news, we believed we would find it. And it's nice to take off for the weekend on the heels of some good news. We announced project wins, promotions, and fun company stories on Fridays. It was a way to make sure we saw all the good that was happening around us amid the stress and pressure of several major construction projects.

Absher's annual year-end gathering was our big bash. Early on in my tenure, I started a tradition of playing a giant game of rock, paper, scissors (RPS) with several hundred team members and their spouses. Everyone would play against me until we got down to approximately eight survivors, who came up on stage for the finals. The RPS winner took home $1,000. The cash was nice, but the bragging rights were a bigger deal. Each year, our annual party team came up with eagerly anticipated twists. One year, we played a video on the history of RPS; one time we explained the worldwide debate on whether you count one, two, throw or one, two, three, throw. It was all a little silly, but fun (and competitive).

Personal Reflection: Coach John Anderson

John Anderson coached Sumner High School football for sixteen years. In that time, his teams won five league championships and two state championships. I was fortunate to have played for Coach Anderson on the undefeated 1975 state championship team.

Coach Anderson was not a win-at-all-cost coach. He strongly believed in winning the right way. As I look back, I see how he led us by embracing the same pillars that were the foundation of The Beatles' success.

His commitment to esprit de corps is what set him apart. He never forgot that football is a game. That is not to say that we didn't work hard, but he set out, with intention, to incorporate fun and humor into that hard work. It kept us loose and sustained us through the hard work.

Coming off a disappointing loss in the state championship game the prior year, Coach Anderson was optimistic about the chances for the 1975 squad. "There is a great motivation to get back," Anderson said. "We don't set a lot of goals around here, but we did set that one. *Our main goal, though, is to have fun and to get as many guys playing as possible.*"

The strength of the 1974 team was a big and talented offensive line, nearly all of whom had graduated. The only returning starter was all-league tackle Mike Linker, who moved to tight end for his senior season (where he became all-state). This meant all five offensive line spots had to be replaced. This wasn't done with transfers; it simply meant the JV linemen from previous seasons became the varsity starters. They were not as big or talented as the previous year, but they played well as a unit.

The day before each game was a noncontact (no pads, helmets) practice to run through the game plan for Friday night's game and get a light workout. He dubbed Thursday practice "Hat Day," and he encouraged us all to wear hats that expressed our personality. As you might imagine, a bunch of sixteen- to eighteen-year-old boys would push the limits with their selections. Most notably, we were excited to see what new outfit star receiver and class clown McGregor Agan would wear to Thursday's practice. To Coach Anderson's credit, he firmly enforced his only rule for hat day—"keep it clean." This habit of keeping it light and having fun on Thursdays kept us relaxed and focused for our games.

During the season, we had team meetings on Sunday evenings to review film of Friday night's game. Coach Anderson emphasized areas for improvement, as well as highlighting outstanding effort. What I remember most, though, is how much fun we had at those film sessions. He approached the lessons with humor; he allowed the team to laugh and be silly. It struck me at the time how much easier it was to remember the teaching points because of the fun and laughter!

This sense of spontaneity and fun infected the team and kept us loose. Football involves a lot of trash-talking, especially in the trenches. In one of our games, a particularly obnoxious trash-talker on an opposing team was calling our guys every name in the book, and some of the guys were getting frustrated by him. At one point, he called one of our linemen "a pantywaist." Our captain and all-league quarterback Carl Boush found the perfect way to inspire the team with fun and humor. Back in the huddle, he told the team that we are going to run right at that guy. When he got to the line of scrimmage, he called out the signals: "Pantywaist, 319 . . . pantywaist, 319 . . . hut." This small gesture relaxed the team, and we ran right over the top of that guy.

The Power of Unity

The Beatles' esprit de corps wasn't merely a pleasant by-product of their collaboration, it was essential to their success. By setting aside individual egos, channeling competitive energy in constructive ways, and maintaining a sense of humor and fun, they created an environment where each member could contribute their best while feeling part of something greater than themselves.

This unity didn't happen by accident. It grew from countless shared experiences: the grueling performances in Hamburg, the rejection from record companies, the meteoric rise to fame, and the constant pressure to innovate. Through it all, they maintained a bond that allowed them to face these challenges not as individuals but as a cohesive unit.

This esprit de corps wasn't just about their music. It was about the spirit they embodied, a spirit that convinced millions of fans around the world that they were witnessing not just four talented musicians but a singular cultural force.

For any team striving for excellence, there is a valuable lesson here. Technical skill and individual brilliance matter, of course. But without the binding force of esprit de corps—the willingness to subordinate ego to the collective good, the productive channeling of friendly internal competition, and the cultivation of joy in the work itself—even the most talented team will fall short of its potential.

As you consider your own teams, whether in business, sports, or any collaborative enterprise, ask yourself: Have we cultivated the esprit de corps that allows each member to contribute their best while feeling part of something greater? Have we created an environment where egos are set aside, competition is friendly and productive, and work is infused with a sense of joy? Are we "all together now"? If not, perhaps there are lessons to be learned from four lads from Liverpool who changed the world—all together.

Conclusion: The Blueprint for Team Unity

The Beatles' esprit de corps wasn't accidental; it was cultivated through conscious choices that prioritized collective success over individual glory. From John's decision to invite the talented Paul into his band, despite potential rivalry, to their willingness to share chocolate bars and credit equally, they demonstrated that true excellence emerges when egos serve the group rather than individuals.

Their approach offers a masterclass in building team spirit that transcends ordinary collaboration. Setting egos aside didn't mean diminishing individual contributions; it meant amplifying them through collective energy. Their friendly competition pushed each member to new heights while their shared sense of humor relieved much of their daily stress. The result was that magical "all together now" spirit that convinced the world they were witnessing something unprecedented.

The lesson extends beyond music. Whether you're leading a construction crew, managing a corporate team, or coaching athletes, the principles remain the same. Esprit de corps requires intentional cultivation: creating space for friendly competition, infusing work with humor and joy, and consistently choosing group success over individual recognition. It's the difference between having talented people and having a team that achieves something truly extraordinary.

As we'll see in the chapters ahead, even the strongest esprit de corps faces inevitable challenges as circumstances change, and success brings new pressures. Understanding how to maintain this precious team chemistry through growth and transition becomes critical for sustained excellence.

Applying the Lessons of Chapter 5

Have you ever been part of a team where the energy was palpable? Where the whole group seemed to be operating on the same wavelength, supporting each other toward a shared goal? That magical dynamic is what the French call "esprit de corps," and it's perhaps the most powerful yet elusive element of sustained excellence.

The Beatles weren't just four talented musicians; they were a unified force with a remarkable team spirit. Even at the height of "Beatlemania," when their fame reached unimaginable proportions, they remained grounded through their connections with each other.

Coach John Anderson's approach to his state championship Sumner High School football team mirrors this same principle. By establishing "Hat Day" practices and introducing humor and fun into training sessions, he created an environment where hard work and joy coexisted—resulting in an undefeated season and a state championship.

The Beatles' story, along with these supporting examples, offers four key principles for building esprit de corps:

1. **Set egos aside for collective success:** Like John inviting the talented Paul to join his band despite potential rivalry, excellence requires prioritizing group achievement over individual recognition.

2. **Channel competition productively:** The Beatles' internal competition, like the creative rivalry that produced "Strawberry Fields Forever" and "Penny Lane," shows how healthy competition can drive innovation when directed toward collective improvement rather than personal glory.

3. **Infuse work with humor and joy:** From their playful press conferences to their irreverent approach to authority, The Beatles never forgot that music was supposed to be fun. Coach Anderson's "Hat Day" practices similarly recognized that even serious pursuits benefit from lightness and humor.

4. **Build a foundation of mutual respect:** Paul's memory of John sharing his chocolate bar highlights how small gestures build the

trust and goodwill that sustain teams through inevitable challenges and conflicts.

TEAM SPIRIT ASSESSMENT: MEASURING YOUR ESPRIT DE CORPS

Rate your team on each element (1–10 scale):

- Ego management:
  How often do team members subordinate
  personal recognition for collective success?   _____

- Healthy competition:
  Do team members inspire better work from
  each other without undermining relationships?   _____

- Fun factor:
  Is there laughter and playfulness
  even during challenging work?   _____

Use this simple assessment as a benchmark of esprit de corps. Take it regularly so you can gauge changes in the esprit de corps of your team or organization.

IMPLEMENTATION GUIDE: BUILDING YOUR TEAM'S ESPRIT DE CORPS

- **Ego check exercise:** Create a "team-first" ritual where members regularly highlight others' contributions.

- **Constructive competition framework:** Establish clear parameters for how team members challenge and reward each other while maintaining psychological safety.

- **Fun audit:** Identify where your team process could incorporate more playfulness without sacrificing productivity, like establishing "Good News Friday" or "Hat Day."

- **Shared experience calendar:** Schedule regular nonwork activities that build camaraderie.

- **Recognition rebalance:** Ensure reward systems emphasize collective achievement alongside individual performance.

CHAPTER 5 PLAYLIST

ESPRIT DE CORPS

This playlist illustrates how The Beatles' success stemmed not only from individual brilliance but from their unique chemistry, mutual support, and the joy they found in creating music together. These are all essential elements of the esprit de corps that defined them at their best.

1. **"All Together Now"**—This lighthearted sing-along from *Yellow Submarine* perfectly captures the band's collective spirit with its childlike simplicity and group vocals. The title itself serves as a rallying cry for teamwork and unity, embodying the essence of esprit de corps.

2. **"Come Together"**—One of their last great collaborations showcases how they could still function as a cohesive unit despite growing tensions. John wrote the song, but each member adds distinctive elements: Paul's iconic bass line, George's subtle guitar work, and Ringo's instantly recognizable drum pattern create a perfect example of their collective genius.

3. **"Paperback Writer"**—Listen closely to the background vocals where they sing "Frère Jacques"—a playful inside joke that demonstrates their willingness to have fun even while creating serious art. The tight harmonies and perfect instrumental interplay show how well they functioned as a team.

4. **"Michelle"**—Born from Paul's playful habit of pretending to be French when talking to girls, this charming ballad showcases their humor translating into serious artistry. The song's elegant French phrases and sophisticated melody earned them a Grammy Award for Song of the Year.

5. **"Taxman"**—George's biting satire opened *Revolver*, showing how the group supported his growing role as a songwriter. Notably, Paul played the guitar solo when George struggled with it—a perfect example of teammates supporting each other and setting egos aside for the greater good.

6. **"Sgt. Pepper's Lonely Hearts Club Band/With a Little Help from My Friends"**—These connected album openers showcase their collaborative genius—creating a fictional band persona while crafting the perfect vehicle for Ringo's vocals. John and Paul's songwriting specifically tailored to Ringo's strengths exemplifies their supportive team spirit.

7. **"Getting Better"**—Another perfect example of John and Paul's complementary viewpoints enhancing each other's work. Paul's optimistic verses are offset by John's sarcastic response—showcasing how their different personalities created a perfect balance.

8. **"All My Loving"**—This song kicked off *The Ed Sullivan Show* on February 9, 1964, and America immediately caught Beatlemania.

John deferred the spotlight to Paul on the show, exhibiting the group-first attitude that was so instrumental in their success.

9. **"Strawberry Fields Forever"**—John's masterpiece became a group triumph through collaboration with each member contributing unique elements. George Martin masterfully merged two different versions, demonstrating a combination of skill and serendipity.

10. **"Penny Lane"**—Paul's response to "Strawberry Fields" illustrates their friendly competition that pushed each other to greater heights. The contrasting perspectives on Liverpool childhood memories show how their different viewpoints enriched their collective output.

CHAPTER 6

PILLAR 4 — THE MAGICAL MYSTERY

W hat do I mean by the "magical mystery"? It is those moments in life when everything clicks. As it relates to a group, a team, or an organization, it is when everyone is locked in and fully present, allowing performance to transcend from the ordinary to the extraordinary. In short, it is those moments where everything flows.

This magical mystery is much more than a clever reference to one of The Beatles' groundbreaking albums. It's that ineffable quality that transforms good teams into legendary ones. When the right combination of people, timing, environment, and purpose creates something that transcends the individual contributions—magic happens. It recognizes the potential for magic in everyday life *and* creates magic, elevating performance to an unparalleled level of excellence.

Derek Taylor, who spent considerable time with The Beatles during their peak years as their press agent, observed: "The magic of The Beatles is timeless and ageless. It has broken all frontiers and barriers.

It has cut through differences of race, age and class. It is adored by the world."[1]

I break down the "magical mystery" into two components: synergy and serendipity. *Synergy* is the internal chemistry that happens when the right people work together in the right way. *Serendipity* is the external fortune: those happy accidents and fortuitous timing that seem cosmically arranged.

Both elements were crucial to The Beatles' ascent to greatness, and both are necessary ingredients for any team or organization striving for excellence. Let's explore how these elements are manifested by The Beatles and how you can cultivate them in your own teams or organizations.

Synergy: Greater Than the Sum of Their Parts

In the book *The 7 Habits of Highly Effective People,* Stephen Covey defines synergy this way: "Simply defined, it means the whole is greater than the sum of its parts. It means that the relationship that the parts have to each other is a part in and of itself. It is not only a part, but the most *catalytic*, the most empowering, the most unifying and the most exciting part [italics mine]."[2]

When it came to The Beatles, this synergy was undeniable. As Sobel wrote in his article for *Strategy+Business*, "The whole of their accomplishment was so much greater than the sum of its parts."[3]

The Beatles' synergy manifested in many ways: from the harmony of their voices to the alchemy of their instrumentation to their collaborative songwriting. Let's take a look at each of those.

The Harmony of Their Voices

One of the most recognizable aspects of The Beatles' sound was their distinctive vocal harmonies. Inspired by groups like the Everly

Brothers, they crafted intricate three-part harmonies that created a rich, layered sound.

"This Boy," an early Beatles track, showcased their remarkable vocal blend. The middle section features a stunning three-part harmony, with John taking the low part, Paul the high part, and George in the middle—creating a sound that was instantly recognizable as uniquely "Beatles."

In their later work, the harmonies became even more sophisticated. "Because," from *Abbey Road*, features exquisite three-part harmony that was recorded three times over, creating a nine-voice effect. The Cirque du Soleil show *Love* features a stripped-down version of this song that highlights just the vocals—a stunning testament to their harmonic capabilities.

What made their vocal synergy special wasn't just that they could sing well together—it was the variety of combinations they could employ:

- John and Paul (the most common pairing)
- John and George
- Paul and George
- Various combinations with Ringo
- Lead vocals with two-part harmony backing

These combinations created different opportunities for synergy and provided listeners with a variety of vocal combinations and sounds that kept their songs fresh and diverse. The lead harmonies of John and George on "You've Really Got a Hold on Me" and Paul and George on some later classics like "While My Guitar Gently Weeps" and "Something" provide a change from the standard John and Paul harmonies but still exude brilliance.

In their early hits, John and Paul's voices blended so perfectly that it was often difficult to tell them apart on songs like "She Loves You" and

"I Want to Hold Your Hand." Their voices intertwined in a way that created something neither could have achieved alone.

For a raw look at the synergy in harmony between John and Paul, listen to them sing "Words of Love" on *On Air—Live at the BBC Volume 2*. This is recorded live on the radio, with no studio tricks like overdubbing or multitracking. This is John and Paul singing live and beautifully in sync.

"Baby's in Black" provides another wonderful example of a John and Paul duet. They seamlessly alternate the melody and harmony between them. The interplay of their voices with George's lead guitar is masterful. In another early song, "I'll Get You," John sings lead, but there are moments of both two-part and three-part harmony that capture the essence of their vocal combinations.

As their career progressed, they began to showcase their individual vocal styles more clearly, but they never lost the ability to come together in perfect harmony when a song called for it—like in "Two of Us," "Because," and "I've Got a Feeling."

The Alchemy of Their Instrumentation

Beyond their vocals, The Beatles created instrumental synergy that was equally compelling. One fascinating example is the duet guitar solo on "And Your Bird Can Sing," where George and Paul played matching guitar parts through the same amplifier. Rather than recording separately and overdubbing, they insisted on playing simultaneously, creating an intertwined sound that couldn't have been achieved any other way.

This approach to dual lead guitar solos influenced many bands that followed, from The Allman Brothers to the Eagles, but The Beatles were pioneers in this technique.

Another example are the songs "Come Together" and "Get Back," where Ringo's distinctive drumming is integral to the songs' identity.

The tom-heavy, hypnotic rhythm in "Come Together" creates the perfect foundation for John's cryptic lyrics and the band's groove. The innovative galloping sound of the drums in "Get Back" is the signature piece of the song. It's impossible to imagine these songs with any other drum parts.

Their Collaborative Songwriting

Perhaps the most remarkable synergy in The Beatles was their collaborative songwriting. By examining it, we can see how their musical influences blended to create something wholly new.

Some of the major early influences on The Beatles were Elvis Presley, Roy Orbison, Chuck Berry, Carl Perkins, Smokey Robinson, Buddy Holly, The Ronettes, the Everly Brothers, and Little Richard. The Beatles loved rock and roll, blues, country, folk, and Motown—especially the Motown girl groups.

Living in Liverpool, they received American records before Londoners did, thanks to Liverpool's position as England's westernmost port. This gave them early access to the latest American music. One of the things that set them apart from other bands in Liverpool and Hamburg was their willingness to discover and incorporate obscure American songs into their repertoire. There were several rock and roll groups floating around Liverpool and Hamburg at the time, and they wanted to stand out. While other bands stuck to traditional, well-known rock and roll and blues tunes, The Beatles were adventurous.

They wanted to play songs that no one else was playing, so they would flip over the latest American releases and learn the B-sides. This led them to a love of Motown tunes, especially groups like The Ronettes, The Shirelles, and The Marvelettes. This infusion of Motown sensibilities gave their music a distinctive quality that infused their songwriting and created a new sound that would create Beatlemania.

When The Beatles got their recording contract with EMI, John and Paul knew that it was time to step up their songwriting game. To achieve their vision of writing their own songs, they had to write songs good enough to be recorded. Paul and John drew on these diverse influences to create a formula for their songs that was both accessible and innovative:

- Up-tempo, energetic arrangements
- Focused on young love
- Clear, memorable hooks
- Brief songs (two to three minutes) to accommodate radio stations
- Build tension throughout the song
- A middle eight or bridge to add variety
- Heavy use of personal pronouns to connect with their audience

This last element—the use of personal pronouns—became a Beatles trademark. Songs like "She Loves You," "I Want to Hold Your Hand," "Love Me Do," "From Me to You," and "Please Please Me" created an immediate connection with listeners, making each fan feel the song was being sung directly to them (especially teen girls).

"Please Please Me," their first UK number one hit, exemplifies their early formula perfectly. Written primarily by John but with Paul's input, it builds tension throughout with minor chords and clever lyrics and features the call-and-response technique they'd learned from American R&B. All the tension that builds throughout the song resolves satisfyingly with a major chord at the end.

As their career progressed, they continued being avid students of other music. They were determined to stay ahead of the times. Some of the later influencers like Bob Dylan, The Beach Boys, Ravi Shankar, and Donovan are evident in their songs from the mid-'60s on.

"Two of Us"

Joshua Wolf Shenk's illuminating book *Powers of Two: Finding the Essence of Innovation in Creative Pairs* investigates the phenomenon that much of human innovation is accomplished in pairs. Shenk argues that creative breakthroughs often emerge not from solitary genius but from the unique chemistry between two minds. John and Paul exemplify this phenomenon perfectly.

As Shenk details, creative pairs typically balance competing forces: One partner might be more experimental while the other provides structure; one more provocative while the other refines. This dynamic tension creates fertile ground for innovation that neither could achieve alone. Shenk explores numerous examples of this phenomenon across various domains: Steve Jobs and Steve Wozniak revolutionizing personal computing, Marie and Pierre Curie advancing our understanding of radioactivity, C. S. Lewis and J. R. R. Tolkien influencing each other's literary masterpieces, and Warren Buffett and Charlie Munger creating extraordinary investment success.

With John and Paul, their differences created a complementary wholeness that defined The Beatles' sound, mirroring these other transformative partnerships. Cynthia Lennon, John's first wife, observed this interdependence with remarkable clarity. "John needed Paul's persistence and attention to detail," she noted. "And Paul needed John's anarchic, lateral thinking."[4] She recognized that, despite their growing creative differences, they fundamentally completed each other. John's raw emotional honesty balanced by Paul's melodic optimism created a partnership that transcended their individual capabilities.

The synergy between John and Paul demonstrates Shenk's core thesis that "the pair is the primary creative unit."[5] Their partnership shows how two individuals, when perfectly matched, can create a third entity—something beyond either of them, something magical that emerges from their interaction. This pattern of creative pairing extends far beyond music, appearing in science, technology, art, and business, making The Beatles not just a musical phenomenon but a template for how transformative innovation often emerges.

At the risk of offending fans of one or the other, the following are some broad generalizations about the differences in the songwriting of Paul and John.

Paul	John
musician first and a poet second	poet first and a musician second
about the music	about the message
cheery/optimistic	reflective/cynical
confident, self-assured	vulnerable, insecure
songs feel immediately familiar like you've heard them before	songs feel uncomfortable, like nothing you've ever heard before

There are some obvious exceptions to these generalizations, but the critical point is that these two tendencies compete with *and* complement each other, creating a broad spectrum of sounds and messages in their music.

These contrasting approaches are starkly evident in two breakup songs that were included on their fourth album, *Beatles for Sale*. The song titles tell the story. Paul's "I'll Follow the Sun" is optimistic even in the face of a failed relationship, while John's "I'm a Loser" wallows in the pain of rejection.

This yin-yang balance created a body of work that addresses the full range of human emotion and experience. When you need to feel optimistic and upbeat, you turn to Paul's songs, like "Good Day Sunshine" or "Penny Lane." When you are feeling reflective or melancholy, John's "In My Life" or "Strawberry Fields Forever" provide the perfect soundtrack.

The synergy extended beyond John and Paul, of course. George, though often overshadowed in the early years, made crucial contributions to the group's sound and identity. He was fascinated by time signatures and frequently suggested changing them within songs to create more interesting transitions between verses and choruses. "We Can Work It Out" is a prime example, where the meter shifts from 4/4 to 3/4 for the middle section, creating a waltz-like transition between sections of the song.

George consistently introduced new instruments to the group, particularly Indian instruments like the sitar, which completely transformed songs like "Norwegian Wood." His guitar work provided distinctive counterpoint to the Lennon–McCartney compositions, with solos that served the songs rather than overwhelming them.

Ringo, meanwhile, created drum parts that were inventive without being flashy. His approach was always to make the song better, not to dominate it. Producer George Martin noted that Ringo had a remarkable ability to maintain a steady tempo without a metronome—a crucial skill in the days before digital recording. His unique left-handed playing on a right-handed drum kit created unusual fills and patterns that became part of The Beatles' signature sound.

Synergy Creates a Classic

The song "A Day in the Life" provides a stunning conclusion to the album *Sgt. Pepper's Lonely Hearts Club Band* and represents perhaps the ultimate example of Beatles synergy. Ultimate Classic Rock praised the song as "one of the most significant songs ever recorded. It was a game-changer at the time, and it still has the ability to amaze based on its technological achievements and pure musicality. It was a once-in-a-lifetime record, and a most fitting finale to the Beatles' masterwork."[6]

What makes this song such a perfect example of synergy is that it fuses two completely different compositions—one by John and one by Paul—into something greater than either could have created alone. If Stephen Covey had been analyzing the recording sessions for "A Day in the Life," he would have recognized a perfect example of his "synergy" principle in action. John's dreamlike verses combined with Paul's contrasting middle section created something neither could have achieved independently—precisely the "third alternative" Covey advocates in his work.[7]

George Martin arranged the orchestral crescendos that linked the sections. Ringo provided the perfect drumming throughout, with fills that complemented rather than competed with the vocals. The result transcends any one member's contribution—it truly is greater than the sum of its parts.

This synergistic approach mirrors what happens in the best businesses and teams. When skilled individuals with complementary strengths come together with a willingness to blend their contributions rather than protect their territories, magic can happen. As Covey notes, synergy is "the highest activity in all life—the true test and manifestation of all the other habits put together."[8]

"A Day in the Life" stands as perhaps the clearest example of what made The Beatles exceptional. It wasn't just four talented musicians; it was four talented musicians who created something together that none could have created individually. The whole was truly greater than the sum of its parts—the definition of *synergy* and the essence of what makes great teams and organizations excel beyond their competitors.

Serendipity: The Happy Little Accidents

While *synergy* describes the internal magic that happens when the right people work together in the right way, *serendipity* encompasses the external factors that seem to align just perfectly. Serendipity is defined as "the occurrence and development of events by chance in a happy or beneficial way."[9] The Beatles' story is filled with these fortunate accidents and coincidences that helped propel them to greatness.

John and Paul Meeting

What are the chances that two of the greatest songwriters, musicians, and rock and roll singers of all time would grow up so near each other? When their mutual friend, Ivan Vaughan, introduced John and Paul, it set in motion a series of events that changed the world. This serendipitous occasion led to George, another uber-talented musician, joining them soon after. Without question, the three of them fed off each other to reach their level of excellence, but serendipity brought them together.

The Perfect Producer

One of the most serendipitous events in The Beatles' career was finding their perfect producer in George Martin. After The Beatles were rejected by Decca Records in January 1962, Brian Epstein continued to search for a record label and eventually booked them an audition with EMI's Parlophone label in June of 1962.

Parlophone assigned them to George Martin, a classically trained musician who had been producing primarily comedy records and sound effects albums. Martin was patient, experimental, and open to unconventional ideas—qualities that would prove essential as The Beatles pushed the boundaries of popular music.

As Mark Lewisohn, Beatles biographer, noted: "They lucked into the only producer in London who shared their resistance to convention, the only man with a reputation for sound experimentation and a strong knack for the unusual, and he'd lucked into The Beatles. And if The Beatles had signed to Decca, they'd have had none of this. Chances are they'd have been saddled with a producer doing a standard job, resistant to their views and publishing and pushing formulaic Tin Pan Alley songs on them to the exclusion of their own."[10]

This fortunate pairing of experimental artists with an experimental producer created the perfect environment for innovation.

A Cultural Moment

Another remarkable moment of serendipity occurred on October 5, 1962. On this date, two significant cultural phenomena were launched: The Beatles released their first single, "Love Me Do," and the first James Bond film, *Dr. No*, premiered.

As John Higgs notes in his book *Love and Let Die: James Bond, The Beatles, and the British Psyche*, these two cultural forces would go on to become defining symbols of British culture worldwide. "The Beatles were about to become the most successful and important band in history. Not to be outdone, James Bond would go on to become the single most successful movie character ever."[11]

This coincidence reflects a broader cultural moment. Britain, having ceded its world-power status to the United States and Soviet Union after World War II, was searching for a new identity. Bond and The Beatles provided it, revitalizing Britain's cultural significance on the global stage. The fact that they emerged simultaneously seems almost cosmically arranged.

Paul would later write one of the most successful James Bond themes, "Live and Let Die"; The Beatles' film *Help!* drew inspiration from the spy movie genre; and Ringo married Bond girl Barbara Bach—further evidence of the uncanny cultural intertwining of these two phenomena.

The Ed Sullivan Connection

The Beatles' breakthrough in America might never have happened without another stroke of serendipity. On October 31, 1963, Ed Sullivan was visiting London when he witnessed firsthand the phenomenon of Beatlemania at Heathrow Airport. A crowd had gathered to welcome The Beatles back from a tour in mainland Europe.

Sullivan, intrigued by the hysteria, asked what was happening and was told about this group called "The Beatles." Whether Sullivan reached out to Brian Epstein first or vice versa is unclear, but shortly thereafter, Epstein flew to New York to meet with Sullivan, resulting in an agreement for The Beatles to appear on his show starting February 9, 1964.

This appearance—watched by seventy-three million people—catapulted The Beatles to unprecedented fame in America. Had Sullivan not been at Heathrow that day, or had he been unimpressed by the crowd's reaction, the trajectory of The Beatles' American invasion might have been very different.

Ringo's Wordplay

Ringo was known for his malapropisms—accidentally jumbling words in amusing ways. Sometimes these verbal slips would find their way into Beatles lyrics and even song titles.

Paul reflected on this bit of serendipity in the documentary to "A Hard Day's Night":

"Ringo had this happy knack of getting things wrong—little malapropisms. And it was always better than the real one. Someone said to him, 'You look a bit tired today' and he said, 'Yeah, I've had a hard day's night' and he meant it. And we all went 'A hard day's night—that's great!"[12]

Thus, "A Hard Day's Night" was born.

Similarly, the phrase "Tomorrow Never Knows" (the title of an experimental Lennon song) came from one of Ringo's expressions. These happy linguistic accidents became part of The Beatles' legacy.

Marsha Albert's Persistence

A remarkable bit of serendipity came through a fifteen-year-old girl named Marsha Albert, from Baltimore. In December 1963, she had heard about The Beatles from a friend in England and began persistently requesting that her local radio station play their music.

The DJ eventually found someone who could bring a copy of "I Want to Hold Your Hand" back from England and asked Marsha to introduce the song on air, making this the first time a Beatles song was played on American radio.

What makes this especially significant is that Capitol Records (the US subsidiary of EMI) had been refusing to release Beatles records in America for about eighteen months, despite EMI's urging. Within six weeks of Marsha's introduction of the song, it reached number one in the United States, becoming the best-selling single in American history to that point.

While The Beatles likely would have broken through eventually (especially with the planned *Ed Sullivan* appearance), Marsha's persistence accelerated their American success and ensured they had a number one single by the time they appeared on television.

Songwriting Coincidences

Even some of The Beatles' songs have serendipitous origins. "Eleanor Rigby," by Paul, tells the sad story of an old woman who died alone. Remarkably, in the cemetery at St. Peter's Church near Liverpool—the very place where John and Paul first met—there is a tombstone for a real Eleanor Rigby.

Paul insists he made up the name, having no knowledge of the real Eleanor Rigby buried there. He later suggested that perhaps he had a subconscious memory of it, possibly having seen the name while walking through the cemetery. The coincidence is striking—that Paul would invent a character with the exact name of a woman buried at the significant location where the band's journey began.

Another extraordinary coincidence involves the song "She's Leaving Home." Paul wrote this song after reading a newspaper article about a young woman named Melanie Coe, who had run away from home. Paul didn't realize that, three years earlier, he had been a guest judge on the TV show *Ready Steady Go*, where he had selected Melanie as the winner of a dance contest. Without knowing it, he had written a song about someone he had previously met. It wasn't until several years later that someone made the connection.

Technical Serendipity

Even in the recording studio, serendipity played a role in creating The Beatles' distinctive sound. John's song "Strawberry Fields Forever" exists in its final form thanks to an incredibly fortunate bit of technical serendipity.

During recording, John couldn't decide between two very different versions of the song—one more acoustic and the other more heavily orchestrated. He told producer George Martin and engineer Geoff Emerick that he wanted the beginning of the acoustic version and the ending of the orchestrated version. "John, we'd be glad to do that," said George Martin, "the only thing that stands in our way is the fact that the two versions were played in different keys and at different tempos."[13] In other words, this was technically an impossible request.

As Martin later recalled: "The gods smiled down upon us, even though the two takes John wanted spliced together were recorded a week apart and were radically different in approach. After some trial-and-error experimentation, I discovered that by speeding up the playback of the first take and slowing down the playback of the second, I could get them to match in both pitch and tempo."[14]

This "impossible" splicing ended up creating one of The Beatles' most innovative recordings, a happy accident that became a classic. If you want to listen for the splice, it occurs just after one minute into the song.

Conclusion: Embracing the Magical Mystery

The fourth pillar of impact, the magical mystery, might seem the most elusive of all, but it's often what separates truly exceptional teams from merely good ones. It's that special something that happens when all the other elements align perfectly: the right people, in the right roles, working toward a compelling vision, with a strong spirit of camaraderie.

When these conditions exist, synergy emerges naturally. The team becomes more than the sum of its parts. Ideas flow freely, creativity flourishes, and achievements exceed what anyone might have predicted based on individual talents alone.

When teams operate with this kind of synergy, they also position themselves to benefit from serendipity. They recognize and capitalize on fortunate coincidences. They see connections that others miss. They transform lucky breaks into lasting advantages.

The Beatles exemplified this magical mystery throughout their career. From the extraordinary blend of their voices to the alchemy of their instrumentation, from the complementary nature of their song-writing to the fortunate accidents that helped propel them to fame, they embodied both synergy and serendipity in remarkable ways.

As you seek to build excellence in your own team or organization, don't neglect this fourth pillar. While you can't force magic to happen, you can create conditions where it's more likely to emerge. Build teams with complementary talents. Foster open collaboration. Allow for experimentation. Create space for deep work together. Balance structure and freedom.

Stay alert for those magical moments when everything just flows. They might be rare, but they're worth pursuing because it's in those moments that ordinary teams become legendary ones, just like four ordinary lads from Liverpool became The Beatles.

Applying the Lessons of Chapter 6

Have you ever experienced those rare, magical moments when everything just flows? When team members seem to read each other's minds, when happy accidents lead to unexpected breakthroughs, and when the whole truly becomes greater than the sum of its parts? These moments of magic aren't just lucky accidents; they can be cultivated through deliberate practices that foster both synergy and serendipity.

The magical mystery of synergy and serendipity isn't exclusive to The Beatles. Every truly exceptional team or organization experiences these phenomena in some form. The question is: Can they be cultivated, or are they purely matters of chance?

I believe that while you can't manufacture magic, you can create the conditions where it's more likely to occur.

Creating Conditions for Synergy

1. **Seek complementary talents and perspectives**
    The Beatles weren't four identical musicians; each brought different strengths and viewpoints. In your team or organization, look for people who complement rather than duplicate each other's skills.

2. **Establish a culture of open collaboration**
    The Beatles had active brainstorming sessions and immediate feedback loops. Create environments where ideas can be freely shared, critiqued, and improved.

3. **Allow for experimentation**
    The Beatles consistently pushed boundaries and tried new approaches. Foster a culture where failure is seen as a stepping stone to innovation rather than something to be punished.

4. **Create space for deep work together**
    From 1960 to 1966, The Beatles spent nearly all their time together—touring, recording, and living in close proximity. While that exact model isn't practical for most organizations, creating dedicated time for teams to work intensively together can foster similar synergy.

5. **Balance structure and freedom**
    George Martin provided the technical knowledge and structure that allowed The Beatles' creativity to flourish. Establish clear frameworks and processes that support rather than restrict creativity.

Positioning for Serendipity

1. Stay open to unexpected opportunities
   The Beatles said yes to opportunities even when the outcome was uncertain. Cultivate a mindset that recognizes potential in unusual places.

2. Build diverse networks
   The Beatles benefited from connections that crossed industries and social spheres. Expand your network beyond the obvious channels related to your field.

3. Embrace "happy accidents"
   When something unexpected happens, ask, "How might this be useful?" rather than immediately trying to correct it. Some of the greatest innovations come from mistakes.

4. Create margin in your schedule
   Serendipity rarely happens on a tight timeline. Build buffer time that allows for exploration and following interesting leads.

5. Share your work widely
   The more people who see what you're doing, the more opportunities arise for unexpected connections. The Beatles' manager Brian Epstein worked tirelessly to get their music heard by influential people.

IMPLEMENTATION GUIDE: NURTURING SYNERGY AND SERENDIPITY

This quick team exercise can be added to the end of any monthly or quarterly meeting to help maintain the collaborative flow that makes great work feel effortless. Just as The Beatles regularly checked their creative chemistry, successful teams need to periodically assess where their magic is working and where it might be getting stuck.

The Monthly Magic Check (ten to fifteen minutes)

Each person briefly shares:

- **Flow Blocker:** What's one thing that prevented great collaboration or killed creative momentum this month? How can we overcome it?

- **Synergy Spark:** What upcoming opportunities do we have for synergy? What can we do as a team to facilitate that opportunity for synergy?

- **Finding Serendipity:** What happened this month (or quarter) that we might be viewing negatively, but if we changed our perspective, could actually be an opportunity or positive development?

Record the results and do a progress check at the next meeting.

CHAPTER 6 PLAYLIST

THE MAGICAL MYSTERY

This playlist illustrates how the Beatles created magic through their uncanny synergy and the serendipitous moments that seemed to guide their creative journey, producing music that transcended the sum of its parts in ways that continue to inspire and mystify.

1. **"We Can Work It Out"**—The ultimate demonstration of their collaborative spirit, with Paul's optimistic verses balanced by John's philosophical middle section. George contributed the transition between the two parts with a change of time signature.

2. **"You Really Got a Hold on Me"**—This Smokey Robinson cover showcases John and George's rare vocal harmony partnership. Their voices merge with a raw emotional quality that demonstrates the magic that emerged from different combinations within the group.

3. **"Words of Love"**—The *Live at the BBC* recording of Buddy Holly's composition showcases John and Paul's harmony locked

in "live" for the radio audience. This is a glimpse of two remarkable voices magically locked in as one.

4. **"This Boy"**—An early masterclass in three-part harmony demonstrates the magical synergy of their voices. The middle section features John's passionate solo, beautifully contrasting with the harmonized verses.

5. **"If I Fell"**—This sophisticated early ballad features some of John and Paul's most intricate vocal harmonies, with Paul singing a challenging high harmony part while John carries the melody. The close intervals and perfect blend create a sound that seems almost impossible to achieve—pure vocal magic.

6. **"Baby's in Black"**—An early example of John and Paul's perfect vocal blend, singing together in close harmony throughout the entire song rather than trading verses. Their voices intertwine seamlessly, demonstrating their natural musical chemistry.

7. **"Eleanor Rigby"**—A tombstone at the St. Peter's Church where John and Paul met bears the name "Eleanor Rigby." Paul claims he was unaware of this incredible coincidence when he wrote the song, saying it was a name he invented. Perhaps it subconsciously lodged in his brain?

8. **"She's Leaving Home"**—Another crazy bit of serendipity. The song was inspired by a newspaper article about a teen girl who ran away from home. Unknown to Paul, it was the very same girl he met previously on a British TV show called *Ready, Steady, Go*. Paul was the celebrity judge of a dance contest and selected her as the winner.

9. **"And Your Bird Can Sing"**—This *Revolver* track features one of the most magical guitar duets in the Beatles catalog, with Paul

and George playing interlocking lead guitar parts that create a harmonized effect greater than either could achieve alone.

10. **"A Day in the Life"**—Considered one of the greatest rock songs ever. It is the ultimate example of Beatles magic—John and Paul's separate compositions merge into something greater than either could have created alone, bridged by an orchestral crescendo that seems to bend reality itself.

PART 2

DERAILMENT— "WHY DID IT DIE?"

I n part 2, we explore the root causes of the breakup of The Beatles and ask the questions: What derailed them? What external and internal forces led to this breakup? Or, in Paul's words, "Why did it die?" (original title of the song "For No One.")

I use the term "derailment" to describe the process and ultimate breakup of The Beatles. Derailment is an apt term. I imagine The Beatles' train rolling along the track of musical superstardom, when it all ends abruptly (at least from a public perspective). From the perspective of business, derailment is when a successful company loses its way, often due to a failure of leadership.

We need to remember some challenges in reflecting upon these issues. The credibility of witnesses comes into question for several reasons:

- The Fab Four were usually guarded in their dealings with the press—often misleading them for humor or self-protection.

- The Beatles themselves have differing memories of what happened at certain times. Example: When they heard they had their first number one hit in the USA, they all have different memories of which of them was sick at the time.

- Drugs and alcohol are not conducive to precise memory.

- The passage of time between the events and the time most of the books were written creates hazy memories. In some cases, the advantage of time has added perspective and more reliability to the stories, but in some cases the opposite is true.

- People in The Beatles' universe have told their stories from their unique perspective, and everyone's perspective is a little different. For example, the retelling of having a session drummer (Andy White) play the drums on "Love Me Do" is completely different from George Martin's perspective and Ringo's perspective.

- Many who told the stories embellished their role in The Beatles' success.

- Others told stories in a way to minimize mistakes and errors in judgment.

When noted Beatle biographer Philip Norman was interviewed in 1987 about credibility challenges, referring to George, he said, "He's the one that we're going to have to ask about The Beatles. There's no one else to ask now. McCartney won't tell you; Ringo can't tell you; and John isn't here." When asked what he meant about Paul, he clarified, "He rewrites history all the time." And asked to clarify his comment about Ringo, he said, "He doesn't know. He just drank the drinks, smoked the joints, had the girls and drummed the drums. That was Ringo."[1] Whether this harsh critique of the surviving Beatles is fair or not, it certainly makes it difficult to rely solely on one source when piecing together The Beatles' history—even if that source is one of The Beatles.

With these challenges in mind, I have done my best to draw from dozens of books, interviews, session logs, documentaries, and the music itself to form my opinions about their breakup. In response to the popular myth that Yoko broke up The Beatles, I say rubbish. In my opinion, those most responsible for breaking up The Beatles were John, Paul, George, and Ringo—probably in that order. To be fair, all four of them, in their own way, contributed significantly to the breakup. In the following chapters, we will analyze what went wrong by revisiting each of the Fab Four Pillars of Impact.

Contrary to many opinions, it was not inevitable that they would break up. There were things that each of them could have done to keep the band together or get the band back together. I dive into that speculation in chapters 11 and 12, which also provide a blueprint for avoiding derailment.

CHAPTER 7

THE TRAIN DERAILED

To understand how The Beatles' train derailed, we must first look at how the original business structure created problems. John, Paul, George, and Ringo knew nothing about business and were happy to allow Brian Epstein to design their business structure. It's easy to fault Brian for the early mistakes, but no one could have anticipated how The Beatles would revolutionize the music industry.

Following are the three companies Brian Epstein set up that were the backbone of The Beatles' business empire, with a brief explanation of how they evolved into Apple Corps:

Beatles Ltd (Beatles and Co.): This was the company formed by Brian Epstein, specifically for The Beatles' business. It continued to exist after Epstein's death as Apple Corps, but without his crucial management guidance, it struggled. This lack of oversight created a power vacuum that contributed to the group's eventual business disputes. The ownership was divided equally among the four Beatles members and NEMS, Brian Epstein's company (each holding 20 percent).

NEMS Enterprises: NEMS (North End Music Stores) was the

Epstein family business that became The Beatles' management company. Brian was the majority shareholder (owning 70–80 percent).

Northern Songs: Northern Songs was established in 1963 as the publishing company for Lennon–McCartney (and Harrison) compositions and went public in 1965. The ownership structure was divided as follows:

- John Lennon: Initially 20 percent, later diluted to about 15 percent when the company went public

- Paul McCartney: Initially 20 percent, later diluted to about 15 percent when the company went public

- Brian Epstein: Initially 10 percent, later about 7.5 percent through NEMS

- Dick James, music publisher, and Charles Silver, his silent partner: Initially 50 percent, later about 37.5 percent

- Public shareholders: About 25 percent after the company went public

There is some dispute as to whether George and Ringo owned any of Northern Songs. The most reliable authorities on the matter indicate that George and Ringo owned a small amount (about .8 percent each). When George wrote a song in the early days, he was essentially a contracted songwriter to Northern Songs. This arrangement sheds light on the meaning of The Beatles' song composed by George called "Only a Northern Song."

While these complex business arrangements would eventually contribute to their derailment, the essential character of The Beatles as a performing and recording unit remained remarkably stable through their first several years of success. Up to this point, they had maintained clearly defined roles that served them well during their meteoric rise. However, as we'll see next, subtle but significant shifts in these roles began to emerge in 1966, between the recording of *Rubber Soul* and *Revolver*—shifts that would eventually transform the very foundation upon which their success was built.

The Beatles' Snapshot Revisited

In chapter 3, we took a snapshot of The Beatles on June 1, 1966. At that time, they were the most successful band in the world (and perhaps of all time). John was the clear leader of the band. Their relentless touring schedule was about to come to an end. *Rubber Soul*, their latest album, was number one in both the UK and the US. It spent six to thirteen weeks at number one (depending on the chart). Their latest single "Paperback Writer"/"Rain" had just been released and was climbing the charts on the way to number one.

Rubber Soul represented a watershed moment in The Beatles' artistic development. The songwriting demonstrated newfound maturity and sophistication, with complex harmonies, introspective lyrics, and innovative instrumentation.

The album introduced folk-rock elements and showed the first significant influence of Bob Dylan on their lyrics. John's classic song "Norwegian Wood" featured the first use of the sitar on a Western pop record, showing George's growing interest in Eastern music and philosophy. In 2012, *Rolling Stone* ranked it as the fifth greatest album of all time.[1] This critical acclaim validated their artistic ambitions and set the stage for even bolder experimentation to come.

Remember the creative output at this time: John had written thirty-one of the songs and Paul twenty, they had cowritten twenty, and George had written only four. June 1, 1966, marked a subtle change in the band.

From this point forward, Paul became more of the leader, especially regarding musical direction. In addition, both he and George entered a particularly fertile songwriting period.

The next Beatles album, *Revolver*, released in August of 1966, shows remarkable growth and maturity. Five of the songs on the album deal with themes of death or dying. This preoccupation with mortality represents another significant shift in their songwriting, moving from the young love–focused lyrics of their earlier work to more existential themes.

Consider Paul's contributions to the album: "Eleanor Rigby"; "Here, There, and Everywhere"; "Good Day Sunshine"; "For No One"; "Got to Get You into My Life"; and coauthorship of "Yellow Submarine" for Ringo to sing. Those songs would be a career for most artists. For me, this is Paul at his creative best.

Not to be left out, for the first time, George had three songs on this album, including "Taxman," the impressive lead-in song (first song on the album), a place of honor for the band.

This is not to say that John's production was slacking off; he continued to create great songs at this time, but Paul was at his peak, and George was improving rapidly. This created a new dynamic in the band.

Who's on the Train?

When we consider the changes within the core group of people "on the train," we must look first at the most dramatic change in their time together as a band. On August 27, 1967, The Beatles and their significant others were in Bangor, Wales, attending a seminar on Transcendental Meditation led by the Maharishi. At the seminar, they received word that their manager, Brian Epstein, had died. It was ruled to be an overdose, but some speculated that it was suicide. Conventional wisdom is that it was an accidental overdose, but there is no question that Brian was going through some bouts of depression and self-doubt.

Note the difference between the reactions of The Beatles:

John: "I knew that we were in trouble then. I didn't really have any misconceptions about our ability to do anything other than play music. I was scared, you know. I thought we had f---ing had it."

George: "There was a huge void. We didn't know anything about, you know, our personal business and finances. You know, he was taking care of everything. And I suppose it was chaos after that."

Paul: "We were kind of managing ourselves really. It was sad, you know, it was very sad to lose an old mate under those circumstances, but I don't think the major worry was what are we going to do now, we haven't got a manager because we had been moving away from that."

Ringo: "We were suddenly like chickens without heads. What are we going to do? What are we going to do?"[2]

Curiously, as soon as the four lads received the tragic news, Paul immediately went back to London, leaving the three others in Bangor to face the press in a state of shock. This could simply have been how Paul processed the grief, but it certainly wasn't a case of "all for one and one for all."

This left a clear void on The Beatles' team. For the most part, business decisions and touring schedules were left to Brian Epstein. When Paul said they had been moving away from him as their manager, there is some truth to that. After they stopped touring in August of 1966, there was not as much for him to manage, but he clearly remained in charge of The Beatles' business. Paul's statement displays a lack of appreciation for the scope of The Beatles' business enterprise.

Overnight, the four lads were faced with the question: Who is going to manage The Beatles? And perhaps more importantly, whom could they trust? As you might imagine, being the biggest group on the planet, many people wanted to have a piece of The Beatles' empire. This resulted in growing tension among the four Beatles.

Finding the Right People

The situation The Beatles faced in losing Brian Epstein bears a striking resemblance to the challenges many organizations face when there's a leadership vacuum. Consider how Alan Mulally approached the troubled Ford Motor Company when he took over as CEO. Like The Beatles after Brian Epstein's death, Ford was in disarray, with executives unsure of their roles and the company's direction.

> Bryce Hoffman writes in *American Icon*:
> Mulally was quick to appreciate the immense—and too often untapped—pool of talent that surrounded him at Ford. When he found someone who knew what was going on and was not afraid to say so, he brought that person to his office and listened— sometimes for hours.[3]

Mulally, like The Beatles, needed to decide who belonged "on the train" and who didn't. But unlike The Beatles, who struggled to find consensus on how to manage their business after Brian Epstein's death, Mulally established clear guidelines to help him identify the right people. He posted ten rules on the wall of the meeting room, including:

- People first
- Everyone is included
- Compelling vision
- Clear performance goals
- One plan
- Facts and data
- Propose a plan, "find-a-way" attitude
- Respect, listen, help, and appreciate each other
- Emotional resilience . . . trust the process
- Have fun . . . enjoy the journey and each other[4]

By observing his leadership team work with these guidelines, Mulally learned who the right people were. Imagine if The Beatles had established similar guidelines that they could rely on as they tried to build their management team after Epstein's death. Would their story have ended differently?

Quitting Time

The stress of Beatlemania on the four members of the band was immense. They were in the eye of the storm and couldn't get out. George once said about their fans, "They gave their money, and they gave their screams. But The Beatles kind of gave their nervous systems. They used us as an excuse to go mad, the world did and then blamed it on us."[5]

This stress along with other factors caused each of the four Beatles to quit at one time or another. By looking at the circumstances around those decisions, we can see the tensions that were pulling on the four of them.

RINGO

The first to quit was Ringo, on August 22, 1968, while they were record-ing the White Album. They had just returned from Rishikesh, India, and Ringo felt like an outsider. He stayed in India the least amount of time and came back early. He felt that the other three were all in sync and he was the odd man out. Since they were busy recording at the time, they had to keep moving forward with their schedule. Two songs on the White Album feature Paul as the drummer: "Back in the USSR" and "Dear Prudence."

The other three, to their credit, did not want Ringo to quit and let him know that. Each of them talked to Ringo. Ringo tells the story that when he talked to George, he said, "It just feels like it's you three and I'm out on my own," and George replied, "Oh, I thought it was you three." When he approached John with the same issue, John said similarly, "Oh, I thought it was you three," and the very same thing happened when he approached Paul. They all got a chuckle out of that and convinced Ringo to return to the band and the studio. When Ringo arrived at the studio, his whole drum kit was covered in flowers with the sign that said, "The greatest rock drummer in the world."[6]

GEORGE

The next to quit was George, on January 10, 1969, while they were recording the film *Let It Be* (later renamed *Get Back*). George was becoming increasingly disgruntled with his minimal role in the group, especially his inability to get many of his songs on the albums. He was particularly frustrated that John and Paul didn't give the same attention to his songs that they all gave to their songs. So, George famously quit in the middle of those sessions.

It was more difficult convincing George to rejoin the band. They had a meeting with the four of them a few days later that did not go well. The next attempted meeting went better; they convinced George to rejoin the band, but they had to agree not to do the big live concert they were considering.

JOHN

On September 20, 1969, after they had just signed a new record deal, John announced to Paul and Ringo at the signing of the new record contract that he would be quitting the band. Interestingly, George was not present at this signing, so he didn't even know that John had "quit" for several months. From the outside, there was no indication that The Beatles were breaking up.

John was becoming more active politically, starting to do more things away from the group, and even wrote and recorded a couple of songs in the next few months on his own. These two songs were "Give Peace a Chance" and "Instant Karma," which were released as singles by John and Yoko, not as part of The Beatles.

PAUL

The final Beatle to quit was Paul, on April 10, 1970. From Paul's perspective, he was not quitting the band—he was merely announcing it to the public. In Paul's defense, he took John's comments in September of the previous year seriously and believed The Beatles were broken up. Paul wanted to get ahead of the public relations disaster and get it out there as he prepared to release his solo album. (By this time, John had already released two solo singles.)

Some serious questions remain that will never be answered: When John quit in September of '69, why didn't he announce it to the public or get the four Beatles together to discuss how they would announce it to the public? It is entirely possible that John had some doubts, and by not announcing it to the public, he left the door open for them to get back together. On the other hand, I certainly understand Paul's desire to get it out in the open so they could all start moving on. Based on everything I've read and heard, Paul was the one who least wanted The Beatles to break up, and he was having a difficult time facing it.

Building a Culture of "Right People"

In September of 2006, Boeing executive Alan Mulally took over as president and CEO of a floundering Ford Motor Company. Mulally's knack for identifying the right people and getting them in the right seats was paramount to his leading a successful turnaround at Ford.

The Beatles' story of each member quitting at different times reveals the eroding trust among the group. Compare this with how Mulally created an environment at Ford where executives could be honest about problems without fear of retribution.

As Hoffman writes in *American Icon*, there was a pivotal moment when Mark Fields, head of Ford Americas, had to make a tough decision about delaying the launch of the Ford Edge due to a quality issue. Mulally had identified a core issue among the executives—a lack of transparency. If the executive team cannot be transparent, how can they work together to address problems?

At one of the executive meetings, Fields shared a projection for the Ford Edge launch that showed it in the red (losing money). The others in the room probably thought he was crazy to share that bad news. As the rest of the room sat in stunned silence, Mulally started clapping and praised Fields for delivering the kind of transparency that was needed. "'Mark, that is great visibility,' he beamed. 'Who can help Mark with this?' This moment transformed Ford's culture."[7] With this new commitment to transparency, challenges were worked on as a team.

Mulally later called this "the defining moment in Ford's turnaround."[8]

When The Beatles agreed to hire Brian Epstein as their manager, they deferred all business decisions to him. Though understandable because of their age and lack of business experience, it was a critical mistake not to learn more about their business situation. Had Brian Epstein and The Beatles created a similar environment to what Mulally did at Ford, where they regularly met to discuss financial goals and results, they would have had sufficient knowledge and experience to identify the "right people" to replace Brian Epstein. As it was, they floundered—not knowing whom to trust.

Changing Roles

In chapter 3, we saw how clearly defined roles facilitated rapid improvement and growth. Up until the final Beatles concert on August 29, 1966, at Candlestick Park in San Francisco, those defined roles remained solid. Before we look at how this began to change the roles, let's look at why The Beatles stopped touring.

After August of 1966, The Beatles could no longer rely on generating magic through live performances. What started as four lads rocking Hamburg clubs had morphed into something unrecognizable—stadiums of screaming fans who could only hear screaming, death threats in the Philippines and America, and the constant pressure of being "on display" like museum pieces rather than musicians. As George later put it, "We'd become performing fleas."[9] At live concerts, the band couldn't even hear themselves play anymore!

Remember that The Beatles formed when they were teenagers. As they grew into their twenties, there were major changes in their lives:

marriages, children, and home ownership. Understandably, their priorities changed. What was an exciting whirlwind in the early days became an annoyance as they tried to create a life with their families.

John was already married to Cynthia when The Beatles had their first hit. Ringo married Maureen Cox on February 11, 1965, and George married Pattie Boyd on January 21, 1966. Paul remained single until he married Linda in 1969.

Ringo, George, and John all bought homes for their new families outside the city of London. Paul, on the other hand, bought a home in London, within walking distance of the EMI studios (now Abbey Road Studio). This provided bachelor Paul with quick and frequent access to the studio. These two facts dramatically changed the group dynamics.

During their touring years, the four of them lived together virtually nonstop, creating a camaraderie and a closeness that was not possible when they all lived in their own homes. It particularly changed the way John and Paul wrote music together. There was very little face-to-face songwriting at this time. They did, however, continue to collaborate, but the way they collaborated had changed. One of them would have the foundation of a song and take it to the other one for comments and refinement.

When they walked offstage at Candlestick Park on August 29, 1966, there was a collective sigh of relief. This monumental decision opened an opportunity for a reshuffling of the seats on their train. When they were touring, the "right seats" were clearly defined by necessity—there simply wasn't time for anything else. As George observed: "Some of those years where we did maybe a tour of England; a tour of Europe; a tour of America; two albums; and about four EPs; and three singles; and made a movie all in the same year—Jesus, how did we do that?"[10]

When they stopped touring, it gave George more time to develop as a songwriter. And the studio environment allowed George to push for more of his songs to be included, changing the traditional Lennon–McCartney–dominated albums. As George improved as a songwriter, he naturally wanted a different seat on the train—no longer content with the standard one or two songs per album.

What About George?

George had the unenviable task of having to learn how to write songs in front of the world and in front of two of the greatest songwriters of all time. In the early days, he wasn't that interested in writing songs, but eventually, he developed a passion for it. Fittingly for an introvert, his first song to appear on a Beatles album was called "Don't Bother Me."

George was on a quest for inner peace; the crazy touring years had taken their toll on him. This piqued his interest in Indian culture and religion. In an interview with *Guitar World*, George discussed his spiritual awakening: "It was like I had a sudden flash, and it all seemed to be happening for some real purpose. . . . And now the rest of my life as a person and a musician is about finding out what that reason is, and how to build upon it."[11]

As a member of the biggest rock group in the world, George was a celebrity everywhere he went. He had become friends with Eric Clapton and other musicians. When he was in their presence, he was the biggest rock star. The only place George played second fiddle was when he was with John and Paul. This was exacerbated by the fact that John and Paul were both very strong personalities, and George was an introvert.

To give you an idea of how focused Paul was on The Beatles as an entity and his own career, here is a snippet from the 1995 interviews for *The Beatles Anthology*:

Paul: "We lived quite near each other in Liverpool. In fact, we were just a bus stop away from each other. I'd get on the bus and then the stop afterward, George would get on. So, being quite close in age, we'd sit together and we'd talk about stuff and that. In fact, he was, I think, about one and a half years younger than me. That's quite a big age difference at that time. So, I suppose I used to talk down to him a little bit, as you do to a sort of kid who's one and a half years younger than you—when he's sort of fourteen and a half and I'm sort of sixteen. It might have been a failure of mine to tend to talk down to him because I had known him as a younger kid."

George: "He was always nine months older than I. Even now, he's still nine months older than I."[12]

For the record, George was born eight months and one week after Paul. The fact that Paul was not aware of their age difference, even after years of reflection, indicates a stunning lack of familiarity and appreciation for George. He practically lived with him nonstop for several years and didn't know his birth date, nor their age difference? The whole world seemed to know George's birth date, but not his bandmate (and the guy who was best man at his first wedding)? Paul was so focused on the next project and his own role in it that he missed an opportunity to create a deeper bond with his bandmate and a chance to make The Beatles even stronger.

As mentioned previously, George got the lead-in song on *Revolver*. When it came time to do the guitar solo in the middle of "Taxman," George attempted it several times. Geoff Emerick, the sound engineer for the song recalled, "So George Martin went into the studio and, as diplomatically as possible, announced that he wanted Paul to have a go at the solo instead. I could see the look on Harrison's face that he didn't like the idea one bit, but he reluctantly agreed."[13] Paul, of course, nailed it quickly and ended up having the lead guitar solo on the song George wrote, even though George's clearly defined role in the band was lead guitarist. There are conflicting reports on how much this incident bothered George; however, to his credit, I've never heard an interview where he complained about it.

As The Beatles became more of a studio band, experimenting with a wide variety of instruments, it changed the early dynamic when the four of them would play together, each on their own instrument, to record a song. This culminated on *Sgt. Pepper's Lonely Hearts Club Band*, where they experimented with many different instruments and sounds and didn't rely nearly as much on the traditional lineup of instruments.

George continued working on his songwriting and started creating a backlog of songs to be considered for Beatles albums (or a future solo career). Despite his increased output, his songs were routinely relegated to a maximum of one per side.

The Importance of Recognizing Talent

Alan Mulally understood that identifying and nurturing talent was essential to turning Ford around. He didn't just rely on established executives but sought out those who truly understood the business, regardless of their position or whether they agreed with him.

The key to Mulally's success at accomplishing this was a willingness to listen and learn. He recognized that he had within the walls of Ford an abundance of knowledge, experience, and talent. All he had to do was learn how to tap into it. This approach stands in stark contrast to how The Beatles, particularly John and Paul, failed to fully recognize and utilize George's growing talents as a songwriter.

George Martin's Role

As The Beatles became more adept at producing their own music and having their own ideas for arranging the songs, George Martin's role began to diminish. Paul's appetite and energy for work never diminished. Living so close to the studio, he could stop by anytime to work on their songs. To a lesser degree, George also became interested in producing music. In fact, one of the purposes of setting up their business, Apple Corps, was to give them an opportunity to produce other artists. With the death of Brian Epstein and the selection of a new manager still unresolved, the other figure who provided discipline to the band, George Martin, found his role reduced as the band started asserting more leadership in the studio.

Replacing Brian Epstein

From the time of Brian Epstein's death in August of 1967 until 1969, The Beatles were more or less self-managing. They launched Apple Corps as an attempt to bring their management under one roof. It was not going well at Apple Corps. They were getting a lot of business advice from various factions, and nobody really knew who was in charge. One thing they agreed on was that they needed to hire a manager.

John had become enamored with Allen Klein, a New York–based manager who had been managing The Rolling Stones and got them a great record deal. He had an unscrupulous reputation in self-dealing but was also a tireless worker who got results.

John wanted to hire Klein to be their manager. George and Ringo agreed, despite his poor reputation, pointing to his success in getting The Rolling Stones a much better record deal than they had. Paul did not like the idea and voted against it. Paul wanted the band to hire Lee and John Eastman, Paul's father-in-law and brother-in-law, who were entertainment lawyers from New York. Paul's best argument for hiring them was that they would work at an hourly rate and not take a percentage of the profits. Klein insisted on a 20 percent share of the profits (the same that Epstein received).

Paul failed to appreciate how the conflict of interest of having his family represent the band would sour the others on the idea. They ended up hiring Klein, who immediately started cleaning up the mess at Apple Corps. He fired many longtime friends of The Beatles who were previously comfortably employed. He succeeded in controlling expenses and landed them the lucrative record deal he'd promised.

So who was right? No one! Klein was unscrupulous and lined his own pocket handsomely. However, he did turn the bleak financial picture around. He aggressively represented the band in dealings with several others who had been taking advantage of them. No one will know if the Eastmans could have accomplished the same.

Hindsight being what it is, they should have sought a third option.

Making the Tough Decisions

Like The Beatles facing the challenging decision of replacing Epstein, Mulally had to make difficult choices about who stayed on his team at Ford. Hoffman describes Mulally's relationship with his CFO, Don Leclair:

> Mulally was worried about how negative Leclair was. He was not convinced anybody could save Ford, and his pessimism would only increase as the company's finances deteriorated. However, Mulally's biggest concern about his hardworking CFO was Leclair's apparent inability to work with the rest of the leadership team. "Don knows the business better than anybody,"

Mulally thought as he listened to Leclair. "But he's not a team player, and he never will be. He's smart, but he can't join me in pulling everyone together." As a result, Mulally knew Leclair's days at Ford were numbered.[14]

Mulally recognized that technical expertise alone wasn't enough. Team cohesion was essential.

Mulally dealt with Bill Ford's brother-in-law, Steve Hamp, in a similar way. Mulally had inherited him as his chief of staff, a position he did not think was needed. Despite the political implications, Mulally worked with Bill Ford to remove Hamp from his position. The Beatles might have benefited from similar decisive leadership when choosing between Klein and the Eastmans—or better yet, finding that elusive "third option."

Conclusion: The Importance of Unity

The story of The Beatles' derailment is a cautionary tale about what happens when ego creeps in—a team loses trust and its sense of unity. Their inability to agree on fundamental business decisions, their failure to fully utilize each member's talents, and their deteriorating personal relationships all contributed to their downfall.

Contrast this with Mulally's approach at Ford, summed up in his encouragement to his team:

At the end of one meeting, Mulally got up and walked to the screen. It displayed a financial chart showing a long, steep decline followed by a modest rise at the end. It looked bad, he acknowledged, but he told the team he had seen worse at Boeing. "Guys," he said, pointing to the trough, "let's get to the bottom as quick as we can, because let me tell you, the ride up is a lot of fun."[15]

Unlike The Beatles, who never found their way back after derailing, Mulally created an environment where Ford could acknowledge its problems, work together as a team, and find its way back to success. It's a powerful reminder that even when the bus derails, with the right leadership and teamwork, it's possible to get back on track and enjoy the ride together.

Applying the Lessons of Chapter 7

When a high-performing team falls apart, the cost isn't just measured in dollars—it's calculated in unrealized potential and personal regret. The Beatles' derailment represents perhaps the greatest "what might have been" in creative history.

By 1969, The Beatles' carefully constructed team dynamic had deteriorated beyond repair. The departure of manager Epstein in 1967 created a leadership vacuum that was never adequately filled. More critically, the original right-people-in-right-seats configuration that had served them so perfectly through their rise no longer fit their evolving needs and ambitions.

Five critical warning signs appeared long before their formal breakup:

1. **Role rigidity:** George remained confined to a limited creative contribution despite his growth as a songwriter.

2. **External influences:** Yoko Ono's presence in the studio broke their unspoken boundary between personal and professional life.

3. **Leadership vacuum:** After Brian Epstein's death, no trusted adviser could mediate their increasingly fractious relationships.

4. **Competing priorities:** Film projects, side ventures, and family commitments created scheduling conflicts.

5. **Misaligned incentives:** Business arrangements created financial tensions that undermined their shared purpose.

These warning signs manifest in specific, observable behaviors that leaders should watch for in their own teams.

DERAILMENT DIAGNOSTIC: TEAM ROLE WARNING SIGNS

For each team member, assess whether these statements have become true:

- Frequently expresses frustration about contribution limits ("I'm not valued for all I can do")
- Shows declining engagement in collective work while increasing investment in side projects
- Refers to past role definitions to resist taking on new responsibilities
- Brings external relationships into team dynamics in disruptive ways
- Prioritizes individual financial gain over collective benefit

Three or more "yes" answers suggest your team configuration may be heading toward derailment.

TEAM ASSESSMENT TOOL:
THE COMPLEMENTARY TALENT AUDIT

This Complementary Talent Audit helps teams identify each member's unique strengths and optimal roles. By documenting both current positions and ideal placements based on capabilities, teams can discover misalignments that may be preventing peak performance. Just as The Beatles maximized their impact by putting each member where they could contribute most effectively, this tool helps organizations ensure their talent is positioned for success.

For each team member (including yourself), identify the following:

- Primary strength: _____
- Secondary strength: _____
- Key personality attribute: _____
- Current role: _____
- Ideal role based on strengths: _____

Where gaps exist between current and ideal roles, you may have the right people in the wrong seats.

IMPLEMENTATION GUIDE:
BUILDING YOUR OPTIMAL TEAM

This five-step process provides a structured approach to identifying individuals who have hidden talent or have outgrown their current role. Rather than making abrupt changes, it guides you through thoughtful evaluation, collaborative discussion, and experimental adjustments—mirroring how The Beatles evolved their lineup and responsibilities over time. The guide helps teams move beyond simple personnel decisions to create the chemistry that turns individual talents into collective excellence.

1. **Talent assessment:** Evaluate team members on both current performance and future potential—just as John saw Paul's future contribution.

2. **Role definition workshop:** Have team members identify where they contribute the most value and where they struggle.

3. **Strengths mapping:** Create a visual representation of how team members' strengths complement each other.

4. **Gap analysis:** Identify missing capabilities that might require bringing in new talent.

5. **Ninety-day role experiment:** Test new role assignments before making permanent changes.

CHAPTER 7 PLAYLIST

THE TRAIN DERAILED

This playlist follows the emotional journey of The Beatles' derailment, from the earliest cracks appearing to the eventual acceptance of their dissolution, while showcasing each member's perspective on what was happening to their once-unbreakable bond.

1. **"Help!"**—The perfect opening track that foreshadows the troubles to come, with John's admitted cry for help disguised as an upbeat pop song. The lyrics reveal his growing sense of isolation and uncertainty at the height of fame, capturing the beginning of derailment.

2. **"You've Got to Hide Your Love Away"**—This Dylan-influenced acoustic number reflects the increasing isolation members felt even while still together. John's vulnerable delivery hints at the emotional walls being built between bandmates as they began retreating into separate worlds.

3. **"I'm Looking Through You"**—Paul's song about seeing someone differently once you truly know them—symbolic of how the band members began seeing each other. Its spiky energy conveys the frustration of watching close relationships change and deteriorate over time.

4. **"I'm So Tired"**—John's exhaustion with fame and the band shows through in this White Album track. The weariness in his voice reflects the toll that years of relentless pressure and deteriorating relationships had taken on all four members.

5. **"While My Guitar Gently Weeps"**—George's masterpiece speaks to the sadness he felt watching relationships disintegrate around him. The mournful guitar work (featuring Eric Clapton) perfectly captures the quiet pain of seeing something precious slowly falling apart.

6. **"Don't Pass Me By"**—Ringo's first solo composition for The Beatles, its country-influenced style stands apart from the others, reflecting the diverging paths each member was beginning to take. The title symbolizes Ringo's plea to the group as they headed for derailment.

7. **"Don't Let Me Down"**—John's plaintive cry not to be disappointed or abandoned—exactly what each member ultimately felt. John's raw vocal performance reveals the vulnerability beneath his tough exterior and his fear of being let down by those closest to him.

8. **"Only a Northern Song"**—George's sardonic commentary on his contractual obligations and limited creative control within Northern Songs publishing company. The deliberately rough production and dismissive lyrics reflect his frustration with the

business arrangements that ultimately contributed to the band's dissolution and his marginalized status.

9. **"Fixing a Hole"**—Paul's metaphorical song about repairing what's broken perfectly captures the band's attempts to patch up their differences. The dreamy, philosophical tone suggests the importance of each person finding a safe space.

10. **"Get Back"**—The final single released before their breakup ironically urges a return to basics. Its deceptively simple structure belies the complexity of their situation—they wanted to recapture their early magic but found that it was fleeting.

CHAPTER 8

COMPETING VISIONS

B y the late '60s, John and George were inclined to take a break or stop altogether while Paul continued to push for more. This created a tension among them: a crisis of vision.

A catalytic vision serves as rocket fuel for organizations and creative collaborations. It unites diverse talents toward common goals, inspires extraordinary effort, and provides direction when obstacles arise. However, what happens when that vision is achieved? Or when the individuals who once shared that vision begin to develop different priorities? This is where many otherwise successful ventures begin to falter.

In this chapter, we'll explore how even the most successful collaborations can be derailed when their catalytic vision splinters or is fulfilled without a clear path forward.

The Beatles: Vision Achieved

In chapter 4, we noted that The Beatles' ambition was anything but modest ("the toppermost of the poppermost"). This catalytic vision—to be the biggest band in the world—drove their relentless work ethic through grueling performances in Hamburg, years of steadfast work, and the early challenges of Beatlemania. But what happens when such a vision is actually achieved?

By 1966, The Beatles had unquestionably reached the "toppermost of the poppermost." They had conquered America, played record-breaking stadium concerts, received MBEs (Member of the Order of the British Empire—an honor awarded by the British monarchy for distinguished service) from the Queen, and revolutionized popular music. Their albums and singles dominated charts worldwide. They had, by any measure, fulfilled their original vision.

Yet they never stopped to consider: What would they do once they achieved it? With their primary goal accomplished, what would be their next mountain to climb? This vacuum of shared purpose created space for individual visions to emerge—visions that would ultimately prove incompatible.

The Fundamental Challenge

There exists a fundamental difference between creating something revolutionary and maintaining it over time. This explains why so few music groups have maintained their original lineup throughout their careers. Among the mega-bands, The Rolling Stones have perhaps come closest, though even they have experienced significant lineup changes over the decades.

Similarly, in business, the skill set of a great entrepreneur differs vastly from that of a professional manager leading a mature, successful company. Very few entrepreneurs who start successful businesses can effectively transition to professionally managing those enterprises for the long-term, especially once they achieve significant scale. The qualities that make someone excel at identifying opportunities, taking risks, and building something from nothing are often at odds with those required for systematic growth and operational excellence.

In sports, especially in the modern era, we see the same challenge. Getting to the top is one thing, but remaining on top is quite another. There are many forces going against sustained excellence: changing personnel, complacency, egos, and distraction, to name a few. The closest recent examples of sustained excellence in sports often involve one superstar with generational talent, surrounded by a changing supporting cast, which creates a new set of risks.

Changing and Competing Visions

As The Beatles' original shared vision was fulfilled, individual visions began to emerge and eventually compete. Understanding these divergent paths helps illuminate why their collaboration, despite its extraordinary success, ultimately proved unsustainable.

JOHN'S VISION

As early as 1966's *Rubber Soul* album, we begin seeing glimpses of John's evolving vision. His lyrics started to focus on broader themes of love, peace, and social consciousness. For John, The Beatles had become a platform—an opportunity to influence people at a level far beyond mere entertainment.

John's evolution toward a more message-driven approach can be traced back to songs like "The Word," from 1965's *Rubber Soul* album. In this early philosophical piece, John begins expressing what would become a central theme in his later work—that love is the answer to society's problems. The song contains lines where John positions himself as a messenger, suggesting he's there to lead people to a better way and spread the message of love. This missionary approach continued developing in songs like "Rain," where John adopts the stance of someone who can show you a different perspective, positioning himself as a guide. His psychedelic-era compositions like "Tomorrow Never Knows" invite listeners to consider a higher level of consciousness, further establishing John as someone offering wisdom and direction.

By the time of "All You Need Is Love," John had fully embraced his role as a cultural messenger, distilling his philosophy into an almost mantra-like simplicity. These songs represent milestones in John's journey from pop songwriter to cultural commentator, revealing his growing desire to lead rather than merely entertain.

John clearly understood the cultural power he wielded. In 1969, shortly before The Beatles officially disbanded, he wrote and performed "Give Peace a Chance." Just three months later, this song was chanted by a crowd of over five hundred thousand people at a peace rally on the Washington, DC, Mall. That same year, the BBC named him "Man of the Decade."

John's vision had expanded from creating innovative music to using his influence to promote social change and peace. He saw himself as someone with the responsibility to lead his followers to enlightenment. This missionary zeal, however sincere, created friction with bandmates who didn't necessarily share his specific social agenda or his methods of pursuing it.

PAUL'S VISION

Paul's vision for The Beatles' next phase remained closest to their original shared purpose. Paul enjoyed being a rock star and cherished his creative partnership with John. He remained driven to create innovative music and wanted The Beatles to continue as the primary outlet for his prolific creativity.

In 1969, as the band was falling apart, Paul continued to push his bandmates to take on new projects, make live appearances, and create more music. During this period, Paul was experiencing exceptional creative fertility that needed expression. He remained committed to that outlet being The Beatles.

Several of Paul's songs during this time reveal the inner turmoil he felt watching The Beatles crumble. "Let It Be," when considered in the context of this breakup, becomes particularly poignant. While many assume Paul is referring to Mary, mother of Jesus, he was actually thinking of his own mother, Mary, who passed away when he was a teenager. The song reflects someone struggling with painful circumstances, hearing a comforting voice telling him that everything will eventually be all right.

Another revealing song is "Two of Us." Though Paul maintained it was written for his wife, Linda, many of the lyrics seem more applicable to his relationship with John. The song takes on special significance when viewed as a reflection on their lengthy partnership.

Paul was heartbroken watching The Beatles dissolve around him. He tried everything he could think of to hold the group together, but his solutions—which typically involved working harder and taking on more projects—backfired. What seemed to Paul like enthusiasm and dedication felt to others, especially John and George, like pressure they couldn't sustain.

GEORGE'S VISION

George's vision was more complex, intertwined with his spiritual journey and his frustration at being undervalued within The Beatles. For

George, the path forward involved seeking spiritual enlightenment and building a life with priorities he considered more meaningful than fame or commercial success.

As we saw in the previous chapter, George grew increasingly frustrated with his secondary status in the band, particularly regarding his songwriting contributions. After years of developing his craft, George had become an exceptional songwriter, creating some of The Beatles' most beloved songs, including "Something" and "Here Comes the Sun." His creativity had flourished to the point that his first solo album, *All Things Must Pass*, was released as a triple album to accommodate his backlog of quality material.

It's worth noting that "Here Comes the Sun" is now the most streamed Beatles song of all time.[1] Frank Sinatra famously called "Something" the greatest love song in the last fifty years.[2] Perhaps nothing exemplifies George's status, compared to John and Paul, more than the unintentional slight that Sinatra often called "Something" a Lennon–McCartney song.[3]

George's songs provide clear insights into his evolving vision. His focus had shifted from The Beatles to spirituality, inner peace, and healthier relationships. The song "All Things Must Pass" hints at his recognition that The Beatles' era was ending. "My Sweet Lord" demonstrates George's reorientation toward spiritual matters. This song functions almost as a mantra or prayer for healing and direction. In "Isn't It a Pity," we see George reflecting on the sadness in human relationships. The song could easily be interpreted as commentary on the deteriorating relationships within The Beatles.

Rita Coolidge, who toured with George for a short while, once said, "George was such a profoundly gentle man and at the same time so charismatic . . . almost like a religious leader in a sense. He had such a magnetic kind of energy around him. But he was so soft spoken. To me, he was like a holy man, just his energy, his aura, everything about him was more beautiful than probably anybody else I had ever met."[4]

RINGO'S VISION

While John pursued political activism, Paul focused on maintaining The Beatles' commercial success, and George deepened his spiritual journey, Ringo developed his own divergent vision: becoming a film star. Ringo had received the most critical acclaim among the four for his natural performance in The Beatles' films. His deadpan delivery and understated charm in *A Hard Day's Night* prompted director Richard Lester to give him an expanded role in *Help!* Film critics consistently praised his on-screen presence.

This new vision became reality when, during the tumultuous *Let It Be/Get Back* sessions in early 1969, Ringo accepted a role in Peter Sellers's film *The Magic Christian*. The timing was revealing—rather than postponing film work to focus on The Beatles' increasingly troubled dynamic, Ringo prioritized his acting aspirations, creating scheduling conflicts that further strained the band's cohesion.

Ringo claimed he knew his priorities. "I am a Beatle," he said ahead of the film's opening night. "If it comes to a toss between doing a film and making a Beatles album, I'll do the album. But I don't mean the film business is just a hobby to me. I'm deadly serious about it."[5]

The situation highlighted a fundamental challenge of maintaining a catalytic vision over time: As team members develop individual interests and identities, their personal visions can drift from the collective purpose that once united them. While Ringo maintained that he would have stayed with the band, his actions revealed the natural tension between group commitment and personal growth.

Unlike George, who directly confronted Paul about creative differences, or John, who dramatically announced his departure, Ringo's vision shift was more subtle. His growing passion for acting didn't manifest as overt conflict, yet it still represented a crucial strand in the unraveling of The Beatles' shared purpose. For any team facing changing priorities, Ringo's example demonstrates how even the most supportive team members may develop competing visions that gradually redirect their energy and attention away from collective goals.

First Solo Singles Show the Changing Vision

One of the most revealing examples of the band members' divergent visions appears in the first solo singles released by each Beatle. These debut songs are absurdly appropriate statements about their changed priorities:

John: "Give Peace a Chance"

George: "My Sweet Lord"

Ringo: "Beaucoups of Blues"

Paul: "Another Day"

John launched with a protest song focused on social justice and antiwar sentiment. George released a spiritual song expressing his yearning for divine connection. Ringo opted for a melancholy country tune. And Paul, despite the turmoil in his life and sad lyrics, maintained outward positivity with an upbeat melody with a Scarlett O'Hara approach to life's troubles—it's just "Another Day."

These distinct artistic statements perfectly encapsulate the divergent paths each member had begun to travel, making continued collaboration increasingly difficult despite their immense collective success.

Nike's Changing Vision

Nike was faced with a challenge similar to what The Beatles faced when they had achieved their vision. However, Nike was able to successfully change (expand) their vision. Their original vision was to "Crush Adidas." While I am not a fan of a negative vision, it certainly is compelling and left no doubt where they were headed. At the time, Adidas was far and away the world leader in the athletic shoe market.

Once Nike had replaced Adidas at the top, that vision no longer resonated. Their new vision was to "Bring Inspiration and Innovation to Every Athlete in the World." This positive vision qualifies as a Jim Collins BHAG ("every athlete in the world"!). As with their earlier vision, it provided the catalyst for Nike to expand their reach around the world and beyond shoes.

Personal Reflection: The Vision Tree

The challenges faced by The Beatles reveal a universal truth: Without a shared vision that evolves as circumstances change, even the most successful collaborations can falter. This understanding informs how forward-thinking organizations approach vision and purpose.

After discovering our core purpose at Absher Construction, we recognized the need to effectively communicate it and gain buy-in throughout the organization. With ambitious growth plans, enhancing our leadership development became a priority.

This led my brother, Tom, to develop what he called "the Vision Tree," a framework that became our standard approach for communicating the importance of vision to our team. The Vision Tree encompasses core ideology, mission, and envisioned future, serving as the foundation for our annual strategic planning sessions.

The Vision Tree concept combines insights from Jim Collins and

Jerry Porras's *Built to Last* with lessons from other sources and, most importantly, our practical experience in leading and managing people. It proved effective because it made abstract concepts accessible to everyone in the organization, not just the leadership team. Through this visual metaphor, team members at all levels could understand how their daily work was connected to our larger purpose.

Components of the Vision Tree

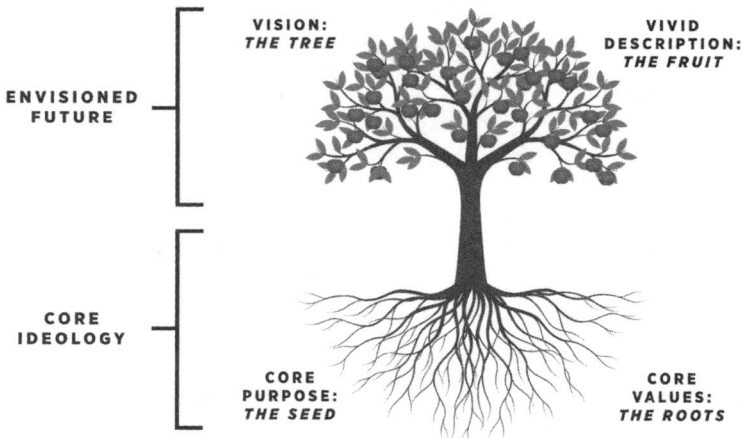

Credit: rolandtopor © istockphoto.com

Core Ideology =
Core Purpose + Core Values (the Why)

The Core Ideology answers the question *Why?* Why does the team or organization exist? That question is answered by understanding the core purpose and values of the organization.

CORE PURPOSE = THE SEED

At the root of the Vision Tree lies the core purpose—the seed from which all else springs. A core purpose

- Is the organization's fundamental reason for being (the "why")
- Captures the soul of the organization
- Might never be fully fulfilled but is always pursued
- Is not merely a description of products or customers

Examples of powerful core purposes include 3M's "To solve unsolved problems innovatively" and Walt Disney's "To make people happy." These statements transcend specific products or services to articulate why the organization exists.

CORE VALUES = THE ROOTS

The roots of the Vision Tree represent the organization's core values— fundamental guiding principles that are distinctive to the organization. Core values

- Are true about the organization (they may or may not align with aspirational written values)
- Are few (typically three to five) and timeless
- Require no outside justification and remain unswayed by external forces

Just as a tree cannot thrive with weak or damaged roots, an organization cannot sustain success without a solid foundation of values that guide decision-making at all levels.

Envisioned Future = Catalytic Vision + Vivid Description (the What)

An effective envisioned future

- Combines its Catalytic Vision with a Vivid Description
- Articulates dreams, hopes, and aspirations in a visible, vivid, and tangible way
- Consists of long-term goals that stretch beyond current capabilities
- Describes what it looks like to fulfill the organization's purpose according to its values
- Stretches the whole organization

VISION = THE TREE

The tree is the Catalytic Vision, an aspirational long-term goal or BHAG. When people look into the future and picture the tree in full maturity, it is sufficiently exciting to propel a team of people forward.

VIVID DESCRIPTION = THE FRUIT

The fruit of the Vision Tree are the specific details of the envisioned future. For The Beatles, "the tree" was getting to the "toppermost of the poppermost," while the vivid description included writing their own music, redefining fashion, and creating innovative music.

The fruit of the Vision Tree:

- Is unique (a differentiator)
- Consists of long-term goals that stretch beyond current capabilities
- Is a vibrant, specific description of what it will be like to achieve the vision
- Transforms the vision from words to a clear image

The Vision Tree framework helps organizations maintain alignment as they grow, ensuring that daily decisions and long-term strategies remain connected to the organization's fundamental purpose and values.

A critical principle of the Vision Tree (and one missed by The Beatles) is that it is annually renewed with our planning sessions. Each year, we confirm our Core Ideology, only occasionally tweaking it. The Envisioned Future can and should change over time. Significantly, we focus on how to keep the roots of the tree healthy, so that it will continue to produce excellent fruit well into the future.

The Beatles' Withering Vision Tree

Returning to The Beatles, we can see how the absence of such a framework contributed to their dissolution. Their initial vision—becoming the biggest band in the world—had been achieved. Without a renewed Envisioned Future, individual visions took precedence, ultimately pulling the collaboration apart.

They failed to address "the roots" of the empire. If they didn't keep the roots healthy, eventually the tree would wither and die. Of course, one of the primary threats to the roots of the tree was the vastly different vision for the future among the individuals in the band.

Imagine if The Beatles had taken time to articulate a new shared vision after achieving their initial goal. Perhaps they could have defined a purpose beyond commercial success—something like "to continuously reinvent music and expand its possibilities." Such a purpose might have provided direction while accommodating their individual creative interests.

Instead, they found themselves at cross-purposes. John wanted to use their platform for social change. Paul wanted to continue creating innovative popular music as The Beatles. George sought spiritual fulfillment and recognition for his contributions. And Ringo wanted to continue making music together while pursuing an acting career.

Lessons for Modern Organizations

The parallels between The Beatles' experience and modern organizational challenges are striking. Companies frequently struggle after achieving initial success, particularly when founding entrepreneurs must transition to professional management roles or when original missions are fulfilled without clear succession plans.

Organizations that endure through multiple generations typically develop mechanisms for renewing their shared vision while honoring their core purpose and values. They understand that vision is not static—it must evolve as circumstances change and initial goals are achieved.

The Vision Tree provides one such framework for this renewal process. By clearly distinguishing between unchanging elements (core purpose and values) and evolving aspirations (envisioned future), organizations can maintain continuity while adapting to changing circumstances.

Practical Applications

How can modern organizations avoid the fate of The Beatles—extraordinary success followed by dissolution due to divergent visions? Several practices emerge from our exploration:

1. **Distinguish between purpose and goals:** Understand that achieving specific goals (like having a top-selling song in the US) doesn't fulfill an organization's purpose. Purpose provides the "why" that sustains motivation beyond any particular achievement.

2. **Regularly renew shared vision:** Schedule time for key stakeholders to reflect on and renew their shared vision, especially after achieving significant milestones.

3. **Create frameworks for communication:** Develop accessible frameworks like the Vision Tree to ensure everyone in the organization understands how their work connects to the larger purpose.

4. **Balance individual aspirations with collective vision:** Create space for individual growth and expression within the context of shared purpose, recognizing that talented people need room to develop.

5. **Plan for success:** Anticipate what will happen after achieving major goals, ensuring the organization doesn't lose momentum or direction when initial targets are reached.

Conclusion: Importance of Vision Alignment

Even the most successful collaborations can be derailed when catalytic vision splinters or is fulfilled without a clear path forward. The Beatles, despite their unprecedented success, ultimately dissolved because they lacked a renewed shared vision to guide them after achieving their initial goals.

Modern organizations face similar challenges but can benefit from frameworks like the Vision Tree to maintain alignment as they grow and evolve. By clearly articulating core purpose and values while regularly renewing their envisioned future, organizations can avoid the fate of The Beatles—extraordinary success followed by dissolution.

The lesson is clear: Vision isn't simply something you define at the beginning of a journey. It requires ongoing renewal and communication as circumstances change and initial goals are achieved. Without this renewal process, even the most successful collaborations can find themselves derailed, with individual visions pulling in different directions despite a history of shared achievement.

In your own organization or creative partnership, take time to ask: What happens after we achieve our current goals? How do our individual aspirations align with our shared purpose? And most importantly, how can we maintain a catalytic shared vision that continues to inspire our collective best work, when some of the team is saying "stop" and another group is saying "go, go, go"?

Applying the Lessons of Chapter 8

When a once-unifying vision splinters, even the most successful organizations can lose momentum and direction. The Beatles' derailment wasn't just about personality conflicts—it represented a fundamental crisis of purpose that ultimately proved insurmountable.

By 1969, The Beatles had achieved their original vision of reaching "the toppermost of the poppermost." Without a renewed shared purpose, individual visions began to emerge and ultimately compete. These divergent paths created a fundamental tension expressed perfectly by the song "Hello, Goodbye." Paul was enthusiastically ready to keep going, but the others were ready to stop or at least take a break.

Five warning signs appeared as their catalytic vision fractured:

1. **Mission accomplished syndrome:** After achieving their initial goal, no compelling shared future was articulated.

2. **Competing personal goals:** Individual aspirations began to overshadow collective purpose.

3. **No "specific little aims":** The team or organization has stopped setting short-term goals.

4. **Value conflicts:** Spiritual, political, and family priorities became increasingly incompatible.

5. **Implementation disagreements:** Even when goals aligned, approaches differed dramatically.

DERAILMENT DIAGNOSTIC: VISION ALIGNMENT CHECK

For your leadership team, assess whether these statements have become true:

- Team members give different answers when asked about priorities for the next six to twelve months.
- Conversations about future direction frequently end in stalemate or superficial agreement.
- Success metrics are interpreted differently by different team members.
- Members are more enthusiastic discussing personal projects than collective goals.
- The organizational "story" has become fragmented or contradictory when told by different leaders.

Three or more "yes" answers suggest your vision may be fracturing in ways similar to that of The Beatles.

PREVENTION STRATEGY: VISION RECALIBRATION PROCESS

1. **Acknowledge significant achievements:** Formally recognize when original goals have been accomplished rather than simply setting new targets.

2. **Vision renewal retreat:** Schedule dedicated time away from operations to redefine shared purpose.

3. **Individual aspiration mapping:** Have each leader articulate their personal vision, then find common ground.

4. **Shared articulation drill:** Ensure every leader can express the renewed vision in nearly identical language.

RECALIBRATION: THE VISION TREE EXERCISE

Even organizations experiencing vision fracture can recover through structured recalibration. The Vision Tree exercise—developed by my brother, Tom—provides a powerful tool:

- **Confirm core ideology:** Get back to your "roots." What is the "why" of your organization? Confirm team buy-in of your core purpose and core values.

- **Refresh the vision:** Does your team still picture the same tree? Reset the vision if necessary.

- **Develop vivid description:** Describe the "fruit" of your efforts. Make the future tangible through specific, motivating details.

By distinguishing between unchanging elements (core purpose and values) and evolving aspirations (envisioned future), this framework creates continuity while adapting to new circumstances.

CHAPTER 8 PLAYLIST

COMPETING VISIONS

This musical journey traces the splintering paths that eventually led to The Beatles' breakup, as explored in chapter 8, "Competing Visions." Each song represents a critical moment where individual aspirations began to overshadow their shared purpose. From Paul's "Hello, Goodbye," with its prescient lyrics about opposing directions, to the revealing solo debuts that followed their dissolution.

1. **"Hello, Goodbye"**—The perfect opening track symbolizing the fundamental conflict within the band. Paul's cheerful opposition lyrics inadvertently foreshadowed the competing directions that would pull the group apart, particularly between Paul and the other three.

2. **"The Inner Light"**—One of George's most spiritually significant songs, serving as an early indicator of his deepening interest in Eastern philosophy and his personal quest for meaning beyond fame. This B-side to "Lady Madonna" showcases George's vision moving toward inner peace and spiritual fulfillment.

3. **"Nowhere Man"**—A reflective piece about directionless existence that takes on new meaning in the context of the band's
   later years. As their original vision of becoming "the biggest
   band in the world" was achieved, they found themselves without a unified purpose—nowhere men making nowhere plans
   for nobody.

4. **"The Fool on the Hill"**—This song represents the isolation and
   misunderstanding that can come with unique vision. Ironically,
   the song (and video that accompanied it) were created almost
   completely by Paul without input from the others.

5. **"Act Naturally"**—Ringo's country-western cover about someone
   destined for movie stardom perfectly aligned with his growing
   interest in acting. By 1969, while the band was deteriorating,
   Ringo was pursuing film roles like *The Magic Christian*, represent-
   ing his vision diverging from the group's musical focus.

6. **"Revolution"**—John's political anthem represents his growing
   vision to use music as a platform for social activism. The song's
   creation sparked heated debates about the band's political stance,
   highlighting how their individual visions for what The Beatles
   should represent were increasingly at odds.

7. **"Give Peace a Chance"—John Lennon and the Plastic Ono
   Band**—John's first official solo single, clearly demonstrating
   his vision to use his platform for social activism and peace.
   Released while The Beatles were still technically together, it
   signaled John's determination to chart his own course with or
   without the band.

8. **"My Sweet Lord"—George Harrison**—George's declaration
   of spiritual devotion became the first song to reach number

one by a solo Beatle. This song perfectly encapsulates his vision for what mattered most to him beyond The Beatles—connecting with God and finding inner peace. The massive success validated his frustrations about limited opportunities within the band.

9. **"Beaucoups of Blues"—Ringo Starr**—Ringo's foray into country music demonstrated his desire to explore different musical styles away from The Beatles. The melancholic tone reflects the sadness he felt as the band dissolved, while showing his adaptability and willingness to reinvent himself.

10. **"Another Day"—Paul McCartney**—Paul's first solo single depicts ordinary life continuing despite personal turmoil. The song reflects his practical approach to the breakup—treating it as just "another day." The cheerful melody stands in contradiction to the sad lyrics.

CHAPTER 9

"I ME MINE" —
THE EROSION OF
ESPRIT DE CORPS

In chapter 5, we explored how The Beatles' esprit de corps—their collective spirit of enthusiasm, devotion, and honor for the group— propelled them to unprecedented heights. That spirit didn't vanish overnight. Instead, it eroded gradually through a series of events, decisions, and changing dynamics that transformed their once-unbreakable bond into something increasingly fragile and, ultimately, unsustainable. Sadly, the root of many of the problems was business.

To keep the esprit de corps level strong, The Beatles leveraged three critical elements: setting egos aside, friendly internal competition, and sense of humor/fun. When growing business challenges and personal differences emerge, each of those elements becomes strained. Once ego or pride creeps in, competition becomes less friendly, and it becomes difficult to maintain a sense of humor or fun.

Business arrangements were at the heart of most of their bruised egos, leading them dangerously close to losing it all.

The Business of The Beatles

The initial business structure that Brian Epstein established for The Beatles (laid out in chapter 7) had cracks in its foundation. These cracks ate away at The Beatles' remarkable esprit de corps. Since they deferred all business matters to Brian Epstein during their rise to the top of the industry, they were not prepared to sort it out when he died.

Many excellent books have been written about what happened to the business of The Beatles. For a comprehensive look at the business of The Beatles, their finances, and the legal actions related to their breakup, I refer you to *You Never Give Me Your Money: The Beatles After the Breakup* by Peter Doggett and *And in the End: The Last Days of The Beatles* by Ken McNab.

For purposes of this book, here is a brief summary of what became of the three major business entities in The Beatles' empire.

Apple Corps (Formerly Beatles Ltd): The Promise and the Problems

Before Epstein's death, in August 1967, a new business structure was already in place to replace Beatles Ltd, with an expanded vision of The Beatles' empire—an organization called Apple Corps. Brian's death left that ship without a rudder, starting a series of events that cost The Beatles untold millions.

In January 1968, The Beatles officially announced the formation of Apple Corps, which would oversee all their business interests. This consolidation was a great idea in concept, but a lack of discipline and focus created tremendous turmoil.

Apple Corps had four main divisions: Apple Retail, Apple Electronics, Apple Publishing, and Apple Records. From a business perspective, the flaw in their reasoning was apparent. Apple Publishing and Apple

Records were within their wheelhouse—they had enough expertise among themselves and those around them to make these divisions successful. However, they had no experience in retail (after Brian Epstein's death) or electronics.

On May 14, 1968, John and Paul held a press conference in New York City at the Americana Hotel to promote their new enterprise, Apple Corps. A few snippets from that press conference reveal the folly of their otherwise commendable vision:

Q: "What is Apple, John?"

John: "It's a business concerning records, films, and electronics. And as a sideline, whatever it's called . . . manufacturing, or whatever. But we want to set up a system whereby people who just want to make a film about (pause) anything, don't have to go on their knees in somebody's office. Probably yours."

Paul: "We really want to help people, but without doing it like a charity or seeming like ordinary patrons of the arts. We're in the happy position of not really needing any more money. So for the first time, the bosses aren't in it for profit. If you come and see me and say 'I've had such and such a dream,' I'll say 'Here's so much money. Go away and do it.' We've already bought all our dreams. So now we want to share that possibility with others."

Q: "If a youngster has a group, or their group thinks that they've got something going, what's the best way you'd recommend for them to get in touch with you to let you hear their stuff?"

Paul: "Just get the address and send it, you know. That's it. Just send the stuff to Apple at Baker Street in London."[1]

The Beatles' altruistic approach to business was captured in a quote from Paul about Apple: "It's a beautiful place where you can buy beautiful things . . . beautiful clothes, beautiful records . . . It's just trying to mix business with enjoyment."[2]

This statement reflected their countercultural values but made for poor business strategy. Apple became a place where people with ideas could walk in off the street and potentially get funding. "Taking them at their word, London Airport immigration was crammed with Americans identifying The Beatles as sponsors. Apple's philanthropic side was mainly McCartney's baby, but Lennon was, initially at least, willing to lend a hand," writes Ken McNab in *And in the End*.[3]

By the time Allen Klein came on board in 1969, he was shocked by what he found. As McNab writes: "Even before the ink on his contract was dry, Klein had already begun stripping Apple to its core. The company, he reckoned, not without some truth, had become a hippie haven for every freeloader in town. Apple owned cars no one could remember buying, had a portfolio of addresses no one had ever visited—including a townhouse in Mayfair—and retained a charge account at such high-end stores as Harrods and Fortnum & Mason."[4]

The Beatles' diversification through Apple Corps reveals a critical oversight that Jim Collins would later identify in his landmark book *Good to Great*. Collins's "Hedgehog Concept" argues that truly exceptional organizations focus relentlessly on the intersection of three vital questions: What are you deeply passionate about? What can you be the best in the world at? And what drives your economic engine?[5]

The Beatles had mastered this concept intuitively during their rise to fame—they were passionate about creating innovative music, demonstrably the best in the world at crafting memorable songs. They had built a highly profitable model around their recordings and performances. Yet, as they expanded Apple Corps into retail, electronics, and other ventures outside their expertise, they abandoned this clarity, behaving more like Collins's "fox" (pursuing many things) than a "hedgehog" (mastering one defining concept).

This diffusion of focus pulled them away from their core genius exactly when internal tensions demanded even greater clarity of purpose. Had they recognized and recommitted to their Hedgehog Concept—perhaps by structuring Apple purely around nurturing musical and artistic talent—they might have discovered a sustainable model that satisfied their creative ambitions while preserving the partnership that had made them exceptional in the first place.

Over the years, Apple Corps has become a well-run, well-respected organization. For many years it was led by one of The Beatles' childhood friends—Neil Aspinall. Apple Corps has been a fantastic steward of The Beatles legacy, and a successful business owned 25 percent each by Paul McCartney, Ringo Starr, and the estates of John Lennon and George Harrison.

NEMS Enterprises

NEMS (North End Music Stores) was the Epstein family business that became The Beatles' management company. Brian Epstein was the majority shareholder (owning 70–80 percent). In 1967, after his death, his brother, Clive Epstein, inherited his shares, but since the management contract was due to expire soon and Clive had no interest in managing, The Beatles needed a new manager.

From late 1967 to early 1969, the management of The Beatles was in turmoil. John, George, and Ringo had no interest in self-managing, whereas Paul seemed motivated by the challenge. In the face of this uncertainty, their creative juices continued to flow, especially Paul's and George's. However, the strain on the relationships made it clear that they needed to find a new manager.

As mentioned in chapter 7, John, George, and Ringo wanted Allen

Klein to be their manager and Paul wanted Lee and John Eastman (his in-laws). Initially, there was an uneasy compromise wherein Klein would be their manager, and the Eastmans would provide legal counsel.

In early 1969, NEMS still owned about 7.5 percent of Northern Songs (the publishing company that owned the Lennon–McCartney catalog), and Clive Epstein felt compelled to sell it to pay estate taxes. Klein promised The Beatles that he would find a way to get those shares for them for nothing. Clive was then approached by a consortium of merchant bankers with an attractive price, but he was inclined to give The Beatles the first chance to buy it.

Unfortunately, promising negotiations between the parties fell apart. Just as Klein was close to a deal with Epstein for the shares, the Eastmans made a terrible mistake. As McNab describes in *And in the End*, the involvement of the Eastmans created a situation where communication completely broke down. John Eastman, without authority from any of The Beatles, sent a letter to Clive Epstein suggesting impropriety in Brian Epstein's management, stating they should discuss "the propriety of the negotiations surrounding the nine-year agreement between EMI, The Beatles and NEMS."[6]

This accusation deeply offended Clive Epstein and "shattered the delicate alliance between Epstein and Klein."[7]

Shortly thereafter, Clive Epstein agreed to sell NEMS's share of Northern Songs to the merchant bankers, and The Beatles missed out on an opportunity to own a significant piece of their publishing catalog.

Northern Songs

After Northern Songs went public, the ownership breakdown was:

- John: approximately 15 percent

- Paul: approximately 15 percent
- NEMS: approximately 7.5 percent
- Dick James and Charles Silver: approximately 37.5 percent
- Public shareholders: approximately 25 percent

After NEMS sold its shares in early 1969, the "public" shareholder percentage grew to about 32.5 percent. The lads were upset about losing out on the opportunity to own the NEMS shares. There was plenty of blame to go around. Klein promised to get the shares and didn't. The John Eastman letter certainly contributed to the fiasco. And from The Beatles' perspective, the Epstein family owed them the chance to buy their share. This disappointment proved to be minor compared to what happened next.

In March of 1969, John and Yoko were in the middle of their "bed-in for peace." John was probably feeling pretty good about taking a stand for something bigger than himself. Then he picked up the *Financial Times* and saw a headline that devastated him: "ATV takes control of Northern Songs."

Can you imagine that? The songs that poured out of his teenage heart, the melodies he and Paul crafted in tiny Liverpool bedrooms, the very DNA of The Beatles' creative legacy were sold. Without any heads-up, Dick James and Charles Silver had secretly sold their stake in the Lennon–McCartney catalog to Lew Grade's Associated Television (ATV). Adding insult to injury, ATV announced they were planning to buy up public shares of Northern Songs to acquire a majority interest.

John was furious. Dick James wasn't only their publisher; he was also supposed to be their friend. This was the guy George Martin had personally introduced to The Beatles, the one who'd made millions off those songwriting sessions between two Liverpool teenagers.

John and Paul had just lost out on getting NEMS's shares in Northern Songs and now this. "They are my songs and I want to keep some of the end product . . . Dick James? We don't think he was very nice. You'd have thought the first thing he would have done would have been to consult us."[8]

Even George Martin, always the gentleman, called James a rat to his face. When the producer who kept The Beatles grounded and professional loses his cool, you know someone crossed a line that should never be crossed.

An even more significant betrayal came soon after. A betrayal that not only cost John and Paul the chance to own their own music but also their friendship (at least for several years). Hoping to save the day, Klein had proposed that John and Paul submit a competing offer to the outstanding shareholders, which would bring them controlling interest in Northern Songs. At this time, The Beatles were strapped for cash because of the Apple Corps debacle, but Klein had a work-around; he suggested that John and Paul put up their shares in Northern Songs as collateral (Klein also offered to put up shares of MGM that his company owned as additional collateral).

McNab recounts that fateful meeting in *And in the End*: "McCartney, however, on the advice of Lee Eastman, refused to throw in his shares, deeming it a risk too far."[9] What happened next was explosive: Klein revealed that John owned 644,000 shares valued at about £1.25 million, while Paul owned 751,000 shares worth approximately £1.4 million. On the advice of his in-laws, Paul had been secretly buying up public shares of Northern Songs.

According to McNab: "There followed a few seconds of silence before all hell broke loose."[10] John was furious, calling Paul a "bastard" and nearly coming to blows over this perceived betrayal. McNab writes that John was "badly wounded" by this revelation, especially since "their song publishing was the one thing about The Beatles John felt most nostalgic about." John later reflected, "It was the first time any of us had gone behind the other's back."[11]

George and Ringo were also upset by Paul's actions and further entrenched the three-against-one battle. Klein, naturally, took advantage of this to draw even closer to John, George, and Ringo. For John, the one who, as a teen, shared half of his chocolate bar with the younger Paul, this was devastating.

The battle for Northern Songs continued without Paul's shares as collateral—a battle they eventually lost, in large part to John losing his patience with the "men in suits" who were negotiating for control of his creations. Sadly, in October of 1969, John and Paul sold their shares in Northern Songs to those men in suits.

The Northern Songs debacle teaches us the fundamental role transparency plays in any organization. Without transparency, trust erodes. When Paul started secretly buying shares, he probably thought he was being smart, protecting their interests. But by keeping John in the dark, he violated the fundamental trust that had powered their partnership since they were teenagers, writing songs face-to-face.

Now that we've seen what happened to the business of The Beatles, let's look at some of the other interpersonal dynamics that damaged the esprit de corps of the band.

Were the First Cracks in the Pillar "Yesterday"?

Long before their official breakup, subtle cracks had begun to appear in The Beatles' unified front. One of the earliest and most significant instances came with Paul's song "Yesterday" (credited to Lennon–McCartney). This deceptively simple ballad about loss and regret would become one of the most covered songs in music history—and, significantly, it was essentially a solo Paul song.

Paul had dreamed the melody and initially called it "Scrambled Eggs" while he worked out the lyrics. When he brought it to the band, it became clear that there was no obvious role for the others. The song required a string quartet rather than a rock band. Eventually, it was decided that Paul would perform it alone, accompanied only by his acoustic guitar and the string arrangement.

For Paul, the success of "Yesterday" was both a personal triumph and a quiet source of pride. Here was proof that he could create magnificent music without his bandmates. For John, who resisted the "Johnny & The Silver Beatles" name for a group-first mentality, it had to have been particularly strange. And for George and Ringo, it reinforced a hierarchy within the band where they sometimes felt like sidemen rather than equal partners.

During The Beatles' 1965 UK tour, when Paul performed "Yesterday" solo with just his acoustic guitar, it marked one of the first times the song was performed live after its release. The moment highlighted Paul's emergence as a sophisticated songwriter but also created a slightly awkward dynamic since the other three Beatles had nothing to do during the song.

After Paul finished the performance, John and George presented him with fake flowers as a humorous gesture—partly to acknowledge his spotlight moment and partly as a bit of playful teasing. It was a classic example of the group's camaraderie and humor even during their biggest performances. From Paul's perspective, however, it certainly could be seen as a bit of a slight over what was a defining moment in his career.

This moment is particularly significant, as it represents an early public instance of the band not performing as a unified quartet, foreshadowing the more individualistic direction their careers would eventually take. Yet the playful presentation of flowers also demonstrated how they could handle these emerging differences with humor and mutual support at this point in their career.

The Maharishi Retreat and White Album Sessions

From February 1967 to February 1968, The Beatles were remarkably prolific. They released "Strawberry Fields Forever"/"Penny Lane" (double-A sided single), *Sgt. Pepper's Lonely Hearts Club Band* (album), "All You Need is Love"/"Baby You're a Rich Man" (single), "Hello, Goodbye"/"I Am the Walrus" (single), *Magical Mystery Tour* (album and film), and recorded "Lady Madonna" for a March 1968 release.

On the heels of this remarkable year, The Beatles went to Rishikesh, India, in February of 1968, for a retreat at the Maharishi's meditation center. Several other celebrities joined them: Mike Love, Mia Farrow, and Donovan among them.

The retreat showed the individual differences among the four Beatles. For George and John, it was a spiritual and emotional renewal; they both stayed for eight weeks. Paul enjoyed it but was ready to get back to work after five weeks. And Ringo stayed for only ten days (the food didn't sit well with him).

It was a particularly fertile time for all three of the major songwriters. They returned with a wealth of material, a lot of which would be included on their first double album, titled *The Beatles* but commonly known as "the White Album."

During this period, George wrote a masterpiece called "While My Guitar Gently Weeps." In an interview, George referred to this song as "All You Need Is Love, Part Two," and a closer examination of the lyrics reveals why.

The song exposes the fractures emerging in the relationships between George and his bandmates. His message to his friends and bandmates is clear: you have no difficulty preaching to the world that "All You Need Is Love," yet you fail to practice that love with those closest to you. While The Beatles (especially John) used their platform to spread messages of love and peace, George felt isolated, in the corner with his guitar gently weeping.

The *Let It Be/Get Back* Sessions: When Everything Fell Apart

In January of 1969, amid growing tensions, The Beatles launched their latest project. The plan was to create a documentary or film of The Beatles creating and recording an album. The film and the album were called *Let It Be*. The documentary footage included in the film *Let It Be* provides a window into their deteriorating relationships. Because of the negative tenor of the original *Let It Be* film, it was pulled from circulation.

The footage was retained, including hours of previously unreleased material. It was restored by Peter Jackson, of *Lord of the Rings* fame, and released in 2022 as a three-part documentary, now called *Get Back*. (I will now refer to these sessions as the *Let It Be/Get Back* sessions.)

On January 10, 1969, during one of the sessions, George quit the band for a few days after an argument with Paul about his guitar-playing. The cameras captured George's frustration: "I'll play whatever you want me to play, or I won't play at all if you don't want me to play. Whatever it is that will please you, I'll do it."[12] His departure forced the band to regroup at Apple Studios and rethink their approach.

A telling conversation between John and Paul occurred the day after George quit the band:

John: "It's a festering wound that we've allowed . . . and yesterday we allowed it to go even deeper and we didn't give him any bandages . . . the point is now, we both do need—we both do that to George."

Paul: "That's why I think we have the problem now, you know, the four of us. You go one way, George one way, and me another, but I know it'll apply to all of us."[13]

Although both recognized the seriousness of the situation, Paul didn't seem to fully acknowledge John's point about their treatment of George.

The Isolation of George

The division of labor and credit within the band had become increasingly problematic. While Lennon–McCartney received songwriting credit for most of The Beatles' output, George's contributions were often sidelined. During the *Let It Be/Get Back* sessions, George brought in "All Things Must Pass," a song that would later become the title track of his acclaimed triple solo album, yet it received little enthusiasm from his bandmates.

In a reflective moment years later, George shared his perspective on his position within the band:

> You know, I think The Beatles were fantastic. John and Paul were fantastic. You see, the funny position I was in was that, in many ways, this whole focus of attention was on The Beatles, so in that respect I was part of it, but from being in them, an attitude came over which was John and Paul, of, "Okay, we're the grooves, and you two just watch it." Not that—they never said that or did anything, but over a period of time . . . In a way I always felt a bit like an observer of The Beatles, even though I was with them, whereas I think John and Paul were the stars of The Beatles. I mean, on a very personal intimate level, you know—don't forget I spent ten years in the back of a limousine with them.[14]

In a 1988 press conference, he reflected on the challenges he was facing in The Beatles and said, "And my problem was that it would always be very difficult to get in on the act, because Paul was very pushy in that respect. When he succumbed to playing on one of your tunes, he'd always do good. But you'd have to do fifty-nine of Paul's songs before he'd even listen to one of yours."[15]

The tension wasn't limited to George. By this time, John had become increasingly distant, bringing Yoko Ono to studio sessions—breaking their unspoken rule about keeping partners out of the recording space. In footage from these sessions, the other Beatles appear uncomfortable with this arrangement, yet no one directly confronts John about it, revealing how communication had broken down.

Ringo commented about it in a conversation with Elliot Mintz, originally broadcast on August 29, 1977, on American radio on the program *Innerview*:

> Yeah. It would've been easier for me if we'd have come back to the four of us situation—all for one, one for all—instead of all for themselves. It was getting more all for themselves . . . or ourselves. I include me, as well. I wanted to do different things too. But my mood was minor compared to theirs.[16]

The *Abbey Road* Truce

Despite these tensions, The Beatles managed to come together one last time in the summer of 1969 to create *Abbey Road*, an album many consider their finest achievement. They decided to do it like in the early days, using the classic lineup of instruments and with George Martin in charge as the producer.

The sessions were remarkably productive and harmonious compared to the *Let It Be/Get Back* experience. Each member contributed significantly: George with "Something" and "Here Comes the Sun," two of The Beatles' finest songs; John with the raw "Come Together" and introspective "I Want You (She's So Heavy)"; Paul with the melodic "Oh! Darling" and the orchestral vision of the side-two medley; and Ringo with the charming "Octopus's Garden" and his only recorded Beatles drum solo on "The End."

Paul's song, appropriately titled "The End," offered a fitting conclusion to their journey together. As the song winds down, John, Paul, and George each share a moving guitar solo, and Ringo provides his brilliant drum solo. For a moment, they recaptured the magic that had first made them extraordinary. This moment of harmony, however brief, serves as a poignant reminder of what was being lost as the group disintegrated.

Personal Reflection: Leadership vs. Management

The derailment of The Beatles' esprit de corps can be better understood through a leadership and management framework. Early in our careers at Absher Construction, my brother, Tom, and I attended a series of leadership development classes where we learned a commonly used acronym to explain the difference between leadership and management.

The leadership acronym "SAM" stands for

- **Setting direction**—Articulate a clear vision, establish goals, and guide a team toward achieving them by providing clarity and focus.

- **Aligning people and resources**—Ensure the team or organization has the right people and proper resources to accomplish the vision and are aligned properly.

- **Motivating**—Keep the team motivated and inspired behind the vision of the organization and the interim goals that will lead to that envisioned future.

The management acronym "POC" stands for

- **Planning**—Implement short-term, task-oriented plans for people and resources so the team or organization is moving toward its envisioned future.

- **Organizing**—Create and enforce policies and procedures that allow the organization to effectively and efficiently accomplish the tasks necessary to accomplish its plans and goals.

- **Coordinating and controlling resources**—Manage the organization's risks, hold people accountable for results, coach and mentor those reporting to you.

We emphasized that being a leader and being a manager are not mutually exclusive. In fact, most leaders have some management functions, and every manager has an opportunity to be a leader, at least among those who report to them.

This helped our team at Absher Construction understand their roles and responsibilities. More importantly, it helped them see opportunities for growth in both leadership and management.

Followership

After using this model for several years, my brother, Tom, noticed a gap in our training, something he called *followership*, for which he developed an appropriate acronym:

Followership: SIG

- **Supporting**—Take responsibility to know and support the Core Ideology and Envisioned Future of the organization.

- **Implementing**—Implement the tactics and frontline work required to accomplish the mission of the organization, which moves it toward its Envisioned Future.

- **Giving feedback**—Give honest and candid feedback in a constructive way. Ideally, provide balanced feedback—what's going well and what are areas of improvement.

We were surprised to find very little material about the role of the followers in an organization. So, Tom added followership to our personnel development program. We observed that great leaders in healthy organizations spend time on the "SIG" activities. In fact, a leader's willingness and enthusiasm for these activities is often what inspires others to follow her or him.

Here are some key takeaways from our years using this framework for leadership development:

1. While some traits of leadership may be innate ("a born leader"), many leadership skills can be learned and developed.

2. Few people spend their time solely as a leader, a manager, or a follower. In fact, many people spend time in each of these three categories.

3. Even frontline workers have opportunities to lead, particularly when it comes to motivating fellow team members.

4. Many leaders make the mistake of failing to nurture a solid base of followers, often missing the immense value followers bring to a team or organization, especially in providing feedback.

5. We found confusion among leaders and managers who did not understand or appreciate the difference between those two roles.

6. The best leaders show a willingness to take on the role of follower when it is appropriate.

Looking at The Beatles Through the SAM/POC/SIG Lens

By applying this leadership model to The Beatles' experience, we can see clearly what went wrong. Starting at the top, John abdicated his responsibility as the leader without any communication with his bandmates. He began to follow his own vision without getting buy-in from the others; the few attempts he made to align people and resources did not allow room for dissent; and finally, by going his own way, he stopped trying to motivate his bandmates.

Paul clearly wanted the band to stay together. After Brian Epstein died, Paul came closest to being the de facto manager. While he was valiantly trying to Plan, Organize, and Coordinate the band, he failed at replacing John as the leader. He was not good at reading the room. When the others were saying stop, he was saying go. It must have been frustrating for him to have all his creative juices flowing at a time when the others needed a break.

Speaking of creative juices, George's were also flowing, and he was allowed only a small creative outlet within the band. In his frustration, he played the victim and could not find a way to articulate clear boundaries that could have moved the band in a new direction. Neither John nor Paul seemed to have seen this, but as John stepped away from his role in the band, Paul and George could have become musical collaborators.

For his part, Ringo had an opportunity to show leadership in the band but failed to seize the opportunity. He had fewer disputes with his bandmates than any of the others. That put him in a unique position to step forward and be the peacemaker. Granted, that would not have been easy with two alpha males like John and Paul, but he might have been able to get through to them. In his role as a "follower," he did not provide open and honest feedback to the others in the band.

Followership was one of their strengths in the early days. George and Ringo were loyal followers and contributed greatly in that role. Paul and John also knew when to step back and let the other lead or manage. As the strengths and interests of the band members changed, John, Paul, and George were no longer willing to be good followers. They were not supporting each other in the same way. True collaboration began to disappear. They stopped giving each other constructive feedback.

The Breakdown of Communication

Perhaps the most critical element in the derailment of The Beatles' esprit de corps was the breakdown in communication. What had once been open, honest, and supportive dialogue became increasingly guarded, resentful, and ultimately absent.

During their early years, The Beatles would spend hours discussing their music, performances, and plans. They shared hotel rooms, traveled in the same vehicles, and huddled together against the madness of Beatlemania. This enforced proximity ensured that issues were discussed and resolved quickly.

As they matured and established separate lives, the natural opportunities for communication diminished. At the same time, the subjects that needed discussion became more complex—business decisions, creative differences, personal lifestyles, and philosophical divergences.

By the time of the White Album sessions, engineer Geoff Emerick noted that The Beatles would often record separately, with band members dropping in to add their parts when the others weren't present. During the *Let It Be/Get Back* sessions, meaningful conversation was replaced by tense silence and superficial banter.

This breakdown in communication meant that resentment festered rather than being resolved. Small issues grew into major grievances through lack of discussion. And without the ability to talk through their differences, the band could not adapt to their changing circumstances.

The Legacy of Their Falling Out

The irony of The Beatles' breakup is that, despite the collapse of their esprit de corps, they continued to create extraordinary music until the very end. *Abbey Road*, recorded when they knew their time together was limited, stands as one of their greatest achievements.

After the breakup, their relationships remained complex. Paul and John engaged in musical barbs, with Paul's "Too Many People" and John's more direct "How Do You Sleep?" exchanging criticisms. Yet they eventually reconciled to some degree before John's tragic death in 1980.

George maintained a certain distance but collaborated with each of his former bandmates on various projects, especially Ringo. Ringo, true to his nature, remained on good terms with all of them, appearing on their solo records and welcoming them on his.

In their solo careers, each Beatle demonstrated both their individual strengths and what had been lost in their separation. John produced raw, honest work but sometimes lacked polish; Paul created melodic masterpieces but sometimes lacked depth; George finally had room for his spiritual and musical growth but sometimes lacked focus; and Ringo maintained his charm but lacked the musical foundation the others had provided.

Conclusion: Erosion of Esprit de Corps

The erosion of The Beatles' esprit de corps offers valuable lessons for any team or organization. Their journey shows how even the strongest bonds can erode when

- Success changes the dynamic among team members.

- Individual ambitions begin to overshadow collective goals.

- Communication breaks down, leaving issues unresolved.

- Roles become unclear or unsatisfying.

- External pressures create internal tensions.

- Leadership fails to adapt to changing circumstances.

For teams and organizations seeking excellence, maintaining esprit de corps requires conscious effort. It demands open communication, mutual respect, recognition of individual contributions, shared goals, and the ability to adapt roles as circumstances change.

The lessons of their esprit de corps, both in its creation and its eventual derailment, continue to provide valuable insights for any group striving for collective excellence. As we'll see in later chapters, understanding how to avoid or navigate through similar challenges is crucial for sustained success.

Applying the Lessons of Chapter 9

Even the strongest team spirit can erode when trust breaks down and communication falters. The Beatles' journey from unified band of brothers to business adversaries offers a sobering case study in how esprit de corps, once established, can still disintegrate without proper maintenance.

The erosion of The Beatles once-unbreakable team spirit didn't happen overnight but through a series of fractures that gradually under-mined their connection.

1. Business tensions replaced creative collaboration: Abdicating all business responsibility to Brian Epstein kept them from developing the knowledge and experience necessary to keep the train on the rails after he died.

2. Communication breakdown: What began as open dialogue devolved into confrontation, passive-aggressive behavior, and eventually silence.

3. Ego resurgence: The selflessness that characterized their early years gave way to self-protection and individual priorities.

4. Fun disappeared: The playfulness and humor that had sustained them through pressure became increasingly absent.

5. Competitive spirit turned destructive: What had been friendly rivalry evolved into harmful competition.

These warning signs manifested in observable behaviors that leaders should watch for in their own teams.

DERAILMENT DIAGNOSTIC: TEAM SPIRIT EROSION INDICATORS

For your team, assess whether these statements have become true:

• Business discussions consistently generate more tension than creative collaborations.

• Team members communicate more formally and less frequently than in the past.

- Private conversations about other team members have replaced direct dialogue.

- Humor and play have diminished or disappeared from daily interactions.

- Achievements are increasingly claimed by individuals rather than celebrated collectively.

Three or more "yes" answers suggest your team spirit may be eroding in ways similar to that of The Beatles in their final years.

PREVENTION STRATEGY: TRUST PRESERVATION PROTOCOL

1. Transparency agreements: Establish explicit expectations about information sharing, particularly in financial matters.

2. Business boundary setting: Create clear separation between creative collaboration and business decision-making.

3. Regular trust check-ins: Schedule dedicated time to address concerns before they become grievances.

4. Third-party mediation: Identify trusted advisers who can facilitate difficult conversations.

5. Relationship investment: Allocate specific time for team bonding outside business contexts.

IMPLEMENTATION GUIDE: COMMUNICATION RESTORATION PROCESS

1. Role clarity workshop: Have each team member identify which elements of SAM/POC/SIG they currently fulfill.

2. Gap analysis: Identify missing functions that nobody is performing.

3. Feedback reestablishment: Create structured opportunities for safe, honest dialogue.

4. Humor reintroduction: Deliberately incorporate playfulness into team interactions.

5. Relationship rebuilding: Start with small creative collaborations to rebuild trust.

CHAPTER 9 PLAYLIST

EROSION OF ESPRIT DE CORPS

This collection tracks the dissolution of the remarkable camaraderie that once defined The Beatles. As their shared spirit fractured under the weight of business disputes, creative differences, and personal tensions, each song captures a different facet of their unraveling bond. From early warnings to post-breakup reflections, these tracks reveal how even the strongest esprit de corps can erode when trust and communication falter.

1. **"I Me Mine"**—George's commentary on the ego battles within the band during their final years together. The contrasting waltz and rock sections musically illustrate the jarring disconnection between the members as self-interest overtook collective purpose and their esprit de corps completely collapsed.

2. **"Yesterday"**—Paul's solo masterpiece presaged the individual paths each Beatle would eventually take, showing how even

within the group, their individual voices were beginning to emerge. This first significant departure from their unified sound hinted at the autonomy each member would eventually seek.

3. **"Money (That's What I Want)"**—This early cover took on ironic significance as business disputes became central to their breakup. What began as four friends making music together evolved into a complex commercial enterprise where financial conflicts—from Apple Corps to Northern Songs—ultimately tore them apart.

4. **"You Never Give Me Your Money"**—Paul's lament about their business troubles captures the disillusionment that followed their idealistic Apple Corps venture. The song reflects how far they'd come from their youthful optimism and once-unbreakable team spirit.

5. **"Can't Buy Me Love"**—This early hit's message about money's limitations took on ironic significance as financial disputes consumed the band's final years. What began as a simple love song became a painful reminder that their wealth couldn't purchase the harmony and mutual respect that had once defined their relationships.

6. **"Baby You're a Rich Man"**—This prophetic song questioned whether wealth brings happiness, foreshadowing the money-related conflicts that would tear the band apart. Its mocking tone toward the "rich man" lifestyle predicted how financial success would paradoxically contribute to their downfall rather than cementing their unity.

7. **"Piggies"**—George's satirical attack on materialism and social pretension reflected his growing disdain for the business world

surrounding The Beatles. The song's bitter tone toward those who think they own this world mirrored his frustration with the music industry figures who seemed to control the band's destiny.

8. **"Yer Blues"**—John's raw confession of depression and suicidal thoughts during the White Album sessions revealed the emotional toll of their deteriorating relationships. His stark honesty about feeling "so suicidal" showed how far their once-joyful camaraderie had declined into individual suffering and isolation.

9. **"God"—John Lennon**—John's stark declaration on his first solo album marks his psychological break from the group identity that had defined him for nearly a decade. His listing of rejected beliefs reveals his determination to establish an individual identity.

10. **"Wah-Wah"—George Harrison**—Written by George immediately after temporarily quitting during the *Let It Be/Get Back* sessions, this explosive track from his solo album *All Things Must Pass* expresses his frustration with being sidelined and controlled within the band. The title references both the guitar effect and the headache caused by their tense relationships.

CHAPTER 10

THE MAGIC LINGERS

The Beatles' uncanny ability to make magic relied on synergy and serendipity. What happens to that synergy when relationships are strained? In chapter 6, I broke down the magical mystery of The Beatles into two parts: synergy and serendipity. In this chapter, we will examine how a few instances of individual work on some of the early songs set the stage for a more siloed approach to songwriting and recording. This siloed approach literally prevented opportunities for synergy and serendipity in their later years together.

The Seeds of Separation: From Harmony to Solo

The derailment of The Beatles' magical synergy didn't happen overnight. While the White Album is often cited as the beginning of their siloed approach to recording, the seeds were planted years earlier, when they began experimenting with new recording techniques that, ironically, reduced their need to collaborate in real time.

As early as 1964, with songs like "And I Love Her" and "Things We Said Today," Paul began double-tracking his own vocals on some songs instead of relying on John's harmonies. To a lesser extent, John did the same thing, with "I Call Your Name" being a great example.

While the results were beautiful, something subtle was lost—the natural blend that occurred when two distinct voices found harmony together in the same moment. These early experiments with self-sufficiency foreshadowed the more dramatic separation to come.

The album *A Hard Day's Night* includes two of the first love ballads written by them: "And I Love Her" by Paul and "If I Fell" by John. These are two of my all-time favorite Beatles songs. For me, "If I Fell" gets the edge largely because I love to hear John and Paul harmonize.

In the late '60s, The Beatles still created magic, but increasingly it was the magic of individual brilliance combined through technology rather than the spontaneous alchemy of four musicians creating in the moment together. This gradual shift reminds us that even the most seamless collaborations can drift apart, not just through conflict but through subtle changes in process and approach that, over time, fundamentally alter how people create together.

Remarkably, despite the tension, once The Beatles got into the studio, even as the group was falling apart, they were able to rekindle that magic. It is that spark that convinces me that they could have found a way to stay together (or gotten back together) successfully.

The derailment of this pillar came about simply because they were not together in any meaningful way after they recorded *Abbey Road*. If a team or group is not together, it is impossible to create synergy or find the nuggets of serendipity. As we saw in chapter 9, relationships were so strained that they needed a lengthy break from each other.

Yet in the face of this tension, they created some of their best music. With George coming into his own as an extraordinary songwriter, *Abbey Road* provided a glimpse of what might have been. George contributed two of the greatest Beatles' songs ever to the album: "Something" and "Here Comes the Sun." This chapter explores how the magical mystery derailed but also how glimpses of that magic persisted until the very end.

The Last Road Trip: "Two of Us"

The song "Two of Us" represents one of the most poignant moments in The Beatles' later catalog. Officially credited to Lennon–McCartney, it was primarily a Paul composition that appeared on the *Let It Be* album but was actually recorded before *Abbey Road*, during the tumultuous January 1969 sessions.

On the surface, "Two of Us" is a charming song about two people on a journey together, but beneath that simple exterior lies a complex emotional landscape. Paul claims—to this day—that it is a song about a drive in the countryside with his soon-to-be wife, Linda. While I don't doubt that it was the original spark for the song, the lyrics point clearly to it being primarily about his relationship with John. Consider the evidence:

- Paul chose for this to be a duet with John. While this was common early in their career, it was quite rare at this point, especially for McCartney-penned songs.

- A cursory review of the lyrics points overwhelmingly to John, not Linda. There is a distinct feeling of the song being about a long-time relationship. Paul and Linda had only been dating for seven months at this time.

- Many of the references in the lyrics seem to tie to specifics of John and Paul's relationship.

- Listen to Paul's voice when he sings the songs; he sounds like he's on the verge of tears at several points.

By the time they recorded "Two of Us," John and Paul's artistic visions had diverged dramatically. Yet, watching the *Let It Be/Get Back* documentary footage of them performing this song, there's a remarkable moment when they lock eyes and seem to reconnect with the magic that first brought them together. They sing into the same microphone, facing each other as they had in their earliest days, momentarily recapturing the synergy that had made them extraordinary.

The song's lyrics take on a bittersweet quality in retrospect. Were they finding their way back to each other, or was this just a momentary connection on the way to their separate journeys? The magic between them flickered despite their differences, suggesting what might have been possible had they found a way to navigate their artistic and personal differences.

This tender moment stands in stark contrast to the general atmosphere of the *Let It Be/Get Back* sessions, which were characterized by tension and frustration. Even amid strained relationships, their musical chemistry could still produce moments of beauty, proving that the magical mystery was not entirely gone—just increasingly difficult to access.

The Ballad of John and Paul

Even as tensions mounted within the band, moments of synergy still emerged between the core partnership. A remarkable example occurred in April 1969 when John returned from his honeymoon with Yoko Ono, eager to record a new song chronicling their wedding adventures: "The Ballad of John and Yoko."

With George away on holiday and Ringo filming *The Magic Christian*, the band was temporarily reduced to just John and Paul. Rather than wait for the others to return, they decided to record the song as a duo. In a single day's session on April 14, 1969, they captured what would become The Beatles' final UK number one single.

This session revealed the musical telepathy that still existed between them despite their growing personal and creative differences. Paul eagerly stepped in to play drums, bass, piano, and harmonize with John, demonstrating the versatility and cooperative spirit that had been their hallmark. John, for his part, played acoustic and lead guitar while singing about his controversial marriage to Yoko.

What's particularly telling about this session is the effortless way they fell back into their collaborative rhythm. The tension that had characterized recent sessions was temporarily set aside as they focused solely on the music.

The result was energetic and immediate: a rock and roll song that harkened back to their roots while documenting John's current life. That they could still create this magic together, even as the band was coming apart, demonstrates the profound musical connection they maintained despite everything else.

This session stands as evidence that the magical synergy between John and Paul remained intact when they allowed it to flow, suggesting that The Beatles' potential wasn't exhausted—merely interrupted. Had they found a way to harness these moments while giving each other the necessary space, perhaps their creative partnership might have continued in new forms rather than ending completely.

One Last Symphony: *Abbey Road*

After the difficult *Let It Be/Get Back* sessions, The Beatles' decision to create one more album together resulted in what many consider their finest masterpiece. *Abbey Road*, released in September 1969, represents a fascinating paradox: a group at its creative zenith while personally falling apart.

Knowing this might be their last album together, they approached it with renewed purpose and commitment. George Martin returned to fully produce after stepping back during the White Album and *Let It Be/Get Back* sessions. The result was a magnificent farewell, showcasing each member's strengths while achieving a remarkable unity of purpose that seemed impossible, given their personal differences.

The album's production quality is immaculate, with warm, crisp tones and sophisticated arrangements that set a new standard for recorded sound. Sonically, it represents the culmination of their studio experimentation, combining the ambitious production techniques developed on albums like *Sgt. Pepper* with a return to more straightforward rock performances reminiscent of their earlier work.

George's emergence as a songwriter equal to John and Paul is perhaps the most striking aspect of *Abbey Road*. His contributions "Something" and "Here Comes the Sun" rank among the album's strongest tracks. "Something" became a number one hit, while "Here Comes the Sun" has become the most streamed Beatles songs of the digital era. The quality of these songs highlights what had been lost by not creating space for George to be a songwriter.

Had John and Paul been more open-minded earlier in their career, they might have recognized George's potential sooner. Songs like "All Things Must Pass," which George presented during the *Let It Be/Get Back* sessions but was rejected for inclusion on *Let It Be*, demonstrated the depth of material he had accumulated. This song, which later became the title track of his acclaimed triple solo album, could have enriched The Beatles' catalog had they been more receptive to his growth as a songwriter.

Even Ringo contributed a composition in "Octopus's Garden," a whimsical underwater fantasy that George helped him develop. This collaborative spirit, particularly between George and Ringo, showed how band members could support each other's creative growth when ego was set aside.

Despite these individual triumphs, what makes *Abbey Road* truly magical is how it all comes together. The album functions as a cohesive whole, with songs flowing into each other naturally. The sequencing demonstrates remarkable attention to detail, creating a journey for the listener that builds to the extraordinary medley that concludes the album.

The Final Bow: The Medley

The crowning achievement of *Abbey Road*—and perhaps of The Beatles' entire career—is the sixteen-minute medley that comprises most of side two. This sequence of song fragments, mostly written by Paul but with key contributions from John, represents their most ambitious composition and arrangement since "A Day in the Life."

The first part of the medley begins with "You Never Give Me Your Money" and continues through "Sun King," "Mean Mr. Mustard," "Polythene Pam," and "She Came In Through the Bathroom Window." The second part begins with "Golden Slumbers," "Carry That Weight," and ends with "The End," the medley weaving together disparate musical ideas into a seamless whole. This approach allowed them to use song fragments that might not have worked as complete tracks, creating something greater than the sum of its parts—the ultimate expression of their synergistic magic.

The medley's effectiveness relies on each member's distinctive contributions. Paul's piano and bass work provide the foundation, John's rhythm guitar adds texture, George's lead guitar sings with emotion, and Ringo's drumming holds everything together with perfect timing and tasteful fills, particularly on "The End," which features his only recorded drum solo with The Beatles.

Most poignant is how the medley builds to the album's final moments. "Golden Slumbers," with its lullaby-like quality, gives way to

"Carry That Weight," whose chorus acknowledges the burden of their legacy and the tensions between them. This transitions into "The End," featuring a round-robin of guitar solos where Paul, George, and John each take turns, trading two-bar phrases in a musical conversation that symbolizes their individual voices coming together one last time.

And then, after all the instruments fade, comes the final line of "The End" that serves as their epitaph. The final reminder at the end of it all, is that what really matters is love. Their simple statement of karmic balance stands as perhaps the most fitting conclusion to their career. It suggests that despite the arguments, the business disputes, and the personal differences that drove them apart, what ultimately mattered was the love they put into their music and shared with the world.

The fact that they could create something so cohesive and profound while their personal relationships were fracturing demonstrates just how powerful their musical connection remained. Even as the magical mystery was derailing in their personal interactions, it continued to flow through their creative collaboration.

Jeff Jarratt, a sound engineer who worked with The Beatles, recalled advice from George Martin when preparing for the *Abbey Road* sessions: "There will be one Beatle there, fine. Two Beatles, great. Three Beatles, fantastic. But the minute the four of them are there, that is when the inexplicable charismatic thing happens, the special magic no one has been able to explain. It will be very friendly between you but you will be aware of this inexplicable presence. Sure enough, that's the exact way it happened. I've never felt it in any other circumstances. It was the special chemistry of the four of them which nobody since has ever had."[1]

This "inexplicable presence" was that magical quality that elevated them from four talented individuals to a force that changed music history. When it derailed, something precious was lost—not just for them but for all of us.

Personal Reflection: Fun to Dream

Remembering that "All Things Must Pass" was around at this time (the song by George that was rejected by John and Paul), it is fun to dream what they could have done with that song. Imagine if John and Paul had given George more songs on *Abbey Road*. Better yet, imagine if they had elevated George to a place of prominence and allowed "All Things Must Pass" to be part of his final medley right before "The End." The themes overlap and could have been the penultimate Beatles message prior to the famous close.

Placed in this position, George's contemplative ballad could have served as a poignant moment of reflection before the band's final musical statement. Its themes of acceptance and impermanence would create a natural philosophical bridge to the finality expressed in "The End." This placement might have provided a perfect emotional pause—a moment of calm acceptance before the band's concluding statement. The resulting sequence would have given George a more substantial voice in the album's emotional crescendo while reinforcing the bittersweet sentiment that permeates *Abbey Road*'s conclusion, perhaps making the album's farewell even more poignant.

When the Magic Fades: Missed Opportunities

Part of The Beatles' magical mystery was their extraordinary luck—being in the right place at the right time repeatedly throughout their career. But as we've seen in previous chapters, serendipity isn't merely luck; it requires openness to possibility and the ability to recognize and capitalize on opportunities when they arise.

As The Beatles' relationships deteriorated, their openness to serendipitous possibilities diminished. They became less receptive to each other's ideas and less willing to explore unexpected creative directions together.

This closing off significantly reduced the chances for happy accidents and fortunate coincidences that had previously enriched their work.

Several key opportunities were missed during this period that might have altered their trajectory:

1. The Lennon–McCartney partnership revival: Despite their differences, John and Paul occasionally showed flashes of their old chemistry, such as when working on "I've Got a Feeling" during the *Let It Be/Get Back* sessions, which combined two separate song ideas into one cohesive track. Had they deliberately focused on rebuilding their songwriting partnership rather than pursuing increasingly separate paths, they might have rediscovered the collaborative magic that made them extraordinary.

2. George's songwriting evolution: George's dramatic growth as a songwriter could have injected fresh energy into the band had they fully embraced it. His Eastern influences and spiritual themes offered new directions that could have expanded The Beatles' musical palette further. Rather than limiting him to a predetermined quota of songs per album, fully integrating his material could have reinvigorated their creative process.

3. As Paul was desperately trying to hang on to his songwriting partner, he failed to miss what was right in front of him. How serendipitous it was that as John became less interested in collaborating with Paul, a songwriter of George's caliber was emerging. A McCartney–Harrison songwriting collaboration could have created some of the finest music the world has ever heard. They could have balanced each other in much the same way John and Paul did.

4. Alternative working methods: The Beatles had fallen into fixed patterns of studio work that no longer served all members

equally. Exploring different approaches—perhaps rotating leadership of sessions or establishing clearer boundaries between projects—might have alleviated tensions and created space for continued collaboration on more flexible terms.

5. Extended break instead of permanent split: Rather than an outright breakup, a clearly communicated extended hiatus might have preserved the possibility of future reunions. Other bands have successfully pursued solo projects while periodically coming back together when the time felt right. The permanent nature of their split closed off possibilities that might have emerged with time and distance.

The most significant missed opportunity, perhaps, was the failure to recognize and directly address the fundamental issues driving them apart. Instead of having honest conversations about what each member needed to continue working together productively, they allowed resentments to fester until separation seemed the only option.

Last Chances: The Final Sessions

The *Let It Be* album (recorded mostly before *Abbey Road* but released after it) was intended as a return to basics—a stripped-down approach that would reconnect them with their roots as a live band. The original concept, suggested by Paul, was to film the creation of an album from rehearsal to performance, culminating in their first live concert since 1966.

This vision never fully materialized, partly because the chosen setting—the cavernous and cold Twickenham Film Studios—created an uncomfortable environment that exacerbated tensions. George temporarily quit the band during these sessions, returning only when they agreed to move to the more familiar surroundings of their Apple Studios and abandon plans for a live concert.

Despite these challenges, the sessions produced moments of genuine magic. The rooftop concert, their final public performance, demonstrated they could still create electrifying music together when the circumstances were right. Their renditions of "Get Back," "Don't Let Me Down," and "One After 909" (a song dating back to their earliest days) showed that their ability to lock in as a performing unit remained intact.

The title track, "Let It Be," emerged as one of Paul's most enduring compositions, a gospel-influenced ballad inspired by a dream about his mother. Similarly, John's "Across the Universe," with its transcendent lyrics and ethereal quality, ranks among his most beautiful songs. Even in this difficult period, their individual creativity remained at a remarkably high level.

Yet the sessions failed to rekindle the collaborative spirit that had defined their greatest work. They were increasingly working on their own material separately, coming together only to provide backing for each other's songs rather than genuinely cocreating. The serendipitous sparks that happened when they fully engaged with each other's ideas were becoming increasingly rare.

What might have happened had they approached these sessions differently? If, instead of attempting to force a return to their early days, they had acknowledged their evolution as artists and found new ways to work together that accommodated their individual growth? The magic might have evolved rather than derailed.

The Unrealized Potential: What Might Have Been

When we consider what brought an end to The Beatles' magical mystery, it's natural to wonder what might have been possible had they found a way to preserve it. Their solo careers provide tantalizing glimpses of collaborations that never happened.

Imagine John's raw emotional honesty combined with Paul's melodic sophistication on more tracks like "A Day in the Life." Envision George's spiritual depth and distinctive guitar work enriching more of John and Paul's compositions, or their talents elevating more of his. Consider how Ringo's steady presence might have continued to provide the perfect foundation for their collective creativity.

Had they stayed together but established more equitable terms—perhaps allowing more space for solo projects within the band framework, or rotating leadership of albums—the 1970s might have produced a series of varied Beatles albums that reflected their maturing perspectives while maintaining their collective identity.

Even after the breakup, there were moments when reunion seemed possible. The closest they came was in 1974 and 1975, when all four ex-Beatles were simultaneously in Los Angeles. Despite rumors and reported near misses, no full reunion materialized. Had they overcome their differences, even temporarily, they might have discovered that the magical mystery could be rekindled.

Conclusion: Enduring Magic

Though the magical mystery eventually derailed, its impact continues to resonate. The Beatles' chemistry—that ineffable quality that elevated their music beyond the sum of their individual contributions—remains the gold standard for creative collaboration. Even in their final recorded work, that chemistry produced moments of transcendent beauty.

Abbey Road stands as testament to what was still possible even as their personal relationships frayed. The closing medley, with its triumphant guitar interplay and final philosophical statement at "The End" offers both a fitting conclusion to their journey and a lasting message about what truly matters in creative partnerships.

The Beatles may have broken up, but the magic they created hasn't diminished with time. If anything, it has grown more remarkable as subsequent generations discover their music and marvel at what four individuals from Liverpool accomplished together. Their magical mystery tour continues to take new listeners away to unexpected places of wonder and inspiration.

As we consider how to build and sustain our own creative teams, we can learn as much from how The Beatles' magic derailed as from how it flourished. By understanding both their triumphs and their challenges, we can better navigate the delicate balance of personalities, ambitions, and circumstances that either sustain or undermine creative synergy.

In the end, perhaps the most powerful lesson is that even magical partnerships have natural life cycles. The Beatles gave us twelve studio albums in seven years—an extraordinary output by any measure. Though we might wish for more, perhaps the intensity that made their work so magical could never have been sustained indefinitely. Sometimes, the most beautiful fireworks are those that burn brightest and then fade, leaving their pattern imprinted on our memories rather than slowly dimming into obscurity.

Applying the Lessons of Chapter 10

When the magic disappears from a once-extraordinary team, the loss extends beyond measurable metrics. The Beatles' final chapter reveals how even the most talented collaborators can lose the ineffable chemistry that once made them exceptional and how glimpses of that magic can persist even amid deteriorating relationships.

The Beatles' magical synergy—their ability to create something greater than the sum of their parts—didn't disappear overnight. It faded gradually through missed opportunities and changing dynamics:

1. **Collaborative creativity became isolated production:** Band members increasingly recorded separately rather than together.

2. **Serendipitous moments went unrecognized:** Opportunities for "happy accidents" diminished as openness decreased.

3. **Musical cross-pollination declined:** The willingness to build on each other's ideas gave way to territorial boundaries.

4. **Flow state experiences became rare:** Sessions felt like work rather than inspired creation.

5. **Collective identity fractured into individual brands:** Solo identities began overshadowing the group identity.

These warning signs manifested in observable behaviors that leaders should watch for in their own teams.

DERAILMENT DIAGNOSTIC: MAGIC LOSS INDICATORS

For your team, assess whether these statements have become true:

- Team members prefer to work separately rather than collaboratively.

- Creative sessions feel forced rather than flowing naturally.

- Unexpected ideas or outcomes are met with resistance rather than exploration.

- Team members are more protective than generous with their contributions.

- References to past successes outnumber excited discussions about future possibilities.

Three or more "yes" answers suggest your team's magical chemistry may be eroding in ways similar to that of The Beatles in their final phase.

PREVENTION STRATEGY: MAGIC PRESERVATION PROTOCOL

1. **Collaboration diagnostics:** Regularly assess how much work happens in isolation versus true collaboration.

2. **Serendipity sessions:** Schedule unstructured creative time with the explicit goal of exploring unexpected directions.

3. **Cross-pollination requirements:** Establish expectations that team members will contribute to each other's projects.

4. **Flow condition monitoring:** Identify and maintain the conditions that previously created flow states.

5. **Rotational leadership:** Allow different team members to direct collaborative sessions to prevent stagnation.

RECOVERY STRATEGY: REKINDLING THE MAGIC

Even teams that have lost their collaborative magic can experience renewal through deliberate reconnection to their original chemistry.

1. **Origin story revisit:** Nostalgia is a powerful tool. Bring the team together to remember and celebrate what initially created their magic.

2. **Configuration reset:** Temporarily return to previous physical and operational arrangements that worked well.

3. **Success re-creation:** Identify the conditions present during peak experiences and deliberately re-create them.

4. **Relationship renewal:** Focus on personal reconnection before attempting creative collaboration.

5. **Small win design:** Create opportunities for quick, low-pressure collaborative successes.

IMPLEMENTATION GUIDE: MAGIC RENEWAL PROCESS

1. **Identify magic moments:** Have team members share when they last experienced true flow and synergy.

2. **Condition analysis:** Determine what specific factors were present during those experiences.

3. **Barrier removal:** Systematically address obstacles to recapturing those conditions—even if the obstacle is a person.

4. **Microexperiment design:** Create short, contained opportunities to experience collaborative flow.

5. **Reflection ritual:** Regularly discuss what is enhancing or impeding the team's magical chemistry.

THE MAGIC LINGERS

Despite their deteriorating relationships, The Beatles still managed to create moments of transcendent magic together, showing how their musical chemistry could overcome even deep personal conflicts. This collection explores both the fracturing of their magical synergy and those remarkable flashes where it still sparked to life. Contrast that to the bitterness evident in the solo offerings.

1. **"Magical Mystery Tour"**—The title track perfectly captures the whimsical, experimental spirit that defined their creative peak, inviting listeners on a journey of discovery. Its invitation to join a mysterious tour parallels how their music continued to take fans on unexpected journeys even as the band's internal relationships became increasingly strained.

2. **"Two of Us"**—Recorded during the tense *Let It Be/Get Back* sessions, this McCartney song about two companions heading home achieves a remarkable intimacy. When John and Paul sing facing each other, harmonizing into the same microphone, they

momentarily recaptured their original magic, despite the band crumbling around them.

3. **"Run of the Mill"**—George's meditation on the band's breakdown poignantly addresses how their relationships deteriorated. He reflects on the importance of personal choice—how it can build up or tear down a relationship.

4. **"Early 1970"**—Ringo's heartfelt reflection on his bandmates' states of mind following their breakup, with verses specifically describing John, Paul, and George. This remarkably honest song shows his continued affection for each of them but shows uncertainty about where he stands with Paul.

5. **"Too Many People"**—Paul's post-breakup attack on John shows how their once-magical songwriting partnership had devolved into musical accusations. Despite the lyrical barbs, Paul's melodic genius remains evident, highlighting how their individual magic continued even as their collective synergy was lost.

6. **"3 Legs"**—Many speculate (unconfirmed by Paul) that this allegorical tale from Paul's *Ram* album uses the metaphor of a three-legged dog to describe the Beatles without him. The playful music contrasts with biting lyrics, demonstrating how their creative powers remained strong even as they channeled them into addressing their conflict.

7. **"How Do You Sleep?"**—Unlike Paul's veiled barbs, John went straight after Paul in this scathing reply. The song features George on slide guitar. The track's undeniable power proves that even their anger could produce compelling art, albeit through conflict rather than harmony.

8. **"Back Off Boogaloo"**—Ringo's second solo single, reportedly inspired by conversations with George, contained veiled references to Paul. The song's infectious energy and production quality demonstrated that even Ringo could channel the group's magical formula into commercial success on his own.

9. **"Sue Me, Sue You Blues"**—George's sardonic commentary on the band's legal battles, directed predominantly at Paul (who had sued his former bandmates), features a brilliant slide guitar performance that showcases his post-Beatles musical growth.

10. **"Abbey Road Medley: You Never Give Me Your Money/ Sun King/Mean Mr. Mustard/Polythene Pam/She Came in Through the Bathroom Window/Golden Slumbers/Carry That Weight/The End"**—Their final recorded masterpiece represents the ultimate example of Beatles magic persisting despite personal animosity. This seamless suite features each member at their best: Paul's melodic vision, John's poetic counterpoint, George's transcendent guitar, and Ringo's perfect rhythmic foundation, culminating in their perfect epitaph.

PART 3

BUILDING ENDURING EXCELLENCE

P art 3 focuses on managing the critical risk that change—both internal and external—plays in teams and organizations. One certainty in life and business is that things do not remain static. How a team or organization handles change is critical to its long-term health and success. Enduring excellence requires awareness, resilience, and flexibility in the face of change. Without these qualities, a team, organization, or individual will likely be derailed.

The Beatles' story provides both a cautionary tale and a blueprint for prevention. Having examined how they achieved greatness in part 1 and how they lost it in part 2, we now turn to the lessons their journey offers for sustaining excellence through inevitable transitions and challenges. This final section of our exploration addresses the universal question that follows any derailment: How can we prevent this from happening to us?

In his excellent work *The Five Dysfunctions of a Team*, Patrick Lencioni provides a clear lens through which to view the dysfunction of The Beatles in their later years.

Absence of Trust: By 1969, The Beatles had lost their fundamental trust in each other. John no longer trusted Paul's motives after discovering Paul's secret purchase of additional Northern Songs shares. George didn't trust that his songs would get fair consideration. The foundation of vulnerability-based trust that had characterized their early years was gone.

Fear of Conflict: While The Beatles weren't afraid of conflict in general, they increasingly avoided productive conflict that could have addressed core issues. Instead of engaging in healthy debate about their divergent visions, they retreated to passive-aggressive behavior. George's comment to Paul during the *Let It Be/Get Back* sessions—"I'll play whatever you want me to play, or I won't play at all"[1]—perfectly demonstrates this dysfunction.

Lack of Commitment: Without trust and healthy conflict, genuine commitment became impossible. Decisions were no longer embraced by the whole group. John's disengagement during the *Let It Be/Get Back* sessions shows how commitment had eroded. When the group couldn't achieve true buy-in on decisions about management, Apple Corps's direction, or artistic choices, their ability to move forward cohesively was fatally compromised.

Avoidance of Accountability: The Beatles stopped holding each other accountable to shared standards. In the early days, they would push each other toward excellence through friendly competition. By 1969, this accountability had deteriorated. John's absences, George's frustration, Paul's controlling behavior, and Ringo's passivity were all allowed without the kind of peer-to-peer accountability that characterizes great teams.

Inattention to Results: Finally, individual agendas began to supersede collective results. What mattered wasn't the band's success but each Beatle's personal goals: John's political activism, Paul's desire to continue their commercial success, George's spiritual journey, and Ringo's acting career. The collective focus that had made them extraordinary was lost.[2]

In the next two chapters, we will dive more deeply into the tools that The Beatles could have utilized to correct their dysfunction—tools that apply to any team or organization.

In chapter 11, we'll examine the interpersonal dynamics essential for navigating change—know and respect your team, provide space for personal growth and changing roles, and communicate openly with active listening. These human connections form the invisible infrastructure that either supports or undermines excellence during periods of transformation.

Chapter 12 builds upon this foundation by exploring the organizational structures needed for sustainable excellence. Stephen Covey emphasizes in *The 7 Habits of Highly Effective People* that "sharpening the saw" is the habit that makes all other habits possible.[3] Similarly, chapter 12 is a blueprint for continuous improvement and renewal. The keys are strong mentors and/or relationships, a process to recalibrate the vision, and a framework that allows redefining the necessary commitment.

Throughout both chapters, we'll draw not only from The Beatles' experiences but also from contemporary organizational wisdom and personal reflections that demonstrate these principles in action. We'll even imagine what might have been possible had The Beatles implemented these strategies, a tantalizing glimpse of the music and magic the world might have enjoyed had they found a way to work it out.

CHAPTER 11

"WE CAN WORK IT OUT"

When organizations or teams derail, we often look first at organizational issues—faulty strategies, poor execution, or financial problems. But The Beatles' story reveals a deeper truth: Derailment frequently begins with the gradual erosion of interpersonal dynamics. The connections between people—how they see each other, respond to each other's growth, and communicate with one another—form the invisible infrastructure that either promotes or undermines excellence.

Often, before strategies fail or execution suffers, relationships fray. This chapter explores the human side of derailment prevention, examining how knowing and respecting your team members, providing space for their evolution, and fostering healthy communication create the resilience needed to navigate inevitable changes.

As we've seen, underlying the business disagreements that were a major cause of The Beatles' breakup were poor interpersonal dynamics among the four of them. These extraordinary individuals, despite their close friendship and unparalleled chemistry, lost their ability to truly see, hear, and understand each other.

Remember what Steve Jobs said in his *60 Minutes* interview? "They were four guys who kept each other's kind of negative tendencies in check."[1] As ego crept in, they stopped keeping each other's negative tendencies in check—a major cause of derailment of any team.

Drawing lessons from The Beatles' breakup, integrating insights from contemporary leadership thought, and sprinkling in some of my personal experiences, we'll explore three key strategies to create healthy interpersonal dynamics, thereby avoiding derailment:

- Know and respect your team.

- Provide space for personal growth and changing roles.

- Communicate openly with empathic listening.

Personal Reflection:
Lessons in Interpersonal Dynamics

Many times, taking time for interpersonal dynamics is at odds with a catalytic vision. Once the overdrive of a catalytic vision kicks in, there is a sense of urgency that permeates the organization. At times I learned this the hard way. I am reminded of the description of Absher's core value "We do right things," which says "We do not lose sight of the important for the sake of the urgent."

For me, this sense of urgency manifested itself as impatience—especially early in my tenure at Absher. Once I saw the vision, I expected (demanded?) that others enthusiastically embrace it.

This is a common mistake among leaders who are driven by a bold vision or a strong sense of purpose. Balancing that catalytic vision with attention to interpersonal dynamics is challenging but critical to the long-term health of any organization or team. In this chapter, I will give three examples of lessons I've learned: one personal reflection on each of the three key strategies for creating healthy interpersonal dynamics.

Know and Respect Your Team

The Beatles' derailment offers a powerful lesson about the importance of truly knowing and respecting your team members. When Brian Epstein died in 1967, the group lost more than just a manager; they lost someone who understood each Beatle's unique strengths, insecurities, and contributions.

Stephen M. R. Covey's work in *The Speed of Trust* emphasizes that trust is the foundation of any effective team.[2] When trust diminishes within an organization, the consequences are severe and multifaceted. The Beatles experienced this deterioration after Brian Epstein's death, as evidenced by the increasing tension while working together in the studio.

Remember Paul's comment about George's age in chapter 9? Even after all those years, Paul thought he was eighteen months older than George; the truth is he was less than nine months older. At a time when most of the world knew how old George was, somehow, the guy who practically lived with him nonstop for several years did not know. This lack of knowledge and respect for George drove a wedge in their relationship. This is a big reason his "guitar gently weeps."

When George struggled to find the right lead guitar solo for his song "Taxman," George Martin asked Paul to give it a go, and he nailed it in one take. While it is a great solo, and Paul is an incredibly talented multi-instrumentalist, the team dynamic might have been better served by encouraging George to stick with it until he nailed it.

In a similar way, John always looked on George as the young kid whom he let join the band. When a pecking order is established among friends at an early age, it is hard to shake those patterns. It seemed that John could only see George as the fourteen-year-old kid auditioning for him on a bus in Liverpool.

Referring to John in a 1987 interview, George said, "I liked him very much; he was a groove. He was a good lad, but at the same time, he misread me. He didn't realize who I was, and this is one of the main faults of John and Paul. They were so busy being John and Paul, they failed to realize who else was around at the time."[3]

According to Covey, when trust breaks down, team members spend valuable time documenting conversations, double-checking work, and building redundant systems to protect themselves.[4] We see this in how The Beatles began working separately during the White Album sessions, often recording their parts independently rather than collaborating. This is not to say that the songs were substandard. On the contrary, the White Album is a masterpiece, but we begin to see ego starting to creep into the sessions.

Ford CEO Alan Mulally demonstrated this principle perfectly during his turnaround of the struggling automaker. Rather than bringing in an entirely new leadership team, he took time to evaluate existing talent and support those who embraced transparency and accountability.

Avoiding derailment requires regular check-ins with team members about their aspirations, frustrations, and ideas, not just their current projects. When people feel seen and valued for their full potential, they're more likely to invest their creative energy in the organization's success rather than looking for opportunities elsewhere.

PERSONAL REFLECTION:
KNOW AND RESPECT YOUR TEAM

I had been president of Absher Construction for less than a year. The next generation of leaders were anxious to make the changes we saw necessary. Toward that end, I asked the whole team to complete a comprehensive survey on the health of the company, with suggestions for improvements. When the deadline for completion passed, we had received most, though not all, of the surveys.

We got great feedback, but I was frustrated that not everyone had completed the survey. I gave it a couple of days and sent out a "reminder" that was not very diplomatic. One of my all-time favorite members of the Absher team, Jack, came into my office to give me some advice. "Chief," he said, "don't hide behind a memo. If you want to know why my survey is late, come ask me. If you want to scold me for being late, do it to my face." He then proceeded to tell me about all the fires he had been putting out at work. He explained how time sensitive they were. And he told me he had been getting migraine headaches, so if I could give him a few days he'd appreciate it.

Lesson: I did not make the effort to know and respect what was on Jack's plate at the time. I was not aware of his bouts with migraine headaches. Even though I was anxious to implement changes within the organization, I needed to give the team time to get on board. It doesn't really matter where the train is going if no one is on it.

Provide Space for Personal Growth and Changing Roles

By 1968, The Beatles had physically and creatively outgrown their original roles. George was no longer content being the quiet lead guitarist limited to one song per album. John was exploring avant-garde art and political activism. Paul was expanding his vision of what The Beatles could be. Ringo was developing as an actor. Yet their defined roles, established when they were teens, couldn't accommodate these evolutions.

Robert Kegan and Lisa Lahey's work in *An Everyone Culture* provides a framework for understanding this challenge. They introduce the concept of "Deliberately Developmental Organizations" (DDOs), where personal growth is seamlessly integrated with business operations. The Beatles, despite their creative brilliance, failed to create a workplace that put business and individual development—and the way each one supports the other—front and center for everyone, every day.[5]

DDOs recognize that "adults, not just children, can and need to keep growing."[6] This personal growth becomes a competitive advantage. Had The Beatles embraced this approach, they might have created structures that accommodated George's spiritual journey, John's political activism, Paul's ambitious vision for The Beatles, and Ringo's developing interest in acting, all while maintaining their collaborative core.

Organizations that endure know that providing space for growth isn't about promotions, it's about creating flexibility within the system itself. When team members outgrow their initial roles, leaders have two options: Create space for their expanded contributions or watch them take those contributions elsewhere.

PERSONAL REFLECTION: PROVIDE SPACE FOR PERSONAL GROWTH AND CHANGING ROLES

When Stephanie came to work for us, she had no construction experience. One of our project directors knew her from church and saw something in her that could benefit our team. We initially hired her as an entry-level project coordinator. This was at a time when we were shifting our vision from building buildings to serving our communities.

While Stephanie struggled to learn the nuts and bolts of construction, she grasped the impact we were having on the nearby community. She gravitated naturally to being the liaison between the project team and the local community. In addition, much of the work we do has requirements and/or goals for the involvement of small or disadvantaged businesses. Stephanie was well suited to recruit, train, and prepare many of those companies to participate on our projects.

Long before diversity, equity, and inclusion (DEI) became so controversial, Absher developed a program with laudable objectives—to increase participation of women and minorities in the construction industry. Because of Stephanie's leadership, we did it the right way—through outreach, training and education, and mentoring. In doing so, she has become one of the top leaders in our company and the community.

Lesson: Had we not been patient, we might have given up on Stephanie. We would have missed out on the impact Stephanie has had on all our projects. And the construction industry would not have had the benefit of a tireless champion for increased participation of minorities and women in our industry.

Personal Growth and Changing Roles in The Beatles

Recognizing team members' unique talents requires recognition that talents and interests evolve over time. George's growth as a songwriter was a resource the group never fully tapped. By limiting him to one or two songs per album, they inadvertently created frustration that contributed to their eventual breakup. Imagine an alternate timeline where John and Paul had actively nurtured George's songwriting earlier, potentially gaining dozens of additional classics. It is even more exciting to imagine a world where John and George occasionally got together to write songs, or Paul and George did the same.

This highlights a crucial lesson for any organization: People evolve. The quiet one today might become your most innovative voice tomorrow. The rookie with unusual ideas might be developing your next breakthrough product. Respecting your team means not only valuing who they are now but recognizing who they're becoming.

Consider how different things might have been if The Beatles had embraced a more fluid approach to their music after they stopped touring. What if they had pursued occasional side projects while maintaining the core band? What if George had been allowed to develop his songwriting through a solo album that satisfied his creative needs while still preserving the group's identity?

By the time The Beatles broke up, George had dozens, perhaps hundreds, of songs available for recording. What might have happened if his bandmates had created space for more of that creativity? Imagine if they had cultivated and welcomed George's songwriting. Because John and Paul were set on their original roles as the songwriters, they failed to give George the space to grow.

In a lesser way, this applies to Ringo. Though clearly not of the songwriting caliber of the other three, he has shown a flair for writing some great songs, especially when given support—like when George helped him with "Octopus's Garden" and cowrote "It Don't Come Easy" and "Photograph" with him (two of the biggest hits in Ringo's solo career).

Providing space for growth means implementing systems like job crafting (where employees reshape aspects of their jobs to better align with their strengths), cross-training opportunities, innovation time, or mentorship programs. It means having career discussions not only about moving up but moving laterally or even creating entirely new roles that leverage emerging talents.

The lesson from The Beatles' derailment is clear: When people feel constrained by their roles, they'll eventually break free of them—potentially breaking the organization in the process. Adaptive organizations build flexibility into their structures, allowing roles to evolve as the people within them grow.

Communicate Openly with Empathic Listening

Stephen Covey's fifth habit from *The 7 Habits of Highly Effective People*—"seek first to understand, then to be understood"—offers insight into where The Beatles' communication broke down. As Covey explains, "Most people do not listen with the intent to understand; they listen with the intent to reply. They're either speaking or preparing to speak. They're filtering everything through their own paradigms, reading their autobiography into other people's lives."[7]

None of them practiced what Covey calls "empathic listening": listening with the intent to truly understand the other person's frame of reference, feelings, and perspective. Had they mastered this skill—setting aside their own concerns long enough to genuinely understand each other's needs and viewpoints—they might have found common ground from which to rebuild their fractured relationships. Instead, each member increasingly retreated into their own perspective, creating a communication chasm too wide to bridge.

By 1969, communication among The Beatles had deteriorated to the point where George didn't even know that John had quit the band for several months. Contrast this with their earlier cohesion, where ideas flowed freely and collaboration thrived. What changed? They stopped truly listening to each other.

PERSONAL REFLECTION: COMMUNICATE OPENLY WITH EMPATHIC LISTENING

Several years ago, we hired Jae, a student studying construction management at the University of Washington, as a summer intern. He was very bright and painfully shy. His introversion was so severe, I questioned whether he could ever become a project manager or team leader. Even though it was difficult to talk with him, we kept trying because he picked things up so quickly. Our concern was he didn't seem to have any ambition to grow in his career.

Eventually, we built enough trust with him to have open dialogue. This would not have worked had we not been willing to listen when he was finally ready to talk. He admitted to his fear of public speaking and that his shyness was an obstacle for him. However, he believed that someday he would be one of the company's top leaders.

It took time, but over the course of a few years, he worked on it, attending Toastmasters and accepting assignments that forced him out of his comfort zone. One such assignment was a move to Hawaii for an opportunity to lead our work there. He was in charge of the interpersonal dynamics of the team. He embraced the experience and grew immensely as a leader.

Sure enough, Jae worked his way up in the company and leads its most profitable division. I wouldn't say he loves public speaking today, but he does it effectively when needed. And, when he speaks, people listen.

Lesson: We easily could have moved on from Jae early on or pigeon-holed him as a backroom engineer had we not encouraged him to be open about his fears and his potential future. Communicating with active listening helped us realize Jae had the ambition to be a leader in the company. By remaining patient, Jae had the time to grow as a person and has become a well-respected leader.

Communication Breakdown of The Beatles

Healthy communication creates a psychological safety zone for those in a healthy relationship. After Brian Epstein's death, this safety zone rapidly deteriorated. In the early days, they had this. By the time of the *Let It Be/Get Back* sessions, we see examples of Paul's controlling tendencies, John's shirking of leadership responsibility, George's inability to express his frustration in a healthy way, and Ringo's quiet acceptance.

Remember George's memorable comment to Paul during the *Let It Be/Get Back* sessions: "I'll play whatever you want me to play, or I won't play at all if you don't want me to play . . . Whatever it is that will please you, I'll do it." This passive-aggressive statement reveals a complete breakdown in psychological safety.

Empathic listening creates psychological safety—an environment where team members can voice concerns, share ideas, and even disagree without fear of humiliation or retribution. It requires leaders to model vulnerability themselves, acknowledge when they don't have all the answers, and demonstrate that they value input from all levels.

Practical steps include implementing regular check-ins that focus not only on tasks but on how people are feeling about their work, creating structured feedback systems, using a decision-making process that ensures all voices are heard, and building time for reflection into meetings rather than filling every minute with action items.

Had The Beatles maintained regular, honest communication about their frustrations and aspirations—perhaps with a neutral facilitator after Brian Epstein's death—they might have found structural solutions that accommodated their evolving needs while preserving the magic of their collaboration.

PERSONAL REFLECTION: CONSTRUCTION MANAGEMENT CLASS

In the fall of 2023, I jumped at the opportunity to teach construction management classes at Pierce College, a local college with an ambitious construction management program. I have been teaching Construction Industry Relationships and Communication and Conflict Resolution.

As I'm sure you guessed, I routinely use references to music in my teaching—especially The Beatles. I weave several lessons from The Beatles' experience into the classes: leadership and management, conflict resolution, and team-building. The feedback from the students has consistently been that their favorite classes are the ones where I apply lessons from The Beatles.

In the Communication and Conflict Resolution course, one of our main points of emphasis is healthy communication and active listening. I am intrigued by the parallels between the communication challenges among The Beatles and the communication challenges in the construction industry (or most any industry).

The following list of communication challenges in the construction industry comes directly from my class material:

1. Construction projects have unique and complex systems.

2. People on a construction team come from diverse backgrounds and education.

3. Construction projects are built in close quarters, often in poor conditions.

4. Construction projects have strict schedules, budgets, and quality demands.

5. Technical skills in construction and communication skills are very different.

Let's compare the "unique" challenges of communication in construction to what The Beatles faced.

- Unique and complex: Creating a song, album, video, or movie, like a construction project, is unique and complex.

- Different backgrounds: While John, Paul, George, and Ringo had similar backgrounds and education, the other contributors to The Beatles' empire (managers, producers, engineers, accountants, and attorneys) certainly did not. This was one of the major causes of their derailment.

- Working in poor conditions: The conditions under which The Beatles created and performed most of their greatest works were small and very poor—especially early in their career. They had to make do with what was available.

- Strict schedule, quality, and budget demands: The Beatles were constantly under pressure to meet their production schedule with the highest of quality. When they became the biggest band in the world, budget became less of an issue—although poor management of their finances was one of the causes of their derailment.

- Technical skills are not the same as communication skills: Like those with technical skills in construction, being a great song-writer, lead guitarist, singer, or drummer does *not* make you a great communicator. It is a vastly different skill.

To take this one step further, The Beatles, the construction industry, and almost every other industry are faced with similar communication challenges, so these lessons apply universally.

The most important lesson I teach our construction management students is the importance of healthy communication and active listening. Here are some tips for active listening from our class:

- Eliminate distractions.

- Practice good body language.

- Make eye contact.

- Listen for new information.

- Grasp the meaning, don't judge the words.

- Ask open-ended questions.

- Clarify/summarize what you've heard.

Imagine if any of The Beatles actively listened to one of their band-mates. With the benefit of decades of study and contemplation, we can see that none of them felt they were being heard by the others. They were all going through huge life changes under massive pressure—from record companies, accountants, lawyers, the press, the public, and each other. Perhaps if one of them had truly listened to his bandmate, it would have opened healthy lines of communication for all of them.

Conclusion: Interpersonal Dynamics

The three ways to avoid derailment that we've explored in this chapter— know and respect your team, provide space for personal growth and changing roles, and communicate openly with empathic listening— form the foundation for preventing derailment in the interpersonal relationships of an organization. These interpersonal dynamics set the stage for the more structural approaches we'll explore in the next chapter.

The Beatles' story shows that even extraordinary talent can be derailed when these fundamentals are neglected. By truly knowing and respecting each team member, creating space for their evolution, and fostering gen-uine communication, you build resilience into your organization's DNA.

Remember that excellence is not a destination but a journey. The practices that helped you achieve initial success will need to evolve as your people and circumstances change. As we'll see in the next chap-ter, this requires intentional structures for mentoring, recalibrating the vision, and redefining commitment.

Applying the Lessons of Chapter 11

Have you ever been part of a team that gradually lost its cohesion and effectiveness despite having talented members? Or witnessed how relationships within an organization eroded over time, leading to diminished results? The difference often comes down to the interpersonal dynamics that form the invisible infrastructure of any successful team.

When The Beatles reached the height of their fame, they faced a critical challenge that many successful organizations encounter: maintaining healthy relationships amid changing circumstances. Their story offers powerful insights into how interpersonal dynamics can either sustain or derail excellence.

EXERCISE 1: KNOW AND RESPECT YOUR TEAM—YOUNG PRESIDENTS ORGANIZATION (YPO) FORUM MODEL

Purpose

The structured forum approach used in YPO creates psychological safety for team members to truly know each other beyond their workplace roles and provide meaningful support for professional challenges. There are many variations of the forum approach; I recommend the one we utilized in our leadership development program at Absher Construction.

Setup

Create "forum" groups of six to eight people at similar organizational levels who meet bimonthly.

Structure

1. Forum formation (initial meeting)

   a. Groups should be deliberately diverse in terms of departments/functions

   b. Each forum elects a moderator who will

      ○ Schedule meetings

      ○ Prepare agendas

      ○ Ensure time frames are respected

      ○ Guide discussions toward meaningful outcomes

   c. The forum establishes ground rules, with these nonnegotiables:

      ○ Strict confidentiality (what's said in forum stays in forum)

      ○ No judgment

      ○ Equal participation from all members

      ○ Commitment to regular attendance

2. Bimonthly meetings (two to three hours)

   a. Personal updates (forty-five to fifty minutes)

      ○ Each member takes five minutes to share updates from three life domains:

         ▪ Personal

         ▪ Family and friends

         ▪ Work and career

      ○ No interruptions during updates

      ○ Brief clarifying questions only after each update

   b. Deep-dive discussion (thirty to sixty minutes)

      ○ Prior to each meeting, the moderator works with one to

two members to identify specific work challenges they're facing.

- ○ The selected member(s) presents their challenge in detail (ten minutes).
- ○ Forum members ask clarifying questions (ten minutes).
- ○ The presenting member listens without responding while forum members discuss:
  - Similar experiences they've had
  - Potential approaches
  - Resources that might help
- ○ The presenting member reflects on what they heard and identifies next steps.

c. Closing round (ten minutes)

- ○ Each member shares one insight gained from the session.
- ○ Moderator confirms the next meeting date and presenting members.

Why It Works

This approach directly addresses the interpersonal breakdown that derailed The Beatles after Brian Epstein's death. Had The Beatles maintained a structured forum for honest communication with clear ground rules, they might have navigated their transitions more successfully.

The YPO forum model creates a unique blend of personal connection and professional problem-solving that builds the deep trust needed to sustain teams through challenging transitions. By understanding colleagues as whole people, not just their work roles, team members develop the empathy and insight needed to support each other's growth rather than feeling threatened by it.

EXERCISE 2: PROVIDE SPACE FOR PERSONAL GROWTH—THE HIDDEN TALENT EXCHANGE

Purpose

This collaborative exercise identifies team members ready for expanded responsibilities or different roles, creating a structured process for growth like what George needed within The Beatles.

Setup

Gather in teams of no more than four people. Provide forms or digital templates for capturing information.

Structure

1. Self-assessment (ten minutes)

    a. Each person privately completes a structured form addressing the following questions:

    - What responsibility or role would you like to take on that you currently don't have?

    - What specific skills or strengths make you well suited for this opportunity?

    - What support would you need to be successful in this new capacity?

    - What timeline do you envision for this transition or expansion of responsibilities?

2. Peer recognition (ten minutes)

    a. On separate forms, each person identifies at least one team member who they believe

- Has untapped potential for a specific responsibility
- Shows readiness for a leadership opportunity
- Would excel in a different role than their current one

   b. Includes concrete examples that support the recommendation

   c. Specifys what organizational benefit might result from this change

3. Information compilation (five minutes)

   a. A designated facilitator collects all self-assessment and peer recognition forms

   b. Forms are submitted confidentially to a designated Career Team composed of

   - HR representative(s)
   - Department leader(s)
   - Leadership development specialist(s)

4. Career Team assessment (outside the meeting)

   a. The Career Team

   - Reviews all submissions
   - Identifies patterns and matches between self-assessments and peer recognitions
   - Evaluates organizational needs against individual growth aspirations
   - Creates potential growth paths for each team member

5. Action planning (follow-up session)

   a. The Career Team

- ◦ Schedules individual meetings with team members
- ◦ Presents tailored growth opportunities:
  - ▪ Project leadership assignments
  - ▪ Cross-functional training
  - ▪ Mentoring relationships
  - ▪ Formal role transitions
- ◦ Collaboratively develops ninety-day action plans with specific milestones
- ◦ Establishes quarterly check-ins to assess progress

Why It Works

This structured approach addresses the missed opportunity within The Beatles where George's songwriting talents weren't fully recognized until too late. By formalizing the process of identifying hidden talents and growth potential, organizations create pathways for development that prevent the frustration that often leads to derailment.

The involvement of a dedicated Career Team provides objectivity and organizational perspective that might be missing within immediate work groups. It also ensures accountability for follow-through, unlike the informal promises The Beatles might have made to each other about future opportunities that never materialized.

This system creates the space for personal growth that keeps talented individuals engaged and contributing their best work to the organization rather than looking elsewhere to fulfill their aspirations.

EXERCISE 3: COMMUNICATE OPENLY WITH EMPATHIC LISTENING—THE CONNECTION CYCLE

Purpose

This exercise helps team members develop active listening skills essential for preventing derailment through misunderstanding and miscommunication.

Setup

Break into teams of no more than four people. Each team will practice the full Connection Cycle.

Structure

1. Select a relevant work challenge or opportunity the organization is facing.

2. Each team member takes three to five minutes to share their perspective while others practice these active listening techniques:

   a. Eliminate distractions: Put away devices and give full attention.

   b. Use attentive body language: Maintain appropriate eye contact and open posture.

   c. Listen for new information: Focus on understanding, not formulating responses.

   d. Grasp the meaning beyond the words: Notice emotions and underlying concerns.

   e. Withhold judgment: Resist the urge to mentally critique or dismiss ideas.

3. After each person speaks, the other team members take turns

   a. Asking open-ended questions to deepen understanding (e.g., "What makes that aspect most important to you?" rather than "Do you think this is important?")

   b. Clarifying and summarizing what they heard (e.g., "It sounds like your main concern is . . .")

   c. Acknowledging the speaker's perspective before sharing their own

4. Once all perspectives are shared, the team collaboratively

   a. Identifies the deeper purpose or "why" behind different viewpoints (drawing on Sinek's emphasis on understanding purpose)

   b. Seeks solution options that address multiple perspectives

   c. Agrees on next steps that honor the input from all team members

Why It Works

Stephen Covey emphasizes that empathic listening is "listening with the intent to understand."[8] This exercise creates that exact dynamic by requiring team members to demonstrate understanding before contributing their own thoughts.

CHAPTER 11 PLAYLIST

ATTITUDE AND PERSPECTIVE

This collection illuminates the interpersonal dynamics explored in chapter 11, offering musical insights into communication, respect, and personal growth. From direct appeals for understanding to philosophical reflections on connection, these songs demonstrate how The Beatles navigated their complex relationships. They remind us that human connection lies at the heart of all collaborative endeavors and that interpersonal awareness is essential for preventing derailment.

1. **"Let It Be"**—Paul's gentle anthem of acceptance emerged during the band's most fractious period yet offers wisdom about navigating difficult transitions. Its message of finding peace during troubled times reflects the chapter's emphasis on maintaining perspective when interpersonal dynamics become strained.

2. **"Across the Universe"**—John's meditative masterpiece explores how thoughts and words connect us across seemingly unbridgeable

distances. Its cosmic perspective on communication resonates with the chapter's focus on developing deeper understanding between team members, transcending ordinary limitations through genuine connection.

3. **"Hey Jude"**—Paul's epic encouragement to John's son Julian became an anthem of support and empathy. Its evolution from intimate piano ballad to communal sing-along demonstrates how personal connection can expand to create collective harmony—exactly the kind of support dynamic teams need to thrive.

4. **"One After 909"**—One of their earliest compositions, rerecorded during the *Let It Be/Get Back* sessions, this song reconnected them to their shared history. The joy evident in their performance shows how remembering common roots can revitalize strained relationships, creating moments of authentic communication amid larger conflicts.

5. **"Rain"**—This innovative track celebrates perspective-shifting and the power of attitude. John tells us that whether it rains or shines, what is important is our attitude about it. In most situations, the only thing we can control is our attitude.

6. **"Within You, Without You"**—George's philosophical exploration of human connection and separation directly addresses the interpersonal awareness the chapter advocates. Its message about the illusory walls between people provides the perfect metaphor for breaking down communication barriers within teams to prevent derailment.

7. **"I Want to Tell You"**—George's frustration with his inability to properly express his thoughts mirrors the communication challenges many teams face. Its honest acknowledgment of the

gap between what we intend to communicate and what others receive illustrates why thoughtful listening practices are essential.

8. **"Free as a Bird"**—Written by John and posthumously recorded for the *Anthology* special, this track demonstrates how the surviving Beatles overcame decades of hurt to collaborate respectfully with John's vocals. Their willingness to find common ground years later allowed wounds to heal and set them "free."

9. **"Real Love"**—Another posthumous reunion track, turning John's unfinished demo into a complete song. Their willingness to honor his memory while adding their own contributions shows us that "real love" has the power to heal.

10. **"In My Life"**—This reflective masterpiece about valuing relationships above all else encapsulates the heart of interpersonal dynamics. Its tender acknowledgment of how people shape our lives reminds us that at the core of all organizational achievements are the human connections that sustain our work together.

CHAPTER 12

"GETTING BETTER"

While the previous chapter focused on ways to improve interpersonal dynamics to prevent derailment, this chapter explores the organizational structures necessary for sustainable excellence. Covey's "sharpening the saw" principle of balanced self-renewal across physical, mental, social/emotional, and spiritual dimensions offers a valuable parallel to organizational renewal. "It's preserving and enhancing the greatest asset you have—you."[1]

Organizations, like individuals, require intentional practices to preserve their effectiveness and avoid burnout. We have seen that each of The Beatles individually recognized the need for self-renewal, but they neglected to build these structures of self-renewal of the organization, which created crippling dysfunction after Brian Epstein's death. To use our train metaphor from chapter 3, imagine The Beatles as a bullet train. They designed a train like no other, to a destination where nobody had ever been. Once they built the train and it had regularly visited the destination, problems emerged. First, they needed to give the train regular care and maintenance (sharpen the saw), and second, the team needed new destinations to keep them engaged (recalibrate the vision). The following practices complement the personal approaches we examined in the previous chapter and provide the framework within which teams can thrive over the long-term.

For any group seeking enduring excellence, three organizational structures are essential:

- **Establish mentor and/or peer relationships for key leaders:** Creating formal and informal networks that provide feedback, perspective, and accountability

- **Recalibrate the vision annually:** Establishing regular practices to reassess and recommit to shared purpose as circumstances change

- **Redefine commitment when necessary:** Developing explicit agreements about how the organization will accommodate evolving individual needs while preserving collective focus

Together with the interpersonal practices from the previous chapter, these structures create a comprehensive approach to avoiding derailment and sustaining excellence through inevitable changes and challenges. They represent an ongoing renewal process aimed at identifying and preventing derailment.

Establish Mentor and Peer Relationships

As The Beatles' success grew, the accountability mechanisms that had kept them grounded began to erode. By the late 1960s, they no longer "kept each other's negative tendencies in check" (as Steve Jobs pointed out to be their strength). And they were increasingly surrounded by yes-men rather than peers who could provide candid feedback crucial for enduring excellence.

Brian Epstein had served as a trusted external viewpoint, but after his death, no one adequately filled this role. The battle over who would replace him as manager (Allen Klein or the Eastman family) was a battle over two bad choices. Neither of those choices could give The Beatles the kind of candid feedback they so desperately needed. During this turbulent time, they needed a trusted mentor or peer they could trust.

PERSONAL REFLECTION: MENTOR AND PEER RELATIONSHIPS

Throughout my career, I have relied on mentors and peer relationships to keep me grounded and to hold me accountable. I became president of our company at thirty-one years old, so I had a lot to learn. When I changed my career path from law to Absher Construction, I had huge gaps in the expertise and experience needed to run a construction business.

My background in law was helpful since contracts are a big part of being a general contractor. My undergraduate education wasn't much help, as I studied English and political science, not construction management or engineering. I picked up a little of the specialized construction lingo working summers as a laborer for the company. More importantly, I got to know many of the company's top people during those summers.

After a few years practicing law, I came on board as corporate attorney but quickly realized it was not a full-time position for a company of our size (at the time). I gravitated toward our biggest needs—in business development, which made for an odd pairing between law and business development.

The gaps in my knowledge were largely filled by a great team of partners, who had the needed expertise in the technical aspects of construction, estimating, and accounting. Though they provided essential feedback, it did not provide the kind of independent peer feedback and mentoring I needed.

Associated General Contractors (AGC)

Acutely aware of the gaps in my knowledge and experience, I made it a point to learn how the best construction companies operated. Fortunately for me, the company was actively involved in the AGC, a trade association whose members are the best and brightest in the industry. By diving into the organization both locally and nationally, I was able to learn from the top professionals in the industry.

Absher Construction has been a member of AGC for over fifty years. Five different members of Absher have served as president of AGC chapters or districts. Most recently, Absher Vice President Curt Gimmestad served as president of AGC of Washington. We have given a lot to AGC, but we have gotten so much more in return.

As I went through various AGC leadership positions, I was able to meet and learn from some great leaders in our industry. I saw first-hand how companies I admired operated. I learned that safety, quality, and profitability are not mutually exclusive: In fact, they go hand in hand. The same commitment to excellence drives each of those objectives. I also learned that striving for excellence in your company and in the construction industry are not mutually exclusive; on the contrary, they are inseparable.

Thanks to the AGC I learned about the construction industry from a fire hose. By immersing myself in the industry, I gained a solid base of knowledge and developed peer contacts in the industry I could trust.

Outside Board of Directors

Privately owned companies often fail to benefit from the advice and guidance of outside peers. To address this, over thirty-five years ago we changed our board structure to include three outside directors. We have had accountants, developers, consultants, and executives from both inside and outside the construction industry.

We benefited greatly from their input and feedback. However, it wasn't just their feedback that was valuable; having outside directors disciplined us to take a high-level quarterly assessment of the company. This, in and of itself, is an essential practice for any organization aspiring to enduring excellence.

Greg Denk, former executive at Kitchell Corporation, served on our board for twenty years. Not only was he a great board member, but he became my primary mentor when it came to running a construction business. I could not have had a better mentor. He (and Kitchell) checked all the boxes: similar markets (but rarely competed geographically), bigger than Absher Construction but not so big as to be irrelevant, and a family-owned business that converted to an ESOP.

As a board member, he was valuable, but as my mentor, he was indispensable. He had "been there and done that." He gave sage advice when asked, held me accountable when I hesitated to make tough decisions, and listened when I needed to vent. I cannot overstate the importance of top executives having a mentor.

Young Presidents Organization (YPO)

The YPO is a global leadership community of over thirty-five thousand extraordinary chief executives. When I joined YPO twenty-five years ago, the value of peer relationships became more apparent. YPO's strongest attribute is its forum structure. A forum is a group of eight to twelve members who meet monthly to discuss business, personal, and social issues. The forum is an informal board for each other's businesses and, more importantly, a group of peers to hold each other accountable.

These forum mates held me accountable in a way that direct reports could not do. In addition, I was able to bounce ideas off them. YPO brought perspectives from outside the construction industry, which challenged my traditional thinking.

Here is one example of how YPO's forum relationships helped me.

Back in the early 2000s, Absher Construction, as part of a joint venture with JA Jones Construction (one of the largest general contractors in the US at the time), built the new $200 million US Courthouse in Seattle. This twenty-three-story modern courthouse, designed by NBBJ Architects, is one of the more impressive buildings in Seattle.

Halfway through the project, JA Jones went out of business (filed for bankruptcy), leaving us to complete the project on our own. We were a minority partner in the JV (35 percent), and our biggest project up to that point in our history was about $50 million.

With the assistance and support of my YPO forum, we developed an action plan to take over the project. Some of the key action items: Instill confidence in the Absher side of the JV, secure the JA Jones side of the construction team to finish the project, secure bonding company support, convince the US government representatives from General Services Administration (GSA) that we had it under control, convince our subcontractors we had it under control, and do it all without any impact to cost or schedule.

Of course, that was just part of the battle. Once we accomplished all the above, we needed to complete the project, meeting the quality, safety, budget, and schedule expectations we had committed to at the beginning of the project. Thanks to the incredible team on the project, we accomplished all of these goals.

So how did the YPO forum help me? It wasn't just the action plan they helped me develop; it was the moral support they gave me. While I certainly got that from my partners and coworkers, it was a different kind of support from peers. My YPO forum mates were all presidents or CEOs of their respective companies. They were looking at problems from a different angle because they were not in the construction industry, and they were not in the heat of the battle. Because of these peers,

I began to see the challenge not as being insurmountable but as a series of small challenges well within our grasp to conquer.

National Builders Alliance (NBA)

For the last several years of my stint as CEO of Absher Construction, I was a member of a construction industry peer group we called the National Builders Alliance (NBA). We were a peer group of eight similarly sized general contractors from across the country who met regularly in a YPO forum–type setting. They provided me with invaluable assistance through several significant events:

- Buyout of my partners
- A project with a multimillion-dollar loss that threatened the company's existence
- COVID
- Transition to a new president and CEO
- Transition to an ESOP (employee ownership)

NBA provided the best of AGC and YPO. Because these construction companies are not in the same markets, we could share information freely. When any of us had critical issues, the others would be there for them. Over time, we built trust and camaraderie—an esprit de corps—that allowed our conversations to flow. We held each other accountable to our commitments and called each other out when we gave any signs of derailment.

My NBA peers were vital to me as I navigated each of those significant challenges listed above—and never more valuable than when they guided me through a process to select my heir apparent. As a longtime family business, with several qualified candidates, this is more complicated than one might expect. Thanks to the peer group, I kept to a disciplined process with objective criteria.

This resulted in the selection of Jeff Richards as our new president (and eventually CEO)—the first nonfamily member to be president. When I focused on what was best for the long-term health of the company and stuck to the process, the decision became clear over time.

By the time Jeff was named president, it was a surprise to no one; that, to me, is the sign of an effective transition process. Of course, the ultimate success of the transition is now predominantly in Jeff's hands, and I am happy to report he is doing quite well.

NBA Peer Group and Winter Construction: Messaging the Sale of the Company

Tom Nichols is president of Winter Construction of Atlanta, Georgia. Winter was one of the contractors in the NBA Peer Group. Tom agreed wholeheartedly with the importance of having peers, so I asked him for an example of its value. Here's what he said:

> This one was both emotionally and strategically complex. We had just finished an eighteen-month strategic planning process that had brought the team together in a powerful way. We were focused, aligned, and energized. On top of that, we'd brought in thirty-plus new shareholders—most of them emerging leaders in the company—who had bought in to the idea of having a real voice and financial stake in our future.
>
> And then . . . we got an unsolicited offer to buy the company.
>
> We ultimately decided to accept the offer, but that brought on a major leadership challenge: How do you explain to all these people—who just bought into the long-term vision—that you're taking a different path? How do you message something that feels on the surface, like a contradiction?

I took that issue to the NBA peer group. What I found there was a mix of empathy and clear-eyed counsel. They knew the stakes weren't just financial—they were cultural, relational, and reputational. That group helped me process the emotional weight of it all but also work through a communication strategy that was honest, forward-looking, and grounded in respect for the team.

It worked. We didn't lose a single employee. People aligned with the decision. And it reinforced my belief that having a safe space to work through hard things with smart, trusted peers is one of the best assets a leader can have.[2]

APPLYING PEER GROUP LESSONS TO THE BEATLES

Granted, it's not easy to find "peers" when you are the biggest stars on the planet. Early in their career, the members of The Beatles were each other's peers. In addition, Brian Epstein and George Martin provided them with many of the benefits of a mentor relationship.

As their popularity grew, it became more difficult to find anyone to hold them accountable. The truth is they had no peers. Once egos got in the way and trust broke down, the internal peer dynamic evaporated.

In a sense, Yoko and Linda stepped in to provide peer support for John and Paul. However, that is complicated, especially in John's case because of his abandonment issues from childhood. Entangling romantic and family relationships with being a peer on a professional level is fraught with risk.

So, how could the most popular people on earth develop the kind of peer relationships that could have helped them? I don't think it would have worked to ask Mick Jagger, Elvis, or Bob Dylan to help. What they needed was a professional manager whom they could trust. Paul got close to that with his in-laws, but to expect the other Beatles to have accepted peer guidance from Paul's in-laws is absurd. In fact, even their guidance was suspect, due to their hatred of Klein.

Sadly, The Beatles were surrounded by opportunists not looking out for their best interests, but that doesn't mean it would have been impossible to find. As mentioned in chapter 7, their unwillingness to see beyond the clearly defined roles from their early years prevented them from seeing the exciting possibilities available. They had a potential candidate in their midst who could have provided that trusted peer role. One of the few people in their circle of influence with the knowledge and integrity to be a mentor or peer was George Martin, their producer.

I am not saying George Martin could have or should have been their manager, but he certainly could have helped them find a better choice than Klein or the Eastmans. He could have been an independent, neutral peer. Martin wasn't one to push himself on people, which would have made him the perfect peer or mentor.

Organizations seeking to avoid The Beatles' fate should establish structured peer feedback mechanisms, create a culture that values constructive criticism, and ensure that even the most senior leaders have mentors or trusted peers who can provide honest perspectives. Without these accountability systems, the behavioral blind spots that derail leaders will go unaddressed until the damage can be irreversible.

Each Beatle developed blind spots that went unaddressed: John's withdrawal and increasing focus on outside interests, Paul's controlling tendencies, George's resentment, and Ringo's passive acceptance. A mentor or trusted peer could have helped them see through the blind spots.

Recalibrate the Vision

By 1969, The Beatles lacked a shared vision of their future. John was pulling toward political activism. Paul wanted to continue their commercial success with live performances. George desired more creative freedom and spiritual exploration. Ringo sought to expand his acting career while maintaining the band. Without a unified direction, derailment was inevitable.

The Beatles, despite their creative brilliance, struggled to evolve their organizational structure to match their artistic evolution.

Vision recalibration isn't about abandoning core values or purpose but rather adapting to changing circumstances. Nike exemplifies this principle beautifully. Remember from chapter 8 that their original vision was to "Crush Adidas." Once Nike had replaced Adidas at the top, that vision no longer resonated. Their new vision was to "Bring Inspiration and Innovation to Every Athlete in the World," which was a catalyst driving them to a broader market.

Nike recently changed their vision to "No Finish Line." While this is a clever advertising slogan, it doesn't work as a true "vision." Nike has plenty of future goals, so it is not a fatal flaw for them, but "no finish line" implies you will never get there. A vision is more catalytic if you can picture the finish line.

For The Beatles, a recalibrated vision might have acknowledged their individual growth while preserving their collective magic. Perhaps they could have envisioned becoming more like a collaborative collective that allowed for both individual expression and continued partnership— something akin to what Crosby, Stills, Nash & Young achieved with their model of both solo and group projects.

The process of recalibrating the vision requires several key elements: assessing the changing external environment, understanding the evolving capabilities and aspirations within the organization, reconnecting with core purpose and values, creating space for collaborative dreaming about future possibilities, and ultimately articulating a vision that feels both ambitious and authentic.

Organizations should schedule regular "vision check-ups," not to change direction capriciously but to ensure their guiding star still resonates and inspires. These might occur annually with minor refinements or every few years for more substantial recalibration. The key is maintaining the tension between stability and adaptation.

Had The Beatles taken time to deliberately recalibrate their shared vision after their touring years or after Brian Epstein's death, they might have crafted a new model for their collaboration that accommodated their individual growth while preserving their unparalleled creative partnership.

Redefine Commitment

The final factor in The Beatles' derailment involved their implicit contract with each other—the unspoken agreements about what they owed the group versus what they could pursue individually. As they matured, married, had children, and developed divergent interests, they never explicitly redefined what commitment to The Beatles meant in this new context.

William Bridges's work in *Managing Transitions* provides valuable insight into this challenge. Bridges distinguishes between change (external situational shifts) and transition (the internal psychological process people experience). As he explains, "Change is situational. . . . Transition, on the other hand, is psychological."[3]

The Beatles experienced numerous external changes: Beatlemania, stopping live tours, Brian Epstein's death, marriage and family life, and the creation of Apple Corps. However, they failed to manage the psychological transitions these changes required. Bridges emphasizes that "it isn't the changes that do you in, it's the transitions."[4]

Bridges outlines a three-phase transition model that The Beatles needed but failed to navigate:

1. **Ending, Losing, Letting Go:** The Beatles needed to acknowledge that their original structure and way of working was ending. They needed to consciously let go of their previous ways of working together to create space for something new.

2. **The Neutral Zone:** This middle phase represents an in-between time where old patterns are gone but new ones aren't fully operational. The Beatles experienced this discomfort but tried to ignore it or skip through it rather than see it as an opportunity to look at new possibilities.

3. **The New Beginning:** The final phase involves embracing new identities and energy. Like the phoenix rising from the ashes, organizations can experience new life with properly executed transitions. The Beatles never reached this phase together, as they failed to navigate the first two phases successfully. Sadly, for Beatles fans, the new beginning in store for The Beatles were four successful solo careers and a legacy that is still going strong.[5]

Bridges warns that "without a well-executed transition, it is just a rearrangement of the chairs."[6] The Beatles rearranged their chairs repeatedly—creating Apple Corps, hiring new managers, trying new recording approaches—but never addressed the deeper psychological transitions needed to sustain their collaboration.

Organizations that endure excellence over decades understand that commitment needs regular redefinition. What worked during the start-up phase won't work during expansion, and what worked during expansion won't work during maturity. The expectations, sacrifices, and rewards evolve—and they must be explicitly discussed rather than assumed.

Redefining commitment involves several critical conversations: What are our nonnegotiable expectations of each other? What flexibility can we provide for individual growth and interests? How do we equitably distribute the rewards of our collective success? How will we make decisions when tensions arise between individual and group needs?

For organizations seeking to avoid derailment, these questions should be revisited regularly—perhaps annually as part of a "vision check-up" or strategic planning, or during major transitions, or when signs of misalignment emerge. The goal isn't rigid rules but rather shared understanding that evolves as circumstances change.

What might this have looked like for The Beatles? Perhaps a strong manager, whom they all supported. Perhaps a formal agreement allowing each member to pursue solo projects while maintaining a schedule of Beatles recording sessions and limited performances. Perhaps more equitable songwriting credit distribution. And perhaps clearer decision-making protocols for business ventures like Apple Corps.

For them to have made it work, the song distribution on albums would have had to be equal among John, Paul, and George, with the occasional Ringo song thrown in. Of course, the ultimate fantasy is that they would have cross-collaborated on some songs. Imagine an album that included songs written by each of them, plus a few songs by McCartney–Harrison, Harrison–Lennon, or all three of them. I'd even throw in some Ringo tunes; his solo career showed remarkable growth as a songwriter, especially when he collaborates.

This structure would have taken much of the pressure off them and allowed them to create more Beatles' music when the inspiration struck—not when the record company demanded it. An equal distribution of songs and this cross-collaboration might well have been the recipe to heal the pain in their relationships and to rekindle and continue that Beatles' magic.

We, of course, will never know if this hypothesis would have worked. The first step would have been to explicitly redefine their commitment to accommodate their evolving lives and aspirations.

What's certain is that organizations that thrive over decades don't rely on the commitments made at their founding—they deliberately redefine those commitments as they and their environment evolve.

Conclusion: Structure for Enduring Excellence

The Beatles' story reveals a sobering truth about excellence: Even extraordinary talent, compelling vision, and strong team spirit aren't sufficient for sustained success without the organizational structures to support them through inevitable changes. Their remarkable achievements from 1962 to 1966 created the foundation for lasting impact, but their failure to build systems for renewal and adaptation led to dissolution just as they were reaching new creative heights.

This chapter has explored three critical organizational structures that could have saved The Beatles and can help any organization avoid similar derailment. External mentorship provides the objective perspective that internal relationships often can't offer. Regularly recalibrating the vision ensures that shared purpose evolves with changing circumstances rather than becoming irrelevant. And frameworks for redefining commitment create explicit agreements that prevent misunderstandings and unmet expectations that poison even the strongest teams.

The Beatles' organizational failure wasn't primarily about personality conflicts or creative differences; it was about the absence of structures to manage growth, transition, and evolving individual needs. They had no processes for "sharpening the saw," no systems for adapting their vision beyond their initial dream of being "toppermost of the poppermost," and no framework for renegotiating their commitments as they matured from teenagers into adults with families and diverse interests.

Organizations seeking sustainable excellence must learn from both The Beatles' triumphs and their failures. The magic they created remains undiminished but imagine what might have been possible with the organizational discipline to support their continued collaboration. The lesson is clear: Getting better requires more than good intentions—it demands systematic approaches to renewal, adaptation, and growth.

Applying the Lessons of Chapter 12

Have you ever been part of an organization that achieved remarkable success only to watch it gradually lose momentum and direction? Or observed a team that failed to sustain its excellence despite having talented members and initial vision? The difference often comes down to the organizational structures that either support or undermine sustainable excellence.

The Beatles' story reveals that even extraordinary talent, clear roles, compelling vision, and strong team spirit aren't enough to sustain excellence without the supporting organizational structures to maintain them through inevitable changes. Their journey offers powerful insights into how organizations can build systems that promote renewal rather than derailment.

The Beatles lacked organizational structures, contributing significantly to their breakup. Organizations seeking sustainable excellence can learn from their experience by implementing these three exercises.

EXERCISE 1: EXTERNAL MENTORSHIP PROGRAM

Purpose

This structured mentorship program ensures that senior leaders have independent, objective perspectives to help them navigate challenges and grow, preventing the isolation that affected The Beatles after losing Brian Epstein.

Setup

Match each senior leader with a single, high-quality external mentor who can provide objective guidance.

Structure

Note: The structure is less important than the quality of the mentor and consistency of the relationship.

1. Mentor selection process (initial phase)

   a. For each senior leader, identify potential mentors with these characteristics:

      ° Significant leadership experience in a noncompeting organization

      ° No prior close personal or professional relationship

      ° Strong record of organizational success and leadership development

      ° Recognized integrity and ability to maintain confidentiality

   b. Interview process

      ° Two-way interviews to ensure compatibility

      ° Clear discussion of expectations and boundaries

      ° Explicit agreement on confidentiality parameters

      ° Formal mentor agreement with twelve-month initial commitment

2. Structured engagement framework (ongoing)

   a. Monthly check-ups (one hour by phone, virtual, or in person)

    b. Quarterly meetings (two hours in person)

- Extended reflection on leadership growth trajectory

- Strategic thinking about longer-term organizational challenges

- Pattern recognition across recent challenges

    c. Annual meeting (three to four hours in person)

- Structured assessment of mentorship value

- Senior leader self-assessment of growth and impact

- Documentation of specific instances where mentorship influenced decisions

- Review of progress against development goals

- Emergency access protocol

       ▪ Agreement on appropriate circumstances for unscheduled contact

       ▪ Response expectations during critical decisions or crises

Why It Works

This system addresses the fatal lack of trusted external guidance that affected The Beatles after Epstein's death. Had each Beatle maintained a relationship with their own trusted mentor, someone outside their immediate circle who could provide honest perspective without being entangled in their business interests, they might have navigated their transitions more successfully.

The external mentor relationship creates a safe space for vulnerability and honest reflection that is often impossible with internal relationships due to power dynamics and competing interests. External mentors can ask the difficult questions and provide unfiltered feedback that internal colleagues rarely can.

EXERCISE 2:
ORGANIZATIONAL PEER GROUP INTEGRATION

Purpose

This structured program helps organizations establish valuable connections with peer organizations, providing objective perspective and accountability similar to what I found in YPO and the NBA peer group.

Setup

Identify six to eight noncompeting organizations of similar size/complexity in different industries or regions (or join a formal peer program).

Structure

1. Establish the peer group framework (initial phase)

   a. CEO/leadership commitment from all participating organizations

   b. Formal confidentiality agreements

   c. Selection criteria for participating executives

   ○ Similar levels of responsibility

   ○ Commitment to organizational learning

   ○ Authority to implement insights

   d. Designated organizational champion responsible for implementation

2. Quarterly exchange program (ongoing)

   a. Rotating host organization for each quarterly meeting

   b. Pre-meeting preparation

      ◦ Standardized metrics sharing (financial, operational, cultural)

      ◦ Current challenge identification from each organization

      ◦ Success story preparation

   c. Meeting structure (two days)

      ◦ Day one

         ▪ Host organization tour and context setting

         ▪ Facilitated challenge sessions (each organization presents one challenge)

         ▪ Structured feedback from peer organizations

      ◦ Day two

         ▪ Implementation planning

         ▪ Cross-organizational small group sessions

         ▪ Formal commitments for next quarter

3. Virtual monthly check-ins (between quarterly meetings)

   a. Progress reports on commitments made

   b. Emerging challenge discussions

   c. Resource sharing

Why It Works

This structure creates the peer accountability that The Beatles lacked in their later years. Just as my NBA peer group helped me navigate major transitions, this system ensures organizations have trusted outside perspectives during critical moments.

The formalized structure ensures the relationship delivers concrete value rather than becoming merely a networking opportunity. The requirement for preparation and follow-through creates accountability that drives meaningful organizational improvement.

EXERCISE 3: ANNUAL VISION AND COMMITMENT RECALIBRATION

Purpose

This two-part annual process enables organizations to systematically update their vision and redefine commitments as circumstances change.

Setup

Schedule a two-day off-site retreat for key leadership team members annually.

Structure

1. Day one: Vision Tree recalibration (first session)

   a. Review Core Ideology (two hours)

      ◦ Reaffirm core purpose and values

      ◦ Assess continued relevance and authenticity

      ◦ Update language if needed to reflect current culture

   b. Current reality assessment (two hours)

      ◦ SWOT (Strengths, Weaknesses, Opportunities, Threats): An honest evaluation of your organization's internal strengths and weaknesses and external opportunities and threats (a "SWOT" analysis)

- Review of major accomplishments and challenges since last recalibration
- Identification of significant shifts in environment or capabilities

c. Vision refinement (three hours)

- Review current vision against assessment findings
- Facilitated discussion of necessary adjustments
  - What aspects remain compelling and catalytic?
  - What elements no longer resonate or inspire?
  - What emerging possibilities should be incorporated?
- Collaborative reformulation of vision if needed
- Visual update to the Vision Tree

2. Day two: Commitment redefinition (second session)

a. Organizational commitment mapping (two hours)

- What critical capabilities must we maintain or develop?
- What resources must we commit to the vision?
- What difficult choices does our vision require?
- What metrics will demonstrate our commitment?

b. Individual commitment clarification (three hours)

- For each leadership team member, assess
  - What specific contributions align with your strengths?
  - What growth areas must you develop to support the vision?

- What personal flexibility do you need to maintain sustainability?

- What support do you need from others to fulfill your commitments?

  ◦ Formal documentation of mutual expectations

c. Implementation planning (two hours)

  ◦ Communication strategy for vision adjustments

  ◦ Integration into operational plans and budgets

  ◦ Milestone development and accountability assignments

  ◦ Quarterly check-in schedule

Why It Works

This process directly addresses the fatal flaws in The Beatles' organizational structure after they achieved their initial vision of becoming the biggest band in the world. The Vision Tree recalibration ensures the catalytic vision remains relevant as circumstances change, while the commitment redefinition provides the explicit agreements about expectations that The Beatles sorely needed as they matured and developed diverse interests.

The two-day structure reminds the organization of the "why," then addresses the "what" from "how"—first establishing the shared direction, then negotiating the specific commitments needed from the organization and individuals. This prevents the misalignment that occurred when The Beatles had conflicting expectations about their roles and contributions after their initial success.

This system creates what Bridges calls a managed transition—not just rearranging furniture but addressing the underlying psychological adjustments needed when circumstances change.[7] Had The Beatles implemented a similar process, they might have found a way to accommodate both their individual growth and their collective genius, perhaps through a model that allowed both solo projects and continued collaboration.

The power of this approach is that it transforms implicit assumptions into explicit agreements, preventing the misunderstandings and disappointments that ultimately derailed The Beatles. When everyone clearly understands what they've committed to and what the organization has committed to them, excellence becomes enduring rather than fleeting.

CHAPTER 12 PLAYLIST

"NOW AND THEN"

This collection traces the evolution of The Beatles' legacy starting with the anthem "All You Need Is Love" then moving on to solo works that reflect their shared journey, demonstrating how excellence can endure even after structural changes. It includes everything from tributes to fallen bandmates to reflections on their extraordinary shared history through inevitable transitions and transformations.

1. **"All You Need Is Love"**—This anthem, broadcast to the entire world via satellite, represents the universal values that sustained The Beatles at their peak. Its message about prioritizing fundamental connections over complex structures parallels the chapter's emphasis on building organizations around enduring human principles rather than rigid systems.

2. **"When We Was Fab"**—George's nostalgic yet clear-eyed look back at The Beatles era, complete with musical references to their classic sound. His perspective offers both appreciation

for their magical time while maintaining a healthy distance, understanding that organizational excellence evolves rather than remains frozen in time.

3. **"Liverpool 8"**—Ringo's autobiographical journey back to where it all began captures the importance of organizational memory and foundational stories. His honest reflection on both triumphs and challenges demonstrates how acknowledging an organization's complete history creates authentic continuity through inevitable changes.

4. **"Early Days"**—Paul's reflective acoustic ballad directly challenges revisionist histories of the band, asserting the importance of authentic organizational narratives. In many ways this song reflects the resilience leaders need when recalibrating vision through challenging transitions.

5. **"Photograph"**—Ringo's poignant hit cowritten with George becomes even more meaningful after George's passing, demonstrating how organizational memories sustain connections beyond structural changes. Its celebration of preserved moments reflects how shared experiences create lasting bonds that transcend formal organizational structures.

6. **"All Those Years Ago"**—George's tribute to John featuring both Ringo and Paul represents their ability to reconnect around shared values despite their differences. This musical reunion demonstrates the chapter's principle that recalibrating vision around core purpose can bring people together even after organizational disruption.

7. **"Friends to Go"**—Paul's song intentionally written in George's style serves as a touching acknowledgment of his influence,

showing how organizational excellence includes honoring mentors and influences. Its gentle homage demonstrates how the impact of respected colleagues continues to shape work long after formal relationships end.

8. **"Never Without You"**—Ringo's touching tribute to George featuring Eric Clapton completes the circle of loss and remembrance among the bandmates. "Never Without You" affirms that the connections formed through shared excellence continue beyond formal structures, influencing future work and relationships indefinitely.

9. **"Here Today"**—Paul's moving tribute to John after his death, imagining a conversation they never got to have. This beautifully vulnerable song demonstrates how the magical connection between them transcended even death, illustrating how authentic organizational relationships create impacts that endure beyond structural endings.

10. **"Now and Then"**—The final Beatles song, completed decades after John's death using AI to clean up his demo vocals, represents the ultimate expression of the band's continuity. This remarkable technological and emotional achievement demonstrates how excellence can find new expressions when we remain committed to core relationships and purposes despite changed circumstances.

CLOSING THOUGHTS

" T H E   E N D "

I was in college when I first read Wooden's book *They Call Me Coach*. Like The Beatles, the book has had an impact on every aspect of my life. Coach Wooden inspired me to consider and articulate my personal values, something he shared in his book. So, I crafted my personal values nearly fifty years ago, and they are still as relevant for me today as they were then.

When life is hard and I need "Help," I refer to these, my personal values for guidance:

- Make today a masterpiece.
- Love others as you love yourself.
- In everything, give thanks.
- Make friendship a fine art.
- Remember your priorities: faith, family, and friends.
- Choose your life, then live by your choices.
- Contentment is not found in having everything but being satisfied with what you have.

- Build others up; do not tear them down.
- Learn from the past, prepare for the future, but live in the present.
- Dwell on what is good, pure, and excellent.

Like most people, my life has had ups and downs. In the face of these peaks and valleys, it is our personal values that sustain us.

As we learned from Jim Collins, our core purpose needs core values as a moral compass or guiding principles. Part of The Beatles' derailment was due to a lack of articulated core values for the band. Once they accomplished their main vision, they had no core values to fall back on. That does not mean the individual members didn't have values; it simply means that The Beatles as a group and a business did not have agreed-upon and articulated values. Without that, they had no agreed-upon moral compass guiding them through internal and external transitions.

A Suitable Ending

In the summer of 1969, The Beatles stepped back in the studio for what would become the final album they recorded together. Appropriately, they left us with a final song, appropriately titled "The End." It is a poignant reminder of the importance of love. This simple yet profound truth serves as both the culmination of The Beatles' journey and a perfect summation of the lessons we've explored throughout this book. The four pillars that supported their rise to excellence—the right people in the right seats, a catalytic vision, esprit de corps, and the magical mystery that happens when everything flows—all rest on a foundation of love, connection, and genuine commitment to something greater than oneself.

When I had my cardiac arrest in 2020, literally dying on the operating table before being resuscitated, it was a profound reminder that life can change—or end—in an instant. During my recovery, I discovered something remarkable: The story of these four lads from Liverpool wasn't just entertaining; it contained wisdom that transcended music, wisdom about excellence, connection, and purpose.

Throughout my life—from playing on a state championship football team, to coaching a state championship basketball team, to leading a successful construction company, to teaching leadership and construction management classes, to raising six kids—I've seen these same principles of excellence at work. The Beatles' story resonates because it reflects universal truths about human achievement and connection.

While we may not have the talent or opportunity to experience The Beatles' extraordinary journey, we do have opportunities to be better tomorrow than we were today, to collaborate with others, and to strive for excellence in the field of our choosing. We have seen the foundation of The Beatles' excellence—four "fab" pillars that apply universally.

The Right People in the Right Seats

Excellence begins with people—not just talented individuals but the right combination of talents, personalities, and roles. The Beatles weren't simply four talented musicians; they were four complementary pieces that fit together perfectly.

I'm reminded of Coach Ed Pepple's decision to insert Jeff Thompson as the starting point guard for Mercer Island High School's basketball team. Jeff wasn't the most talented player, but he was exactly what the team needed—a steady presence who enabled the stars to shine. Following that adjustment, the team never lost another game and went on to win the state championship.

Similarly, at Absher Construction, our success came not only from individual talent but from finding the right combination of people who complemented each other's strengths and covered each other's weaknesses. As we restructured the business in the 1990s, placing five owners with diverse skills and perspectives in key roles, we created a leadership team greater than the sum of its parts.

The Beatles taught us that excellence is rarely about a single star; it's about creating a constellation where each element shines brightly in relation to the others. John's edge and artistic vision, Paul's melodic craftsmanship and perfectionism, George's spiritual depth and musical exploration, and Ringo's steady reliability and good humor—together, they created something none could have achieved alone.

A Catalytic Vision

Vision doesn't just point to a destination; it provides the energy to get there. The Beatles' ambition to be "the toppermost of the poppermost" drove them to work relentlessly, challenge industry norms, and continuously reinvent themselves.

I remember when we finally articulated Absher Construction's core purpose: "to create and build community with vision and compassion." This wasn't just a slogan; it was a catalytic vision that transformed how we approached our work. Suddenly, we weren't just building structures; we were building communities. This shift in perspective energized our entire company and propelled us to new heights.

My father, "The Dad," understood the power of interim goals when he took our family on that memorable road trip to Disneyland. By building excitement for stops along the way—the Nut Tree Inn and Pea Soup Andersen's—he kept six restless children engaged and moving toward the ultimate destination. The journey became as important as the destination.

Similarly, The Beatles broke down their ambitious vision into achievable milestones: Get a record contract, have a hit in Britain, conquer America. This progressive approach to their vision maintained momentum and provided ongoing motivation.

Esprit de Corps

The third pillar—that spirit of unity, commitment to fun, and a sense of humor—was essential to The Beatles' success and is crucial for any team striving for excellence.

Coach John Anderson's approach to our state championship football team exemplified this perfectly. He never forgot that football is a game. His "Hat Day" practices and humor-infused film sessions kept us loose and joyful even as we worked toward our ultimate goal. As he said, "Our main goal is to have fun and to get as many guys playing as possible." The result? An undefeated season and a state championship.

The Beatles set aside individual egos for the good of the group, channeled competitive energy into productive collaboration, and maintained a playful, irreverent approach that kept them grounded amid unprecedented fame. Their esprit de corps created a safe space for experimentation and growth—the same kind of environment we tried to establish at Absher Construction and that great coaches like John Anderson and Ed Pepple created for their teams.

The Magical Mystery

The final pillar acknowledges the quality that emerges when the stars align perfectly—that flow state where everything clicks and magic happens.

I've experienced this magical mystery in various contexts: when our 1975 Sumner Spartans football team gelled despite having a smaller, less experienced offensive line than the previous year and when the leadership team at Absher Construction found our purpose and suddenly everything flowed toward that vision.

The Beatles experienced this magic throughout their career, from the early Hamburg days when they played marathon sets that forged their musical identity to the studio innovations that redefined what pop music could be. In one of the greatest songwriting partnerships in history, John and Paul connected in a way that allowed the magic to flow. Even in their final sessions, amid personal tensions and impending breakup, all four could still access that magical flow when they played together.

Love Is All You Need

Underlying all four pillars is a fundamental truth that The Beatles first expressed in the song "The Word" and brought to the masses with their anthem "All You Need Is Love"—not romantic love but a deeper commitment to connection, compassion, and shared purpose.

The Beatles demonstrated this commitment in countless ways: when John invited Paul to join his band despite knowing Paul might outshine him, the egalitarian approach to profit-sharing, the willingness to set aside individual preferences for the good of a song, the genuine delight they took in creating together, especially in their early years.

Striving for excellence is a noble quest: one that has driven human achievement throughout history. However, what I hope you take from these lessons is that it isn't just what we accomplish but how we accomplish it—the connections we forge, the joy we create, the love we give and receive along the way. To accomplish this, we must practice it where we are, because if we can't do it there, we won't do it.

The Beatles understood this. Despite their unprecedented success, their music always remained rooted in human connection and emotion. From "Love Me Do" to "The End," they reminded us that beneath the complexities of achievement and ambition lies a simple truth: We're here to love and be loved, to create and share, to find meaning together.

When I look back on my own journey—from a five-year-old watching The Beatles on Ed Sullivan, to a coach, to a teacher, to a business leader, to a husband, father, and now grandfather—I see the same principles at work. The moments of greatest achievement and deepest satisfaction have always involved connection, purpose, and love.

In the corporate world, we often talk about "return on investment." The Beatles remind us of a different kind of return—the love you take is equal to the love you make. The effort, passion, and heart you put into your endeavors come back to you, not only in material success but in the quality of your experience and the impact you have on others.

As you apply the Four Pillars to your own pursuits, remember that beneath them all lies this fundamental equation. Enduring excellence isn't just about achievement; it's about creating something meaningful that enriches both those who create it and those who experience it.

The Fab Four Pillars of Impact do not apply only to musical groups, teams, businesses, and organizations; they can apply to faith, family, and friends. Imagine if we applied the Four Pillars to those relationships. How much deeper could those relationships be?

Imagine

I would be blind not to notice the divisiveness and negativity permeating our political and social landscape. I do not have the solution to that problem. However, I know that divisiveness and negativity are not part of the Fab Four Pillars. In fact, those were a big part of The Beatles' derailment (and perhaps our country's?). When we obsess about the "evil" of the other side, we are not dwelling on what is good, pure, and excellent. When we can't have civil discourse over substantive issues for fear of being "canceled," we are no longer free.

One of the important lessons from The Beatles is that the level of excellence they attained was possible because they did it together. It was possible because of what they had in common *and* because of their differences. They were at their best when they embraced their differences and made them a strength. Imagine if we could do that.

So let me leave you with this thought: Striving for enduring excellence is more fulfilling as part of a family, a team, a group, a business, an organization, or even a country. It is when a group of individuals strive together for excellence that synergy leads to real magic.

Together, teams can create a level of excellence that is beyond the grasp of any individual. More importantly, The Beatles showed us how to do it with a universal message of peace and love. Their legacy invites us to do the same.

And in the end, that's what truly matters.

CLOSING THOUGHTS—
THE FINAL PLAYLIST

"THE BEATLES 2
(THE BLACK ALBUM)"

I magine if The Beatles had stayed together past 1970. Because of the backlog of songs (especially from George), I see a double album sequel to The Beatles, commonly referred to as "the White Album." Let's call it "The Beatles 2." The album cover is all black and will be referred to as "The Black Album" due to its contrasting cover design to the White Album.

In my reimagining of The Beatles in 1970, they were able to "work it out." At this point in their careers, perhaps the only way for The Beatles to stay together would have been for them to agree on an equal split of songs among John, Paul, and George. Accordingly, I have selected seven songs from each of them for this album, with Ringo taking the lead on three: one written by him, one written by John, and one he cowrote with

George. All these songs were written and recorded as solo songs around the time of The Beatles' breakup and would have been available to be on a Beatles' album, had they chosen to make another one together.

Track Listing

Side One

1. **"Instant Karma"** (1970) (Lennon)—John's urgent spiritual awakening anthem transformed with the full Beatles treatment. Paul's melodic bass lines and backing vocals add depth while George's guitar accents and Ringo's distinctive drumming create that unmistakable Beatles energy.

2. **"Maybe I'm Amazed"** (1970) (McCartney)—Paul's raw, emotional tribute to Linda becomes even more powerful with John and George's harmony vocals and a more dynamic arrangement that builds to the kind of crescendo only The Beatles could achieve together.

3. **"What Is Life"** (1970) (Harrison)—George's exuberant question about love retains its jubilant horn section but gains new dimension with John and Paul's backing vocals and their tight rhythm section driving it forward.

4. **"I'm the Greatest"** (1973) (Lennon)—A playful, self-deprecating song written by John specifically for Ringo, performed with the winking humor and camaraderie that characterized their best group dynamics, featuring piano work from John.

5. **"Working-Class Hero"** (1970) (Lennon)—John's stark social commentary reimagined with subtle Beatles touches—Paul's understated bass, George's textured guitar work, and Ringo's

restrained percussion creating a more nuanced backdrop for John's biting lyrics.

6. **"Run of the Mill"** (1970) (Harrison)—George's meditation on friendship and betrayal takes on powerful new meaning as a Beatles track, with John and Paul's harmonies adding poignancy to lines about choosing sides and broken communication.

Side Two

1. **"Junk"** (1970) (McCartney)—Paul's delicate, nostalgic piece becomes a showcase for the band's ability to create magic from simplicity. George adds a gentle slide guitar that intertwines with Paul's melody while Ringo provides the perfect light touch.

2. **"I'd Have You Anytime"** (1970) (Harrison/Dylan)—George's collaboration with Bob Dylan becomes a Beatles gem with John and Paul adding harmony vocals on the chorus, creating the warm invitation of friendship George intended.

3. **"Power to the People"** (1971) (Lennon)—John's political rallying cry gets the full Beatles treatment, combining the raw energy of their early rock with their mature musicianship. The band builds an arrangement that matches the urgency of John's message.

4. **"Beware of Darkness"** (1970) (Harrison)—George's warning against spiritual pitfalls becomes even more powerful with the full band, especially Paul's melodic bass providing a foundation for George's philosophical lyrics and John adding unexpected harmonies.

5. **"Every Night"** (1970) (McCartney)—Paul's intimate song about finding stability grows into a band showcase of restraint

and subtle interplay. John adds a countermelody that complements Paul's lead vocal beautifully.

6. **"Isn't It a Pity"** (1970) (Harrison)—Side two closes with George's epic reflection on human relationships, building to a "Hey Jude"–like climax with all four Beatles creating those transcendent harmonies that defined their legacy.

Side Three

1. **"Uncle Albert/Admiral Halsey"** (1971) (McCartney)—Paul's multipart composition becomes the perfect showcase for The Beatles' studio experimentation and playful side. John adds surreal touches while the band navigates the song's changing tempos and moods as only they could.

2. **"It Don't Come Easy"** (1971) (Starkey/Harrison)—Ringo's philosophical rocker, secretly cowritten with George, gets the full Beatles arrangement it deserves with John and Paul adding backing vocals and George's distinctive guitar work shining through.

3. **"Look at Me"** (1970) (Lennon)—John's introspective acoustic piece gains subtle embellishments from the others—Paul's harmonies, George's delicate guitar accents, and Ringo's light percussion—while maintaining its vulnerability.

4. **"Another Day"** (1971) (McCartney)—Paul's first solo single after The Beatles' breakup captures the mundane rhythm of daily life and the quiet resignation of someone just going through the motions.

5. **"My Sweet Lord"** (1970) (Harrison)—George's spiritual masterpiece retains its uplifting message but with the distinctive

stamp of The Beatles' harmonies, particularly in the "hallelujah" chorus where John and Paul's voices create that signature blend.

6. **"That Would Be Something"** (1970) (McCartney)—Paul's minimalist blues sketch becomes a full band jam, showcasing their ability to take a simple idea and build it into something special through their musical conversation.

Side Four

1. **"Mother"** (1970) (Lennon)—John's raw emotional primal scream therapy becomes slightly more contained but no less powerful with the band's support. The arrangement builds gradually, with George's slide guitar adding emotional texture.

2. **"Behind That Locked Door"** (1970) (Harrison)—George's country-tinged song of encouragement gets the full Beatles treatment with Paul and John adding harmony vocals that enhance its message of friendship and support.

3. **"Early 1970"** (1971) (Starkey)—Ringo's reflection on his bandmates becomes a meta-Beatles moment, with each member playing along to the verses about themselves, creating a self-referential piece about their relationships.

4. **"Too Many People"** (1971) (McCartney)—Paul's thinly veiled criticism of John becomes a more nuanced conversation within the band context, with John adding his own perspective through his guitar parts and background vocals.

5. **"All Things Must Pass"** (1970) (Harrison)—George's philosophical masterpiece finally receives the full Beatles arrangement

it deserved, with John and Paul's harmonies elevating the chorus to transcendent heights.

6. **"Love"** (1970) (Lennon)—The album closes with John's simple but profound statement, expanded with gentle contributions from all four Beatles that create a perfect coda to their final studio statement—a reminder that despite everything, love remained at the core of their message.

ACKNOWLEDGMENTS

This book would not have been possible without my extended family, who not only tolerated but embraced my Beatlemania from the very beginning. First and foremost, to my wife, Daria, who supported me throughout this endeavor. She provided her exceptional editing skills, listened to hours of Beatles songs, and still smiled when I insisted on sharing one more story about The Beatles.

To our children and grandchildren, who have all been a big part of this Beatles journey—whether they liked it or not. They've grown up with these songs as the soundtrack to family gatherings, car rides, and milestones in all our lives. Watching them connect to the music, from listening to "Yellow Submarine" and "Octopus's Garden" as children to incorporating "Here Comes the Sun," "In My Life," and other Beatles songs in their weddings, reminded me why these four lads from Liverpool continue to matter across generations.

To my siblings, my willing participants in this shared Beatlemania that began when we were kids. You understood from the start that this wasn't just music; it was a way of seeing the world. Thanks for being my earliest supporters and most enthusiastic collaborators in decoding what made The Beatles so special.

A special nod of appreciation to my brother, Tom, and my cousin Mike (1955–2024) for sharing their passion for music and The Beatles with me. Our sessions customizing lyrics to Beatles songs to share with our family are among my most cherished memories. Mike, I wish you could see how those creative moments influenced these pages. I think you'd be pleased to know the tradition continues.

To my mom, who allowed The Beatles to be a part of our lives from a young age, even when Grandma thought we'd all go to hell for listening to them. You could have easily dismissed it as just noise, but instead you allowed us the freedom to explore the music we loved.

To my dad (1931–2014), for teaching me many of the lessons that found their way into this book. You taught me the importance of goal setting, honesty, and hard work. The Beatles may have provided the soundtrack to our upbringing, but you built the solid foundation for our family from which to grow.

To the entire team at Absher Construction—past and present—you have shaped and continue to shape the future of the communities we serve. You inspire me with your hard work, passion for the construction industry, and commitment to excellence.

In 2005, Absher Construction formed a leadership development company, Lighthouse Institute, which is still going strong today. Tim Rhoades, a longtime leader at Absher Construction, left to lead Lighthouse Institute. He was instrumental in developing many leaders at Absher (and in other companies). With appreciation, I acknowledge his impact on my leadership philosophy and this book.

Finally, to The Beatles themselves for creating music that continues to teach us about creativity, collaboration, and the beautiful complexity of working together toward something greater than ourselves. Through all the ups and downs of writing this book, when the "long and winding road" seemed endless, your music reminded me that all you need is love.

And a big thank-you to all the family, friends, and coworkers "in my life."

From Me to You, Dan

APPENDIX A

THE PLAYLISTS

*All songs performed by The Beatles and written by Lennon-McCartney unless otherwise noted.

PREFACE PLAYLIST: DAN'S TOP TEN

1. "Strawberry Fields Forever" (1967)
2. "A Day in the Life" (1967)
3. "In My Life" (1965)
4. "Here Comes the Sun" (1969) (G. Harrison)
5. "Here, There and Everywhere" (1966)
6. "While My Guitar Gently Weeps" (1968) (G. Harrison)
7. "Penny Lane" (1967)
8. "I Am the Walrus" (1967)
9. "Let It Be" (1970)
10. "If I Fell" (1964)

CHAPTER 1 PLAYLIST: THE EVOLUTION OF EXCELLENCE

1. "She Loves You" (1963)

2. "I Want to Hold Your Hand" (1963)

3. "And I Love Her" (1964)

4. "Ticket to Ride" (1965)

5. "Norwegian Wood" (1965)

6. "For No One" (1966)

7. "When I'm Sixty-Four" (1967)

8. "Happiness Is a Warm Gun" (1968)

9. "Something" (1969) (G. Harrison)

10. "The Long and Winding Road" (1970)

CHAPTER 2 PLAYLIST: THE BEATLES' EARLY RECORDINGS

1. "That'll Be the Day" performed by The Quarrymen (1958) (Buddy Holly, Norman Petty)

2. "In Spite of All the Danger" performed by The Quarrymen (1958) (P. McCartney/G. Harrison)

3. "You'll Be Mine" (1960)

4. "Ain't She Sweet" (1961) (Jack Yellen, Milton Ager)

5. "Cry for a Shadow" (1961) (G. Harrison/J. Lennon)

6. "Sheik of Araby" (1962) (Harry B. Smith, Ted Snyder, Francis Wheeler)

7. "Hello Little Girl" (1962)

8. "Besame Mucho" (1962) (Consuelo Velázquez)

9. "Like Dreamers Do" (1962)

10. "I'll Be on My Way" (1962)

CHAPTER 3 PLAYLIST: RIGHT PEOPLE, RIGHT SEATS

1. "Three Cool Cats" (1962) (Jerry Leiber, Mike Stoller)

2. "Love Me Do" (1962)

3. "How Do You Do It" (1962) (Mitch Murray)

4. "Please Please Me" (1963)

5. "I Saw Her Standing There" (1963)

6. "Do You Want to Know a Secret?" (1963)

7. "Baby It's You" (1963) (Burt Bacharach, Mark David, Barney Williams)

8. "It Won't Be Long" (1963)

9. "All I've Got to Do" (1963)

10. "Thank You, Girl" (1963)

CHAPTER 4 PLAYLIST: CATALYTIC VISION

1. "Lucy in the Sky with Diamonds" (1967)

2. "The Word" (1965)

3. "Good Day Sunshine" (1966)

4. "Tomorrow Never Knows" (1966)

5. "A Hard Day's Night" (1964)

6. "Eight Days a Week" (1964)

7. "Octopus's Garden" (1969) (R. Starkey)

8. "Tell Me What You See" (1965)

9. "Things We Said Today" (1964)

10. "Glass Onion" (1968)

CHAPTER 5 PLAYLIST: ESPRIT DE CORPS

1. "All Together Now" (1969)

2. "Come Together" (1969)

3. "Paperback Writer" (1966)

4. "Michelle" (1965)

5. "Taxman" (1966) (G. Harrison)

6. "Sgt. Pepper's Lonely Hearts Club Band/With a Little Help from My Friends" (1967)

7. "Getting Better" (1967)

8. "All My Loving" (1963)

9. "Strawberry Fields Forever" (1967)

10. "Penny Lane" (1967)

CHAPTER 6 PLAYLIST: THE MAGICAL MYSTERY

1. "We Can Work It Out" (1965)

2. "You Really Got a Hold on Me" (1963) (Smokey Robinson)

3. "Words of Love" (1963) (Buddy Holly)

4. "This Boy" (1963)

5. "If I Fell" (1964)

6. "Baby's in Black" (1964)

7. "Eleanor Rigby" (1966)

8. "She's Leaving Home" (1967)

9. "And Your Bird Can Sing" (1966)

10. "A Day in the Life" (1967)

CHAPTER 7 PLAYLIST: THE TRAIN DERAILED

1. "Help!" (1965)

2. "You've Got to Hide Your Love Away" (1965)

3. "I'm Looking Through You" (1965)

4. "I'm So Tired" (1968)

5. "While My Guitar Gently Weeps" (1968) (G. Harrison)

6. "Don't Pass Me By" (1968) (R. Starkey)

7. "Don't Let Me Down" (1969)

8. "Only a Northern Song" (1969) (G. Harrison)

9. "Fixing a Hole" (1967)

10. "Get Back" (1969)

CHAPTER 8 PLAYLIST: COMPETING VISIONS

1. "Hello, Goodbye" (1967)

2. "The Inner Light" (1968) (G. Harrison)

3. "Nowhere Man" (1965)

4. "The Fool on the Hill" (1967)

5. "Act Naturally" (1965) (Voni Morrison, Johnny Russell)

6. "Revolution" (1968)

7. "Give Peace a Chance" performed by the Plastic Ono Band (1969)

8. "My Sweet Lord" performed by George Harrison (1970) (G. Harrison)

9. "Beaucoups of Blues" performed by Ringo Starr (1970) (Buzz Rabin)

10. "Another Day" performed by Paul McCartney (1971) (P. McCartney, L. McCartney)

CHAPTER 9 PLAYLIST: "I ME MINE"— THE EROSION OF ESPRIT DE CORPS

1. "I Me Mine" (1970) (G. Harrison)

2. "Yesterday" (1965)

3. "Money (That's What I Want)" (1963) (Berry Gordy Jr., Janie Bradford)

4. "You Never Give Me Your Money" (1969)

5. "Can't Buy Me Love" (1964)

6. "Baby You're a Rich Man" (1967)

7. "Piggies" (1968) (G. Harrison)

8. "Yer Blues" (1968)

9. "God" performed by John Lennon (1970) (J. Lennon)

10. "Wah-Wah" performed by George Harrison (1970) (G. Harrison)

CHAPTER 10 PLAYLIST: THE MAGIC LINGERS

1. "The Magical Mystery Tour" (1967)

2. "Two of Us" (1970)

3. "Run of the Mill" performed by George Harrison (1970) (G. Harrison)

4. "Early 1970" performed by Ringo Starr (1970) (R. Starkey)

5. "Too Many People" performed by Paul McCartney (1971) (P. McCartney)

6. "3 Legs" performed by Paul McCartney (1971) (P. McCartney)

7. "How Do You Sleep?" performed by John Lennon (1971) (J. Lennon)

8. "Back Off Boogaloo" performed by Ringo Starr (1972) (R. Starkey, G. Harrison)

9. "Sue Me, Sue You Blues" performed by George Harrison (1973) (G. Harrison)

10. "Abbey Road Medley: You Never Give Me Your Money/Sun King/Mean Mr. Mustard/Polythene Pam/She Came in Through the Bathroom Window/Golden Slumbers/Carry That Weight/ The End" (1969)

CHAPTER 11 PLAYLIST: ATTITUDE AND PERSPECTIVE

1. "Let It Be" (1970)

2. "Across the Universe" (1969)

3. "Hey Jude" (1968)

4. "One After 909" (1969)

5. "Rain" (1966)

6. "Within You, Without You" (1967) (G. Harrison)

7. "I Want to Tell You" (1966) (G. Harrison)

8. "Free as a Bird" (1995) (J. Lennon, P. McCartney, G. Harrison, R. Starkey)

9. "Real Love" (1995) (J. Lennon)

10. "In My Life" (1965)

CHAPTER 12 PLAYLIST: "NOW AND THEN"

1. "All You Need Is Love" (1967)

2. "When We Was Fab" performed by George Harrison (1987) (G. Harrison)

3. "Liverpool 8" performed by Ringo Starr (2008) (R. Starkey, Dave Stewart)

4. "Early Days" performed by Paul McCartney (2013) (P. McCartney)

5. "Photograph" performed by Ringo Starr (1973) (R. Starkey, G. Harrison)

6. "All Those Years Ago" performed by George Harrison (1981) (G. Harrison)

7. "Friends to Go" performed by Paul McCartney (2005) (P. McCartney)

8. "Never Without You" performed by Ringo Starr (2003) (R. Starkey, Mark Hudson, Gary Nicholson)

9. "Here Today" performed by Paul McCartney (1982) (P. McCartney)

10. "Now and Then" (2023) (J. Lennon)

CLOSING THOUGHTS—THE FINAL PLAYLIST: "THE BEATLES 2 (THE BLACK ALBUM)"

Side One

1. "Instant Karma" performed by John Lennon (1970) (J. Lennon)
2. "Maybe I'm Amazed" performed by Paul McCartney (1970) (P. McCartney)
3. "What Is Life" performed by George Harrison (1970) (G. Harrison)
4. "I'm the Greatest" performed by Ringo Starr (1973) (J. Lennon)
5. "Working-Class Hero" performed by John Lennon (1970) (J. Lennon)
6. "Run of the Mill" performed by George Harrison (1970) (G. Harrison)

Side Two

1. "Junk" performed by Paul McCartney (1970) (P. McCartney)
2. "I'd Have You Anytime" performed by George Harrison (1970) (G. Harrison, Bob Dylan)
3. "Power to the People" performed by John Lennon (1971) (J. Lennon)
4. "Beware of Darkness" performed by George Harrison (1970) (G. Harrison)

5. "Every Night" performed by Paul McCartney (1970) (P. McCartney)

6. "Isn't It a Pity" performed by George Harrison (1970) (G. Harrison)

Side Three

1. "Uncle Albert/Admiral Halsey" performed by Paul McCartney (1971) (P. McCartney)

2. "It Don't Come Easy" performed by Ringo Starr (1971) (R. Starkey, G. Harrison)

3. "Look at Me" performed by John Lennon (1970) (J. Lennon)

4. "Another Day" performed by Paul McCartney (1971) (P. McCartney)

5. "My Sweet Lord" performed by George Harrison (1970) (G. Harrison)

6. "That Would Be Something" performed by Paul McCartney (1970) (P. McCartney)

Side Four

1. "Mother" performed by John Lennon (1970) (J. Lennon)

2. "Behind That Locked Door" performed by George Harrison (1970) (G. Harrison)

3. "Early 1970" performed by Ringo Starr (1971) (R. Starkey)

4. "Too Many People" performed by Paul McCartney (1971) (P. McCartney)

5. "All Things Must Pass" performed by George Harrison (1970) (G. Harrison)

6. "Love" performed by John Lennon (1970) (J. Lennon)

Note: "The Beatles 2 (The Black Album)" is an imagined double album that could have been released had The Beatles stayed together past 1970, featuring an equal distribution of songs among John, Paul, and George (seven songs each), plus three for Ringo.

NOTES

Chapter 1

1. Jim Collins and Jerry Porras, *Built to Last: Successful Habits of Visionary Companies* (Harper Business, 1994), 1.

2. Jim Collins, *Good to Great: Why Some Companies Make the Leap . . . and Others Don't* (Harper Business, 2001), 11.

3. Thomas J. Peters and Robert H. Waterman Jr., *In Search of Excellence: Lessons from America's Best-Run Companies* (Harper Business, 2006).

Chapter 2

1. "George Harrison Is Attacked at His Friar Park Home," The Beatles Bible, updated June 10, 2020, https://www.beatlesbible.com/1999/12/30/george-olivia-harrison-stabbed-friar-park-michael-abram/.

2. "*Mersey Beat* Launches," The Beatles Bible, updated April 12, 2018, https://www.beatlesbible.com/1961/07/06/mersey-beat-launches/.

3. Paul McCartney, "Paul McCartney on George Martin," PaulMcCartney.com, August 3, 2016, https://www.paulmccartney.com/news/paul-mccartney-on-george-martin.

Chapter 3

1. Jim Collins, *Good to Great: Why Some Companies Make the Leap . . . and Others Don't* (Harper Business, 2001), 13.

2. Collins, *Good to Great*, 41.

3. Paul McCartney, *The Lyrics: 1956 to the Present* (Norton, 2021), 235.

4. Brian Epstein, *A Cellarful of Noise: The Man Who Made The Beatles* (Souvenir Press, 1964).

5. Mark Lewisohn, *Tune In: The Beatles: All These Years* (Little, Brown, 2013), 637.

6. Mark Leibovich, "When I'm 84," Magzter, originally from *The Atlantic* (May 2025), 43, https://www.magzter.com/stories/news/The-Atlantic/WHEN-IM-84.

7. Lewisohn, *Tune In*, 763.

8. John Wooden, *Wooden on Leadership: How to Create a Winning Organization* (McGraw Hill, 2005). 197.

9. Wooden, *Wooden on Leadership*, 197.

10. George Martin and Jeremy Hornsby, *All You Need Is Ears: The Inside Personal Story of the Genius Who Created the Beatles* (St. Martin's Griffin, 1994), 130.

Chapter 4

1. David Sheff, "John Lennon and Yoko Ono on Love, Sex, Money, Fame and All About the Beatles," *Playboy*, September 24, 1980, http://www.beatlesinterviews.org/dbjypb.int4.html.

2. Mark Lewisohn, *Tune In: The Beatles: All These Years* (Little, Brown, 2013), 537.

3. George Harrison, "George – Pop Profile – Live at the BBC/30th November, 1965," BBC, aired November 30, 1965, released 2023, https://open.spotify.com/track/51UslSkGPT7TrXYIsEsWAF.

4. Jim Collins and Jerry Porras, *Built to Last: Successful Habits of Visionary Companies* (Harper Business, 1994).

5. Lewisohn, *Tune In*, 537.

6. Jim Collins, *Good to Great: Why Some Companies Make the Leap . . . and Others Don't* (Harper Business, 2001).

7. Malcolm Gladwell, *Outliers: The Story of Success* (Back Bay Books, 2011).

8. Gladwell, *Outliers*, 49.

9. Gladwell, *Outliers*, 49.

10. Geoff Emerick and Howard Massey, *Here, There and Everywhere: My Life Recording the Music of The Beatles* (Avery, 2007), 254.

11. George Martin and Jeremy Hornsby, *All You Need Is Ears: The Inside Personal Story of the Genius Who Created the Beatles* (St. Martin's Griffin, 1994), 128.

12. Martin and Hornsby, *All You Need Is Ears*, 128.

13. Martin and Hornsby, *All You Need Is Ears*, 130.

Chapter 5

1. F. E. Adcock, F. E. Adcock quotes, Quote Fancy, https://quotefancy. com/quote/1629227/F-E-Adcock-That-typically-English-character-istic-for-which-there-is-no-English-name.

2. "Half a Chocolate Bar Started The Beatles," The Daily Beatle, updated December 27, 2024, https://webgrafikk.com/blog/uncategorized/ half-chocolate-bar-started-beatles/.

3. Ian MacDonald, *Revolution in the Head: The Beatles' Records and the Sixties* (Chicago Review Press, 2007), location 485, Kindle.

4. Andrew Sobel, "The Beatle's Principles," *Strategy+Business*, February 28, 2006, https://www.strategy-business.com/article/06104.

5. George Martin and Jeremy Hornsby, *All You Need Is Ears: The Inside Personal Story of the Genius Who Created the Beatles* (St. Martin's Griffin, 1994), 126.

6. Martin and Hornsby, *All You Need Is Ears*, 130.

7. Caroline Hallemann, "Remembering the Night the Beatles Played for the Royal Family," *Town & Country*, October 5, 2017, https://

www.townandcountrymag.com/leisure/arts-and-culture/a10284914/
beatles-royal-variety-performance/.

8. Michael Braun, *Love Me Do! The Beatles' Progress* (Graymalkin Media, 2019), 78.

9. Braun, *Love Me Do!*, 78.

10. Braun, *Love Me Do!*, 78.

11. Braun, *Love Me Do!*, 78.

Chapter 6

1. Derek Taylor, liner notes to *Beatles for Sale*, The Beatles, Parlophone, 1964.

2. Stephen Covey, *The 7 Habits of Highly Effective People: Powerful Lessons in Personal Change* (Free Press, 2004), 262–63.

3. Andrew Sobel, "The Beatle's Principles," *Strategy+Business*, February 28, 2006, https://www.strategy-business.com/article/06104.

4. Joshua Wolf Shenk, *Powers of Two: Finding the Essence of Innovation in Creative Pairs* (HarperOne, 2015), location 78, Kindle.

5. Shenk, *Powers of Two*, locations 228 and 240, Kindle.

6. Michael Gallucci, "The Beatles Cap Their Masterpiece with 'A Day in the Life': The Story Behind Every 'Sgt. Pepper' Song," Ultimate Classic Rock, May 29, 2017, https://ultimateclassicrock.com/beatles-day-in-the-life/.

7. Covey, *The 7 Habits*.

8. Covey, *The 7 Habits*, 262.

9. *Oxford English Dictionary*, "serendipity," accessed July 20, 2025, www.oed.com/view/Entry/176587.

10. Mark Lewisohn, *Tune In: The Beatles: All These Years* (Little, Brown, 2013), 647, 768.

11. John Higgs, *Love and Let Die: James Bond, The Beatles, and the British Psyche* (Pegasus Books, 2023), 2.

12. *A Hard Day's Night*, directed by Richard Lester, July 6, 1964, Pavilion Theatre, distributed by United Artists.

13. Geoff Emerick and Howard Massey, *Here, There and Everywhere: My Life Recording the Music of The Beatles* (Avery, 2007), 139.

14. Emerick and Massey, *Here, There and Everywhere*, 139.

Part 2

1. Philip Norman, interview by Selena Scott, *West 57th*, CBS News, March 27, 1987, https://youtu.be/G1wkRVUlCzM.

Chapter 7

1. Wikipedia, s.v. "Rubber Soul," last modified June 13, 2025, https://en.wikipedia.org/wiki/Rubber_Soul.

2. *The Beatles Anthology*, episode 7, "Seven (June '67 to July '68)," directed by Geoff Wonfor and Bob Smeaton, aired 1995, ITV, https://vimeo.com/517685752.

3. Bryce G. Hoffman, *American Icon: Alan Mulally and the Fight to Save Ford Motor Company* (Crown Currency, 2013), 115.

4. Hoffman, *American Icon*, 106.

5. The Beatles, *The Beatles Anthology* (Chronicle Books, 2000), 342.

6. The Beatles, *The Beatles Anthology*, 336–37.

7. Hoffman, *American Icon*, 123.

8. Hoffman, *American Icon*, 123.

9. George Harrison, *I, Me, Mine* (Chronicle Books, 2002), 95–96.

10. The Beatles, *A Hard Day's Night*, special edition audio CD, 2009, Parlophone/Apple Corps.

11. Sam Kemp, "The Beatles Albums That Saw George Harrison Find His 'Real Purpose,'" *Guitar World*, December 23, 2021, https://faroutmagazine.co.uk/the-beatles-albums-george-harrison-find-real-purpose/.

12. *The Beatles Anthology*, directed by Geoff Wonfor, produced by Neil Aspinall and Chips Chipperfield, November 19, 1995, ITV.

13. Emerick and Massey, *Here, There and Everywhere*, 126.

14. Hoffman, *American Icon*, 115.

15. Hoffman, *American Icon*, 121.

Chapter 8

1. Ashley King, "'Here Comes the Sun' Becomes the First Beatles Song to Hit 1 Billion Spotify Streams," Digital Music News, May 11, 2023, https://www.digitalmusicnews.com/2023/05/11/here-comes-the-sun-becomes-first-beatles-song-to-hit-1-billion-spotify-streams/.

2. Peter Aspden, "Something—Sinatra Called It 'The Greatest Love Song of the Past 50 Years,'" *Financial Times*, September 23, 2019, https://ig.ft.com/life-of-a-song/something.html.

3. Emma McKee, "A Mistake by Frank Sinatra Proved George Harrison's 'Peculiar' Position in The Beatles," Showbiz Cheatsheet, July 6, 2022, https://www.cheatsheet.com/news/mistake-frank-sinatra-proved-george-harrisons-peculiar-position-beatles.html/.

4. Ken Sharp, "The 'Delta Lady' Speaks: Q&A with Rita Coolidge," *Rock Cellar* Magazine, July 8, 2016, https://rockcellarmagazine.com/rita-coolidge-qa-interview-delta-lady-leon-russell-layla/.

5. Ringo Starr, interview by David Wigg, *The Beatles Tapes from the David Wigg Interviews*, January 21, 1970, Polydor.

Chapter 9

1. "Lennon and McCartney Give Interviews in New York," Beatles Bible, updated July 12, 2022, https://www.beatlesbible.com/1968/05/14/lennon-and-mccartney-give-interviews-in-new-york/.

2. "Lennon and McCartney Give Interviews."

3. Ken McNab, *And in the End: The Last Days of The Beatles* (Polygon, 2019), 11.

4. McNab, *And in the End*, 115.

5. Jim Collins, *Good to Great: Why Some Companies Make the Leap . . . and Others Don't* (Harper Business, 2001).

6. McNab, *And in the End*, 42.

7. McNab, *And in the End*, 43.

8. McNab, *And in the End*, 77.

9. McNab, *And in the End*, 100.

10. McNab, *And in the End*, 99.

11. McNab, *And in the End*, 99.

12. *The Beatles: Get Back*, Part 1, directed by Peter Jackson, 2021, Walt Disney Studios.

13. *The Beatles: Get Back*, Part 2.

14. *The Beatles Anthology*, directed by Geoff Wonfor, produced by Neil Aspinall and Chips Chipperfield, November 19, 1995, ITV.

15. Mick Brown, "A Conversation with George Harrison," *Rolling Stone*, April 19, 1979, https://www.rollingstone.com/music/music-news/a-conversation-with-george-harrison-190204/.

16. Ringo Starr, interview by Elliot Mintz, *Innerview*, aired August 29, 1977, broadcast on American radio, http://www.beatlesinterviews.org/db1976.00rs.beatles.html.

Chapter 10

1. Mark Lewisohn, *The Complete Beatles Recording Sessions: The Official Story of the Abbey Road Years, 1962–1970* (Hamlyn, 2021), 174.

Part 3

1. *The Beatles: Get Back*, Part 1, directed by Peter Jackson, 2021, Walt Disney Studios.

2. Patrick Lencioni, *The Five Dysfunctions of a Team: A Leadership Fable* (Jossey-Bass, 2002).

3. Stephen Covey, *The 7 Habits of Highly Effective People: Powerful Lessons in Personal Change* (Free Press, 2004).

Chapter 11

1. Dan Farber, "Tim Cook Maintains Steve Jobs' Beatles Business Model," CNET, June 12, 2013, https://www.cnet.com/tech/tech-industry/tim-cook-maintains-steve-jobs-beatles-business-model/.

2. Stephen M. R. Covey, *The Speed of Trust: The One Thing That Changes Everything* (Free Press, 2008).

3. George Harrison, interview by Selena Scott, *West 57th*, CBS News, March 12, 1987.

4. Covey, *The Speed of Trust*.

5. Robert Kegan and Lisa Lahey, *An Everyone Culture: Becoming a Deliberately Developmental Organization* (Harvard Business Review Press, 2016), 4.

6. Kegan and Lahey, *An Everyone Culture*, 87.

7. Stephen Covey, *The 7 Habits of Highly Effective People: Powerful Lessons in Personal Change* (Free Press, 2004), 239.

8. Covey, *The 7 Habits*, 240.

Chapter 12

1. Stephen Covey, *The 7 Habits of Highly Effective People: Powerful Lessons in Personal Change* (Free Press, 2004), 262.

2. Tom Nichols, personal communication, April 23, 2025.

3. William Bridges, *Managing Transitions: Making the Most of Change* (Da Capo Lifelong Books, 2009), 16.

4. Bridges, *Managing Transitions*, 16.

5. Bridges, *Managing Transitions*, 18.

6. Bridges, *Managing Transitions*, 17.

7. Bridges, *Managing Transitions*.

ABOUT THE AUTHOR

DAN ABSHER is a business leader, teacher, and writer. He spent thirty-two years as CEO of Absher Construction, where he remains as the board chair. He has learned that the greatest lessons in leadership, team-building, and organizational excellence do not come from textbooks but from leading a successful business and a lifelong passion for The Beatles.

After graduating from Stanford University (1980) and Notre Dame Law School (1983), Dan practiced law for two years before joining the family construction business. For the past two years, he has been a professor in the Construction Management Department of Pierce College.

Dan is the founder of The Fab Four Academy, whose mission is to share The Beatles' message of love while developing wildly successful teams and organizations. He has led workshops like "Team-building with the Beatles," "Beatles 101—All You Need is Love," and "Creating the Fab Forum."

Dan lives in the Pacific Northwest with his wife, Daria, and his dog, Ringo, where he writes, teaches, and reflects on why the band that broke up over fifty years ago still has so much to teach us about working—and living—together.